D0064964

Against Liberalism

ALSO BY JOHN KEKES—

A Justification of Rationality

The Nature of Philosophy

Dimensions of Ethical Thought (co-editor)

The Examined Life

Moral Tradition and Individuality

Facing Evil

The Morality of Pluralism

Moral Wisdom and Good Lives

AGAINST LIBERALISM

JOHN KEKES

Cornell University Press

ITHACA AND LONDON

First published 1997 by Cornell University Press.

Library of Congress Cataloging-in-Publication Data
Kekes, John.
 Against liberalism / John Kekes.
  p. cm.
 Includes index.
 ISBN 0-8014-3361-4 (cloth : alk. paper). — ISBN 0-8014-8400-6
(paper : alk. paper)
  1. Liberalism. 2. Liberalism—Moral and ethical aspects.
I. Title.
JC574.K44 1997
320.5′1—dc20   96-44864

Printed in the United States of America

Cornell University Press strives to utilize environmentally responsible suppliers and materials to the fullest extent possible in the publishing of its books. Such materials include vegetable-based, low-VOC inks and acid-free papers that are also either recycled, totally chlorine-free, or partly composed of nonwood fibers.

Cloth printing 10 9 8 7 6 5 4 3 2

IN LOVING MEMORY OF MY FATHER
KÉKES JENŐ
AND OF MY FIRST TEACHER
FENYŐ ANDOR

Contents

Preface

This book is a criticism of liberalism. Its thesis is that liberalism is incapable of achieving its own aims because it is riddled with inconsistencies. Some of these inconsistencies result from the liberal commitment to two incompatible aims, one negative, the other positive. The negative aim is to avoid evils, such as dictatorship, torture, poverty, intolerance, repression, discrimination, lawlessness, and so forth. The positive aim is to create conditions in which individuals can make good lives for themselves.

Liberals think that first among these conditions is individual autonomy, which is fostered if a state guarantees the rights of individuals to make free choices about how they live, equal concern and respect for their endeavors, a just share of the resources they need, and a generous plurality of options.

The evils that it is the negative aim of liberalism to avoid are evils because they endanger good lives. The values of autonomy, freedom, rights, equality, distributive justice, and pluralism that it is the positive aim of liberalism to realize are valuable because they are thought to be necessary for good lives. Liberalism is inconsistent because the realization of these liberal values would increase the evils liberals want to avoid and because the decrease of these evils depends on creating conditions contrary to the liberal values.

Another respect in which liberalism is inconsistent results from the incompatibility of the liberal conceptions of equality, justice, and pluralism with good lives. It is destructive of good lives to create conditions in which good and evil people are treated with equal concern and respect; in which justice is taken to involve the redistribution of resources without regard to whether their present holders and future recipients deserve them; and in which pluralism is restricted to options that conform to liberal preconceptions.

The thesis of this book is developed in ten chapters. Chapter 1 describes the political programs, the basic values (freedom, equality, right, pluralism, and distributive justice), and the core commitment (autonomy) of liberalism. Chapter 2 argues that evil is prevalent, that it results mainly from nonautonomous actions, and that the political programs, basic values, and core commitment of liberalism make it more rather than less prevalent. The thesis of Chapter 3 is that the refusal to hold individuals responsible for the evil they nonautonomously cause leaves liberalism without moral resources to cope with the most frequent kind of evil. Chapter 4 shows that many liberal political programs presuppose collective responsibility, while the core liberal commitment to autonomy excludes it. Chapter 5 criticizes the liberal conception of equality for misdiagnosing the problem it aims to ameliorate, prompting absurd and inconsistent policies for dealing with it, and denying the plain fact of moral inequality among human beings. Chapters 6 and 7 consider and reject the liberal conception of justice on the ground that it excludes the essence of justice: desert. Chapter 8 provides criticisms of the inconsistency between the liberal commitment to pluralism and the central liberal belief that when the basic liberal values and autonomy conflict with nonliberal values, the liberal values should override the nonliberal ones. Chapter 9 examines and shows the failure of the attempt to base liberalism on benevolence, rather than on the more usual Kantian grounds. The case against liberalism is summarized in Chapter 10.

Liberals' first line of defense against these criticisms will be to deny that they hold the views attributed to them. It is therefore necessary to provide extensive citations. The system adopted is that citations in the text advance the descriptive or critical accounts of which they are parts. They are there as steps in the argument, and their sources appear in parentheses. Citations collected as notes at the end of the book support the attribution of particular views to particular authors. Readers need to consult the notes, therefore, only if they want evidence that the attributions in the text are accurate.

Some of my previously published works are recycled in parts of the book. In all cases, they have been revised, often radically, to fit in with the overall argument. Chapter 3 includes some material from chapter 2 of *Moral Tradition and Individuality* (Princeton: Princeton University Press, 1989) and from "The Reflexivity of Evil," *Social Philosophy and Policy* 14 (1997), forthcoming; Chapter 4 draws on "Collective Responsibility as a Problem for Liberalism," *Midwest Studies* 20 (1995): 416–30; Chapter 5 incorporates "A Question for Egalitarians," *Ethics* 107 (1997), forthcoming; Chapter 8 borrows from chapters 3 and 11 of *The Morality of Pluralism*

(Princeton: Princeton University Press, 1993): and Chapter 9 uses portions of "Benevolence: A Minor Virtue," *Social Philosophy and Policy* 4 (1987): 21–36, and "Cruelty and Liberalism," *Ethics* 106 (1996): 834–44.

Wallace Matson, Louis Pojman, and Steven Cahn read the entire manuscript. Their comments helped to correct numerous weaknesses. I am especially indebted to Matson's detailed, sympathetic yet tough-minded criticisms. Jonathan Mandle, Robert Simon, and James Sterba commented on parts of the manuscript. I am grateful for their generous help. None of them, however, should be supposed to endorse my views. In fact, they strongly disagree with many of them. It is even more to their credit, therefore, to have helped to express them better.

Roger Haydon has now been the editor of two of my books. There may be editors better than he, but it would be hard to imagine one. His grace, wit, intelligence, efficiency, and expert midwifery have made it easy and pleasant to transform an insufficiently focused manuscript into the present book. Whether it is now well enough focused is for the reader to say, but that it is better than it was is to a considerable extent Haydon's doing.

My wife, Jean Y. Kekes, had made the work on the manuscript possible by creating many of the conditions in which it could be done, and then she helped to do it by listening patiently to my lucubrations. I am immeasurably indebted to her love, support, and good sense on this occasion, in years past, and, with luck, in years yet to come.

JOHN KEKES

ITHAKA
Charlton
New York

CHAPTER 1

What Is Liberalism?

Contemporary debates within modern political systems are almost exclusively between conservative liberals, liberal liberals, and radical liberals. There is little place in such political systems for the criticism of the system itself, that is, for putting liberalism in question.

—ALASDAIR MACINTYRE, *Whose Justice? Which Rationality?*

A discussion of liberalism ought to begin with a definition that identifies a set of necessary and sufficient conditions that all versions of liberalism must meet. But no such set exists, which makes liberalism elusive. This lack is acknowledged by liberals themselves.[1] In the absence of a satisfactory definition, however, no criticism or justification can hope to apply to all versions of liberalism. The most promising approach appears to be, therefore, to propose an interpretation that embraces as many versions of liberalism as possible, while frankly acknowledging that some versions may still be left out and that other interpretations are also possible. That, in any case, will be the approach followed here.

The subject of this chapter is, then, an interpretation of liberalism. It begins with a brief account of the attractions of liberalism, lists some typical liberal political programs, goes on to an initial description of the basic values that inspire these programs, and then discusses the core of liberalism, which provides the ultimate reason for the basic values and the political programs. In later chapters, individual liberal thinkers will be engaged and greater depth will be provided. It must be emphasized that what will emerge is only one possible interpretation. To avoid repetition and pedantry, "liberalism" from now on will mean this interpretation. It is left to the reader to bear in mind that other interpretations are possible. The

1

present one, however, is meant to be broad enough to include most versions of contemporary liberalism.

1.1 WHY LIBERALISM PLEASES

The history of liberalism has hitherto been a story of success. it began during the Renaissance as a reaction to religious orthodoxy, gained strength throughout the Reformation, and became one of the main political forces in the Enlightenment. In the course of its development, liberalism moved away from being merely a negative reaction and toward a positive political vision that could be appealed to as an alternative to all types of absolute authority. It steadily expanded its opposition to the divine right of monarchs, to aristocratic privilege derived from feudal times, and then to all forms of oppression, whether it be in Czarist Russia, Ottoman Turkey, the Communist Soviet Union, Fascist Spain and Italy, Nazi Germany, or the Greece of the colonels. With the demise of Marxism, it has become the dominant ideology of our time, one sign of which is that even its opponents now couch their defenses of the regimes they favor in evaluative terms that liberals have imposed on political discourse.

Liberalism transcends national borders and historical periods, draws its adherents from many languages, religions, and classes, and intends to give hope for a better future not just to Westerners but to many others throughout the world. It is unlikely, therefore, that it would be formed by a single, easily identifiable historical influence. Economic, intellectual, political, and social factors had to combine to foster its coming to dominance. It is possible to identify three philosophers, however, who succeeded in offering a systematic formulation of some of the key ideas that have been generally recognized as fundamental to liberalism. These philosophers, of course, have predecessors who influenced them and to whom they owe often considerable intellectual debt. But because this book is not about the history of liberalism, it will not attempt to trace the pedigree of these key ideas.

One of the most influential liberal ideas is that the aim and justification of government is to protect the life, liberty, and property of the citizens living under it. The formulation of this idea is John Locke's, although it owes much to Thomas Hobbes. Locke supposed that the means by which the government ought to provide this protection is justice as defined by law. All citizens are equally subject to its authority, and it is reasonable for them to accept it because the law guarantees the rights of individuals to life, liberty, and property. Legitimate authority safeguards these rights, and opposition to authority is justifiable if it transgresses them. Locke's immensely appealing idea is that governments ought to be able to justify their authority to the individuals who are their subjects and that the only reasonable justification is that the rights of individuals are better protected by the system of justice their government maintains than by what they could hope for under different arrangements.

The central importance that liberalism attributes to individuals is greatly enhanced by the idea of autonomy formulated by Immanuel Kant, who was in this respect influenced by Jean-Jacques Rousseau. Kantian autonomy may be understood as the condition in which individuals are free from external determination, such as coercion, force, or various forms of threat and manipulation; their actions are executions of their choices; they are also free from internal causal influences that affect their choices through uncontrolled desires, passions, or prejudices; and their choices are controlled by reason, understood as conformity to universalizable principles. Kant believed that all human beings are equal in their capacity for autonomy, that moral responsibility and human dignity both rest on this capacity, and that morality requires respect for everyone capable of autonomy. He thus articulated the idea that individuals are entitled to equal respect because of their autonomy, interference with which is a violation of an absolute moral prohibition.

John Stuart Mill, influenced by Benjamin Constant and Wilhelm von Humboldt, further strengthened liberalism by arguing that it is morally impermissible to interfere with the actions of individuals even if they are motivated by irrational, destructive, stupid, or emotive considerations, provided only that their actions do not harm others. As Mill might have put it, liberalism is opposed to the coercion even of nonautonomous actions, just so long as such actions are compatible with the autonomous functioning of other individuals. Mill thus opposed paternalistic interference intended to benefit individuals. His opposition was based on the widely accepted liberal view that individuals are likely to know best what is good for them, and even if they are mistaken, it is better in the long run to allow them to make mistakes than to have a government impose an alien conception of the good on them.

As these brief historical remarks make evident, essential to liberalism is the moral criticism of dictatorship, arbitrary power, intolerance, repression, persecution, lawlessness, and the suppression of individuals by entrenched orthodoxies. Reason and morality are on the side of liberals and against their opponents in this moral criticism. Indeed, one of the causes of the triumph of liberalism is that it has attracted the allegiance of many of those all too numerous people who have suffered and are suffering under repressive regimes. An adequate political morality, however, must offer more than moral criticism, even if it consistently opposes what ought to be opposed.

Liberalism also aims to develop a moral theory that concentrates on politics—on the values that ought to govern the political institutions of a state. Liberalism and rival theories of political morality differ over the values they favor. These differences, however, reflect an even deeper one concerning assumptions about human nature and conceptions of a good life in accordance with which the moral and political values are meant to be formulated and justified.

The relevant liberal assumptions are made explicit in the following representative statements. Writing from the liberal left, John Rawls (1993: xxv) identifies "the problem of liberalism" as, "How is it possible that there exists over time a stable and just society of free and equal citizens profoundly divided by reasonable religious, philosophical, and moral doctrines?" And speaking from the liberal right, William Galston (1991: 10–11) says, "The liberal conception of the *good* . . . allows for a wide . . . pluralism among ways of life. It assumes that individuals have special . . . insight into their own good. . . . [T]he liberal account of the human good . . . undergirds the fundamental considerations . . . of distributive justice within liberal orders. . . . Liberalism is committed to equality, but it needs excellence. It is committed to freedom, but it needs virtue."

The assumptions that unite different versions of liberalism are, then, that a liberal state should be guided by values that reflect a plurality of reasonable conceptions of a good life, guarantee the freedom and equality of its citizens, and maintain a just distribution of the goods its citizens need to pursue their conceptions of a good life. These are regarded by liberals as goods to which citizens have rights. And it is assumed that citizens not only can but also should make decisions for themselves about the conceptions of a good life they will make their own as they act autonomously within the private sphere that their rights protect. The basic liberal values may then be identified as pluralism, freedom, rights, equality, and distributive justice. What makes them basically valuable is that they enable individuals to live autonomously. The aim of liberalism is to create and maintain political institutions that foster these values and, through them, autonomy. Versions of liberalism differ because their champions disagree about the interpretation of the basic values, about their respective importance to autonomy, and about how autonomy should be pursued.

1.2 POLITICAL PROGRAMS

The political programs that liberals favor differ, of course, from context to context. The discussion of specific programs must therefore be restricted to a specific context. For the purposes of illustration, it will be restricted here to the contemporary American context and within that to domestic rather than international affairs. These programs are the redistribution of wealth from the rich to the poor; graduated taxation; mandatory participation in the social security plan; strong government control of the economy, including business and finance; the extension of rights protecting freedom to include protecting welfare; greater racial and gender equality; the legal enforcement of integration; multiculturalism; affirmative action programs; the preferential treatment of women and blacks; government-supported universal health care; the widest possible system of secular public education; the mainstreaming of people with physical and mental disabilities, especially children; freely available abortion; the opposition to the legal enforcement of morality, particularly concerning consensual sexual practices among adults; sharp separation of church and state; increased funding for welfare and decreased funding for defense; strong procedural protection of accused criminals; and the aggressive pursuit of these programs by the federal government.

Such political programs reflect deeper attitudes that liberals typically hold. For example, with respect to the redistribution of wealth, they care more about the needs of the recipients than about the rights of the donors; in affirmative action and preferential treatment, they are more concerned with the victims of past injustice than with the present victims of these policies; in criminal justice, they focus more on avoiding the punishment of innocents than on assuring the punishment of the guilty; in education, they prefer special programs for those with low intelligence to special programs for the talented; in regulating pornography, they focus on the importance of free expression rather than on outraging the prevailing sensibility; in the separation of church and state, they stress the freedom not to worship at the expense of the freedom to worship; in welfare legislation, they concentrate on what people need rather than on what they deserve; in multiculturalism, they emphasize the benefits of diversity, while de-emphasizing the harms of lack of unity.

Liberals are not alone, of course, in endorsing these programs and holding these attitudes, and not all liberals need to endorse and hold all of them. Liberals, however, are typically committed to most of them, and most nonliberals are opposed to a good many of them. What is significant for the present purposes, however, is not so much that liberals typically do favor them but rather the justification they give for doing so: that is, in the contemporary American context, these attitudes and the programs that reflect them are the concrete ways in which the basic liberal values are most likely to be realized.

1.3 BASIC VALUES

Because the interpretation of the basic values of liberalism is controversial even among liberals themselves, any proposed interpretation must keep to the middle between the pitfalls of securing the consent of the contending parties by being too vague and of providing a detailed, albeit partisan, account. In trying to keep to a course that avoids both, the interpretation will aim to be specific until it becomes controversial, at which point it will indicate the reasons for the controversy.

Pluralism is one basic value of liberalism.[2] According to it, there is an irreducible plurality of reasonable values and reasonable conceptions of a good life. In a liberal society, individuals ought to be free to adopt any one or any combination of these values, and they ought to be similarly free to construct out of them their own conceptions of a good life and to live according to them. One political implication of pluralism is that the government ought to guarantee the equal treatment of every reasonable conception of a good life, which means that the government ought not to favor any particular reasonable conception over others.

This is often taken to imply that the government should be neutral about the conceptions of a good life its citizens pursue, that it should be equally tolerant of them, or that in the politics of a liberal society the right should be accorded priority over the good. This last implications may be further elaborated as the view that the business of government is to formulate and maintain the rules that enable its citizens to make what they wish of their lives. Conformity to these rules is what is right, whereas the good is what guides citizens in trying to live according to their conceptions of what their lives ought to be. The liberal view is that political morality should be concerned with the right and that it should be left to individuals to decide about the good. Pluralism is thus the liberal value that defines the right political attitude toward the good.

Controversies about pluralism begin because it is unclear whether the right and the good can be sharply separated, whether the neutrality of the government is merely procedural or whether it involves providing some substantive goods that all conceptions of a good life require, whether neutrality extends to antiliberal conceptions of a good life, whether plurality is an intrinsic property of values or merely a symptom of the human incapacity or unwillingness to recognize true values, whether toleration is warranted by genuine equality among conceptions of a good life or by prudential reasons against paternalism, and whether the exclusion of some conceptions of a good life as unreasonable do not simply reflect liberal prejudices. These controversies, however, concern the extent or inclusiveness of pluralism, but they do not weaken the liberal commitment to pluralism itself (see Galston 1991; Hampshire 1983; Kekes 1993; Larmore 1987; Macedo 1990; Moon 1993; and Raz 1986).

All the basic values of liberalism are intertwined, but perhaps none more so than pluralism and freedom. If pluralism is the recognition that there are many different values and conceptions of a good life, then freedom is the political space in which individuals can choose among them. "Freedom," or "liberty," in the political sense of these synonymous terms, is the idea that the citizens of a society ought to be allowed to choose their values and conceptions of a good life without external interference. Freedom conceived in this way expresses a human aspiration that motivates an untold number of people in both the Western world and elsewhere.[3] An often quoted passage from Isaiah Berlin (1969b: 131) captures this aspiration as "the wish on the part of the individual to be his own master. I wish my life and decisions to depend on myself, not on external forces of whatever kind. I wish to be the instrument of my own, not of other men's, acts of will. I wish to be a subject, not an object; to be moved by reasons, conscious purposes, which are my own, not be causes which effect me, as it were, from outside. I wish to be . . . deciding, not being decided for, self-directed and not acted upon by external nature."

Of course, all liberals recognize that the claims of freedom are not unconditional. An obvious restriction on the freedom of the individual is that its exercise should not interfere with the freedom of other individuals. This much is uncontroversial. But a further restriction may also be in order. The absence of external coercion may be accepted as necessary for freedom, but coercion may also be internal. If individuals are ruled by compulsion, addiction, irrational prejudices, or uncontrolled and misdirected passions and if the genuine choices they make are informed by ignorance, stupidity, manipulation, and propaganda, then they lack freedom as much as if they had been subjected to external coercion. People often choose to adopt values that they would not adopt if they were reasonable. Being free from external interference thus falls short of being free to make reasonable choices. And presumably freedom is a basic value because it enables individuals to make reasonable choices among values and conceptions of a good life. Controversies about freedom begin when the question arises of how far it is legitimate to restrict the freedom of individuals to make unreasonable choices. These controversies center around the relation between negative and positive freedom, between the extent to which freedom is the absence of coercion and the extent to which it is the opportunity to make reasonable choices (Berlin 1969c; Kukathas 1993; and Ryan 1979).

Liberal controversies about freedom, however, extend even further. It is common ground among liberals that the value of freedom emerges only under civilized conditions. If starvation, disease, poverty, illiteracy, superstition, ignorance, insecurity, and so forth are rampant, then freedom is an unaffordable luxury.[4] The maintenance of the civilized conditions necessary for freedom being a meaningful value, however, notoriously requires coercing individuals to make choices favorable to it. Securing the conditions of freedom therefore depends on its restriction. And a most controversial question for liberals is, by how much can freedom be legitimately restricted in order to improve health, prosperity, education, security, and similar conditions of it?

A further controversial area is that freedom is only one of the basic values of liberalism. It would be incompatible with pluralism to suppose otherwise. Other basic values of liberalism, however, often conflict with freedom. And freedom may be justifiably restricted by the greater importance that is reasonable to assign in some contexts to the claims of other values. No liberal consensus exists about how such conflicts are to be resolved.[5]

Yet liberals generally agree that freedom is a basic value because it is a necessary condition of individuals' making for themselves what they regard as a good life. This agreement extends to the recognition that the claims of freedom may be legitimately restricted—the disagreements are over the questions of how far and under what circumstances and for what reasons its restrictions may be legitimate (see Swanton 1992 for the fullest and best account).

Rights are another basic value of liberalism. The fundamental idea is that "individuals have rights, and there are things no person or group may do to them (without violating their rights)" (Nozick 1974: ix). The more important is the respect in which protection is needed, the more basic is the right that may be claimed for providing it. The most important protections are thought to be those that individuals need because they are human, not because they have adopted any particular values or conceptions of a good live. The need for such protections is universally human, and individuals are equal both in having the need and in being entitled to its satisfaction. The corresponding rights are referred to as human or basic or fundamental. All human beings are said to have them and to have them equally, because they attach to features of humanity with respect to which human beings are alike.

Human rights are not legal rights because a legal system may be justifiably criticized for failing to protect human rights. A legal system certainly ought to protect human rights, but the rights exist independently of any such system. Human rights may be said to be moral, in the sense that they protect human beings in the enjoyment of benefits and the avoidance of harms that count as such simply because of the physiological, psychological, and social conditions that hold equally for everyone. Human rights thus define areas whose violation is morally impermissible because they constitute minimum requirements of human welfare. There are, of course, legal and moral rights other than human rights, but they vary from society to society and person to person. The rights that are a basic value of liberalism are human.

It is generally agreed by liberals that the justification of human rights is that they protect conditions necessary for the functioning of human beings as such. But this general agreement turns into sharp disagreement as soon as an attempt is made to specify the conditions supposedly necessary for human functioning.[6]

Part of the reason why these disagreements matter is that liberal political programs are strongly influenced by the interpretation of human rights that forms their background. If the liberal state ought to protect the human rights of individual citizens, then it makes a great deal of difference whether the rights are interpreted merely as protections from unwarranted interference with the exercise of individual freedom or as the obligation to provide such substantive benefits as individuals may be thought to require as part of the minimum requirements of their welfare. Some of the sharpest controversies among liberals concern the questions of whether human rights are only negative or are positive as well; if they are positive, what the required benefits are; and how broadly it is reasonable to define those benefits to which individuals are thought to be entitled.

Underlying these often deep disagreements, however, is the agreement that there is a basic protection, defined by the minimum requirements of human welfare, to which individuals are entitled, a protection that the state is responsible for providing, and that one standard by which the moral standing of any state may be judged is how well it provides this protection. An often adduced justification of the liberal state is that it comes closer to meeting this standard than does any other type of state.

Of the basic values of liberalism, equality is the most difficult to pin down and consequently the most controversial. The root idea is the combination of the positive claim that there is some fundamental respect in which all human beings are equal and ought to be treated equally and the negative claim that arbitrary inequality among human beings is morally repugnant. The positive claim, however, is vacuous unless the respect in which equality is supposed to hold is specified, and the negative claim is in a similar position until it is specified what inequality is arbitrary. Liberal controversies about equality are caused by disagreements about the content of the required specification.

Underlying these controversies, however, there is a shared moral vision.

In one expression of this vision, Gregory Vlastos says: "If *A* were a states-man, and giving him relief from pain enabled him to conclude an agree-ment that would benefit millions, while *B*, an unskilled laborer, was him-self the sole beneficiary of the life relief, we would, of course, agree that the *instrumental* value of the two experiences would be vastly different— but not their *intrinsic* value. In all cases where human beings are capable of enjoying the same goods, we feel that the intrinsic value of their enjoy-ment is the same. In just this sense we hold that (1) *one man's well-being is as valuable as any other's.* And there is a parallel . . . in our feeling for freedom. . . . For us (2) *one man's freedom is as valuable as any other's*" (1962:51).

Combining this egalitarian moral vision with the preceding remarks about human rights, one may interpret the positive claim involved in equality as holding in respect to human rights. All human beings are equal and ought to be treated equally insofar as the conditions required for their functioning as human beings are concerned. And similarly for the negative claim against arbitrary inequality: inequality is arbitrary if it illegitimately favors protecting the human rights of some individuals over those of others. This position allows for the possibility that human rights may be legitimately restricted, but there is general agreement among lib-erals that only those restrictions could be legitimate that are required for the protection of the whole system of human rights. Criminals' rights to freedom, for instance, may be legitimately restricted if the freedom of others is thereby protected. The liberal value of equality derives, there-fore, from the moral vision according to which all human beings are equally worthy of having their human rights protected and unequal pro-tection is justifiable only if it is required by the protection of human rights in general.[7]

The sharing of this moral vision, however, does not eliminate sharp disagreements among liberals about what its implementation would con-sist in. Just as there are disputes about whether human rights are merely negative or also positive, so also are there disputes about the specific con-ditions of freedom and well-being with respect to which equality is thought to be desirable. These conditions may be legal, political, eco-nomic, or social equality or equality in respect to education, health care, police protection, and so on. But added to these is one that makes the achievement of a liberal consensus about equality even more difficult. Given the assumption that equality should hold in some specific respect or respects, its protection may require either equalizing everyone's oppor-tunity to achieve the benefit in question or equalizing the outcome of the efforts to make use of the opportunity. The political implications of the alternatives favored are, of course, enormous, and disagreements about which ought to be favored are at the center of current discussions about setting the liberal political agenda.

No basic value of liberalism is more closely allied with a single thinker than justice is with John Rawls. His view is developed in *A Theory of Justice* (1971) and *Political Liberalism* (1993). Since the appearance of the first book, immense interest has focused on the complex issues raised by Rawls. In response to criticisms, Rawls revised his position, and his latest views are put forward in the second book. Rawls's theory is not of justice in general but only of the distributive aspect of it. It is a powerful, complex, and subtle theory. Critical responses to it fall into three not very sharply distinguishable classes (see, for example, Daniels 1975; Kymlicka 1990; and Sandel 1982). To the first belong liberals who by and large accept the theory, although they may differ about its details. The second contains liberals who reject the theory as a whole. The third consists of antiliberals who reject both Rawls's theory and liberalism. The identification of Rawls's theory with liberalism is so strong that the rejection of the theory is often held to amount to the rejection of liberalism itself, to the indignation of anti-Rawlsian liberals.

Rawls explicitly identifies the problem to which his theory of distributive justice aims to be a solution as "the problem of liberalism": "How is it possible that there exists over time a stable and just society of free and equal citizens profoundly divided by reasonable religious, philosophical, and moral doctrines?" (Rawls 1993: xxv). These free and equal citizens are assumed to be reasonable and to want to live according to their conception of the good. They will, therefore, cooperate with one another, because they recognize both that they themselves could not live as they wish without such cooperation, and that the same is true of others.

The question is what the terms of their cooperation should be. But whatever they turn out to be, they will have to include principles that govern the distribution of primary social goods: goods that citizens may reasonably want, whatever their conception of the good may be, such as rights, liberties, income, security, and so on. These goods must be produced and protected, of course, and doing so provides benefits and imposes burdens on the cooperating citizens. The principles of distributive justice state the terms in which these benefits and burdens ought to be distributed among the citizens.

There are two such principles: "a. Each person has an equal claim to a fully adequate scheme of equal basic rights and liberties, which scheme is compatible with the same scheme for all; and in this scheme the equal political liberties, and only those liberties, are to be guaranteed their fair value. b. Social and economic inequalities are to satisfy two conditions: first, they are to be attached to positions and offices open to all under conditions of fair equality of opportunity; and second, they are to be to the greatest benefit of the least advantaged members of society" (Rawls 1993: 5–6). These principles describe an ideal. The political programs of liberalism are designed to make the actual state of affairs in imperfectly liberal societies conform more and more closely to the ideal.

Numerous liberals reject Rawls's theory, while continuing to espouse liberalism. Such critics are committed to justice and to the other basic values, but they deny that Rawls's concentration on distributive justice expresses what is essential to liberalism. Or, even if they agree on the importance of distributive justice, they disagree with the economic egalitarianism that Rawls claims distributive justice involves (see, for instance, Galston 1991: chapter 6; Matson 1983; Nozick 1976; and Raz 1986: chapter 5). But there is no disagreement among liberals about there being some basic, politically procurable minimum required for living according to any conception of a good life and about it being the responsibility of the liberal state to secure whatever that minimum is.

1.4 SOME DISAGREEMENTS WITHIN LIBERALISM

It will deepen this account of the basic values of liberalism to consider some of the main differences between versions of liberalism. Perhaps the best place to begin is with what may be identified as "classical" liberalism. This is the view that the most basic liberal value is freedom, conceived as the absence of external interference with individual activities. Freedom must be limited, of course, because one person's free activities may interfere with another person's similar activities. The classical liberal answer to the question of how these limits can be justifiably drawn is dictated by freedom itself: only those limits of individual activities that protect the opportunities of all individuals to pursue free activities are justified. The role of the government is to do what is necessary to guarantee the most extensive private sphere within which individuals are left free to make of their lives what they please.

Rights define the respects in which individuals ought not to be interfered with; equality holds among individuals in respect to their freedom and rights; justice consists in the legal protection of freedom, equality, and rights; and pluralism is the recognition that free individuals will pursue different conceptions of a good life, each of which may be reasonable and yet incommensurable with the others. This is the liberalism of Mill (1978), Berlin (1969a), Friedrich Hayek (1960), and Robert Nozick (1974), among others. There are moderate and radical versions of classical liberalism, and the more radical versions shade into libertarianism (see Lomasky 1987, Machan 1976, and Narveson 1988).

Classical liberalism has been criticized on various grounds (Gray 1969 and Ryan 1993), but the criticism that is most important to understanding different versions of liberalism focuses on the reluctance of classical liberals to go beyond freedom rights. It is argued against this reluctance that the meaningful exercise of freedom requires adequate economic resources, health care, education, security, and so forth. Equality, rights, and distributive justice must therefore be extended to protect not just freedom but also the conditions required for its exercise. Only if individuals are brought to the position where they can have an equal opportunity to take advantage of pluralism can they be said to exercise their freedom meaningfully. The version of liberalism from which this criticism follows has been called "egalitarian" by some, "deontological" by others.

The core of egalitarian liberalism continues to be autonomy. The autonomous life, however, is seen as requiring both freedom and welfare rights. It requires that individuals should be guaranteed certain basic goods that are needed for living according to any conception of a good life. The role of government, therefore, is to protect not merely freedom rights but also welfare rights. Since the resources required for equal welfare rights are unequally distributed, part of the role of government is to redistribute resources so as to assure that everyone has an equal opportunity to pursue one among the available plurality of conceptions of a good life. Such redistribution will result in curtailing the freedom rights of those who have a larger share of the goods.

The aim of redistribution, however, is not to promote any particular conception of a good life but to provide the resources that individuals need for pursuing whatever conceptions of a good life they choose. Egalitarian liberals therefore insist that the government ought to remain scrupulously neutral regarding the plurality of reasonable conceptions of a good life. The activities of the government ought to be restricted to establishing the procedures and distributing the resources that are the conditions for the individual exercise of autonomy.

Insofar as people are reasonable, they will be in favor of egalitarian liberalism because it leads to a stable political system in which individuals can best pursue their self-interest without having to fear that others in their society are so deprived of the opportunity to do likewise as to have no interest in maintaining the political system. This is the liberalism, for instance, of Bruce Ackerman (1980), Ronald Dworkin (1977a, 1977b, 1985a, 1988b), David Gauthier (1986), Alan Gewirth (1978), Thomas Nagel (1991), and Rawls (1971, 1993), to name some of its best-known representatives. Egalitarian liberalism tends to tilt toward the left, and as it does, it does indistinguishable from socialism (see Lukes 1991, Nielsen 1985, and Ryan 1993).

Egalitarian liberalism has been criticized by classical liberals for being coercive in its policy of redistribution, by socialist liberals for not being egalitarian enough, and by conservative liberals for abandoning moral standards under the guise of neutrality, but the criticism that has been most influential in shaping the development of liberalism has come from communitarians. Some communitarians are themselves liberals, but some are not. It is often very difficult to say whether a dispute between egalitarian liberals and communitarians is between two versions of liberalism or between its defenders and critics. It complicates matters further that communitarianism itself has several versions, ranging from the socialist left to the conservative right. Some representatives of this position are Ronald Beiner (1992), Alasdair MacIntyre (1984, 1988), Margaret Moore (1993), Michael Sandel (1982), Charles Taylor (1985a, 1992), and Michael Walzer (1983).

The focus of communitarian criticisms is the way in which egalitarian liberals understand autonomy. The autonomous life is thought by them to be essentially individualistic, self-interested, rational, aimed at realizing a private conception of a good life, and one of viewing other people and their own society from the vantage point of the role they play in that conception. The trouble with this understanding of autonomy, according to communitarians, is twofold: it misrepresents the moral psychology of rational agents, and it represents, at best, only a particular conception of a good life, which egalitarian liberals champion in violation of their commitment to neutrality.

On the first count, communitarians argue that the requirements of self-interest, rationality, and conceptions of a good life are not defined by autonomous agents but are the products of the moral tradition into which individuals are born and whose ideals, values, conventions, and principles their moral education inculcates in them. Moreover, self-interest is rarely conceived egoistically. Normally, agents identify with their families, friends, colleagues, ethnic groups, coreligionists, or fellow citizens. Their individuality, therefore, is not formed by self-creation but by the multiplicity of influences to which they are subject. Autonomy, on this view, consists in finding a fit between their individuality and moral tradition (Kekes 1989).

On the second count, communitarians point out that the conception of a good life held by egalitarian liberals, to whom autonomy is essential, is only one among many. The insistence on individualism, rationality, and striving for the agents' conceptions of a good life is the product of one strand in the Western tradition that has emerged from the Enlightenment. It is secular, voluntaristic, atomistic, and tinged with a strong dose of Promethean romanticism (Flathman 1992 and Taylor 1989). Egalitarian liberals mistake this conception of a good life for the good life itself. They fail to recognize that there are religious, tribal, ethnic, agrarian, hierarchical, and communal conceptions of a good life to which this, or indeed any, understanding of autonomy is not only foreign but inimical. Egalitarian liberals, therefore, cannot consistently maintain that the government ought to be neutral among conceptions of the good, for they themselves are anything but neutral about antiliberal conceptions.

Liberals of all kinds have taken these communitarian criticisms to heart. In the more recent responses there seems to be consensus that the government cannot be altogether neutral; that liberalism is not a universal human ideal but one restricted to the context of Western, prosperous, industrialized, and democratic states; that individuals are formed in essential ways by the context into which they were born and in which they have been raised; that reasonable conceptions of a good life include ties of affection and solidarity; and that the desires of rational agents do not by themselves define the goods of the agents who have them. More recent liberal thinkers interpret autonomy and pluralism, freedom, rights, equality, and distributive justice in the light of these criticisms; some examples include Galston (1991), Stuart Hampshire (1989), Will Kymlicka (1989), Charles Larmore (1987), Moore (1993), Rawls (1993), and Raz (1986).

1.5 THE CORE OF LIBERALISM

Although pluralism, freedom, rights, equality, and distributive justice are the basic values of liberalism, it must be explained why liberals attach such great importance to them. They protect individuals, but what is the protection for? They provide favorable conditions, but to what are the conditions favorable? They are constituents of or essential means to some end, but what is this end? A second way of making the force of these questions felt is to consider why liberals regard pluralism, freedom, rights, equality, and distributive justice as basic. Why, for instance, are order, prosperity, peace, security, civility, or happiness not as basic? A third way of raising the same issue is to suppose that the citizens of some liberal society are in full possession of the basic values and then to ask whether this possession is compatible with living empty, wasted, misdirected, miserable, boring, or pointless lives. And since the answer is clearly in the affirmative, it becomes obvious that however important these basic values are, something needs to be added to them to explain why they are so highly valued. This something is the true core of liberalism, the inner citadel for whose protection all the liberal battles are waged: autonomy.[8]

Autonomy is an ideal governing how people ought to go about living their lives. Liberals do not regard it as an ideal of a particular conception of a good life but as an ideal of what individuals ought to do to pursue whatever conceptions of life they regard as good.[9] Autonomy is what the basic political values of liberalism are intended to foster and protect. Autonomy is the end of which these other values are constituents or to which they are means. Contrariwise, if autonomy were impossible for some individuals—because they had a mental disorder, were debilitatingly ill, or had been irreversibly brutalized under adverse conditions—then the extent to which the basic values ought to be provided for them would be diminished by an amount proportional to their diminished capacity to attain autonomy.

The essential feature of autonomy is a specific form of control that individual agents exercise over their actions. "By autonomy," states Stanley Benn, "I understand a character trait amounting to a capacity to act on principles . . . that are one's own because one has made them so by a process of rational reflection on the complex principles and values that one has assimilated from one's social environment" (1985: 803); and according to Gerald Dworkin, "A person is autonomous if he identifies with his desires, goals, and values, and such identification is not itself influenced in ways which make the process of identification in some way alien to the individual" (1988b: 61). (See also Christman 1989; G. Dworkin 1988a, 1993; and Haworth 1986.)

Autonomy thus involves choice, but goes beyond it. Making a choice may fall short of real control because the choice may be between alternatives that are forced on the agent, the agent may not have reasonably evaluated the available alternatives, or the agent lacked sufficient understanding of the significance of the choice. Autonomy therefore requires the kind of control that involves an unforced choice among alternatives that the agent has reasonably evaluated in the light of sufficient understanding of the significance of choosing one among the available alternatives.

The nature of this kind of control may then be specified by five conditions.[10] The first condition is *the performance condition,* the agents perform actions. Actions are something that agents do for a reason, which usually involves both a motive and a goal. The motive may be said to be a desire, provided it is understood broadly. The goal is the satisfaction of the desire. Desires, broadly understood, are extremely varied: physiological and psychological, innate and acquired, pleasurable and painful, beneficial and harmful, positive and negative, important and trivial, enduring and transitory, reasonable and unreasonable, good and evil, and so forth. The agents' reasons for choosing the actions then involve the belief that by their performance the goal of satisfying the motivating desire is more likely to be achieved than otherwise.

The second condition is *the choice condition:* the agents choose to perform actions from among a number of alternatives that they reasonably believe are available. Making the choices involves the agents' reasonable beliefs in having the capacity and the opportunity to perform several of the available alternatives. It is sufficient for meeting this condition that the agents should hold the beliefs reasonably; it is not required that the beliefs be true—sufficient control exists for autonomy if the agents unknowingly choose the only actually available alternative. What matters is the agents' internal motivation to perform the actions, not whether they have the capacity and opportunity to perform some other actions.

A further consideration bearing on choice is that this condition of autonomy does not depend on the quantity but on the importance of the choices agents can make. Having ample scope for choices in trivial matters does not compensate for lacking it in important ones that seriously affect how the agents live (Taylor 1985c). The requirement of autonomy, therefore, is that agents should reasonably believe themselves to have the capacity and the opportunity to make significant choices. And significance should be understood in terms of choices that have a formative influence on the life the agents go on to live. Religious affiliation, employment, sexual conduct, political allegiance, and place of residence typically have such formative influence, whereas culinary and color preferences, the choice of teams to root for, or how to spend a vacation typically do not.

Making choices under these circumstances, however, may still fall short of autonomy because further, yet unspecified factors present in the circumstances could prevent agents from exercising sufficient control. To exclude these autonomy-defeating factors, it is necessary to impose both negative and positive constraints on choices so as to be able to distinguish between nonautonomous and autonomous ones. The next three conditions are intended to specify these constraints.

The third condition is *the unforced choice condition,* the choices are between alternatives that are not forced on the agents. This condition imposes two negative constraints on the choice condition by excluding circumstances in which a choice is made but is nonautonomous. One way in which this can happen is if the alternatives among which the choice must be made are forced on the agents, as in having to choose between persecution and conversion. The agents choose, but they can hardly be supposed to have sufficient control.

A choice that is forced in this manner does not indicate diminished control merely because it must be made between undesirable alternatives. The loss of control requires that the alternatives be undesirable not just for that agent in that situation but also for any agent in that sort of situation. The reason for this is that the alternatives between which they have to choose may be forced on agents because of the particular preferences they have cultivated and not because the alternatives themselves are intrinsically undesirable independently of their preferences. If the agents' preferences make some alternatives undesirable, then they need not have suffered a loss of control, provided they have control over their preferences. Agents may have to choose between honor and ambition, but if the ambition is too strong, then the unpleasantness of the choice indicates not loss of control but the agents' failure to exercise the control they have. On the other hand, the choice between persecution and conversion cannot be attributed to the agents' failure to exercise control, because it is a forced choice between intrinsically undesirable alternatives. Unforced choices should then be understood as choices that are not forced on agents by intrinsically undesirable alternatives.

The other negative constraint on the choice condition is that the alternatives available to the agent ought not to be restricted by moral and political values that the agents do not accept. If the available choices exclude some religious, sexual, and aesthetic practices or careers and lifestyles on the ground that they are incompatible with some values, which are not the agents' own, then the choices among the remaining alternatives are not fully autonomous. How far such exclusions actually curtail autonomy does not depend on the strength of the case for their exclusion but on how important it is to the agents that the excluded alternatives be available, if for no other reason than that the agents should be able to reject them freely. This second kind of negative constraint on the choice condition makes it evident that choices can be forced both by having intrinsically undesirable alternatives to choose between and by depriving agents of the opportunity to decide what alternatives are desirable.

The fourth condition is *the evaluation condition,* the agents have favorably evaluated the actions that they choose to perform. This condition imposes a positive constraint on the choice condition by requiring the agents to have a particular kind of reason for making their choices, if they are to be autonomous. If the agents choose to perform actions unthinkingly, without considering the consequences and without weighing the reasons for the various alternatives, then they have still made choices, but there was no reason for them. This is not to deny that there may be reasons for spontaneous actions. Actions may be spontaneous because their agents have done all the required thinking, considering, and weighing in the past, so they can now afford spontaneity. It is possible, therefore, to have reasons for actions even if they are not rehearsed at the time of acting. What is needed is for the agent to have reasons, which could be provided, even if they are not present in their minds.

These reasons, however, must be of a certain kind to qualify for autonomy. If the reason for choosing an action is that the agent is an addict
and needs a fix, then the agent has a reason but it is not sufficient for the
control that autonomy requires. The appropriate kind of reason derives
from the agents' beliefs about the kinds of desires that ought to be satisfied. A felicitous way of expressing this is that the satisfaction of the
agents' first-order desires should conform to their second-order desire to
live the kind of life in which some first-order desires are satisfied and
some others are not (see, for example, Frankfurt 1988a and Taylor 1976).
It may then be said that the evaluation condition requires agents to have
identified with, accepted, and approved the desires their chosen actions
aim to satisfy.

The firth condition is *the understanding condition,* the agents' favorable
evaluation of their chosen actions must be based on sufficient understanding of the significance of these actions. This condition strengthens
the positive constraint on the choice condition by requiring that the evaluations made by agents should take account of certain features of the
chosen actions. One of these features is that the agents should see their
actions under the aspect of objectively acceptable descriptions. A description is objectively acceptable if reasonable people who are familiar with
the context would agree with the agents' description of it. Agents' descriptions may fail to be objective because of self-deception, inattention,
delusions, self-centeredness, fanaticism, fantasy, stupidity, and so forth.
These ways of failing in objectivity are themselves chosen, unchosen, or
somewhere in between. The extent to which they are unchosen is the
extent to which the agents' lack of objectivity renders their actions nonautonomous.

Another feature is that the agents should see their chosen actions from
the perspective of their past patterns of action. The agents should be able
to say, if the need arises, whether their chosen actions continue or deviate
from their usual conduct. Are the actions characteristic for the agents,
and if they are, is their pattern one that the agents think is reasonable to
continue? If it is a deviation from the pattern, what is the reason for it,
and is the reason a good one? It is not, of course, that actions can be
autonomous only if the agents have laboriously asked and answered all
these questions. What autonomy requires is that the agents should be
alive to the significance of their chosen actions and be ready to face the
questions if there is reason to believe that they call for serious reflection.

One last feature that needs to be mentioned in this connection is the
agents' awareness of the moral standing of their chosen actions. The requirement is not that autonomous actions must be morally praiseworthy,
for morally blameworthy actions can also be autonomous. The require-

ment is not even that the moral standing of the chosen actions should be uppermost on or even important to the agents' minds, for the agents may subordinate moral considerations to others. The requirement is that agents should recognize the relevance of moral considerations to the evaluations of their actions. This requires agents to accept good and evil as one of the aspects under which the significance of their chosen actions must be viewed, even if the agents' chosen actions turn out to be evil when so viewed.

In summary, each of these conditions is necessary and they are jointly sufficient for an action to be autonomous. Agents may be said to be autonomous to the extent to which their actions are autonomous. And insofar as they are exercising the kind of control over their actions that these conditions depict, they may be said to be making autonomous choices. Since conformity to the last three conditions is a matter of degree, because the forces influencing choices and the extent of the agents' evaluation and understanding of them can be greater or lesser, agents, choices, and actions can be more or less autonomous.

These five conditions require that autonomous actions be both free and based on the agents' judgment. It may be said, therefore, that autonomy has a freedom and a judgment component. The performance, choice, and unforced choice conditions jointly form the freedom component. The evaluation and understanding conditions constitute the judgment component. Autonomous actions consequently must be free, because they must be chosen and the choices must not be forced, but free actions may not be autonomous, because the agents may not have favorably evaluated them or understood their significance.[11]

It is crucial to understanding the liberal conception of autonomy, however, that it is committed not merely to the need to conjoin the freedom and the judgment components but also to a particular view of how the judgment is to be exercised. The judgments must be the agents' own, and they must be based on the agents' critical reflection on their own choices, actions, and conceptions of a good life. This excludes the substitution of the judgment of some political, religious, moral, charismatic, or whatever authority for the agents' own. And it excludes as well the agents' judgments being based on indoctrination, compulsion, unexamined prejudice, uncontrolled passion, and the like. Autonomy requires that the agents should judge how they should exercise their freedom and that their judgments should involve the application of some standards that they have come to accept as a result of critical reflection on them and on how they should live.

Just as liberals disagree over basic values, so also do they disagree about the degree of autonomy that is required for agents, choices, and actions to qualify as autonomous. Their views range from what is perhaps the minimal requirement defended by Rawls (1993: 72–88) to a fuller one endorsed by liberal perfectionists such as Raz (1986: 369–99). The weaker the requirement is, the less it insists on the connection between autonomy, on the one hand, and truth and goodness, on the other. It is sufficient for minimal autonomy if the agents have reasons to believe that their beliefs are true and their aims are good. The requirements of fuller autonomy are more stringent: the agents' beliefs about the truth of their beliefs and the goodness of their aims must be rational. Defenders of fuller autonomy believe that there are objective standards to which beliefs about truth and goodness ought to conform and that autonomy involves at the very least a rational effort to conform to them. Defenders of minimal autonomy do not require conformity to objective standards or that the efforts to be rational should succeed.

This gap between the minimal and the fuller requirements of autonomy leaves open such obvious questions as the extent to which autonomous actions must be rational; how differences over the rationality of various desires, choices, and evaluations can be settled; what effect the vexing problem of determinism has on autonomy; how much control is needed before autonomy can be ascribed to individuals; how serious must the loss of autonomy be to warrant diminishing the rights of individuals; what is the appropriate moral and political reaction to the episodic and to the systematic misuse of autonomy; how individuals should be treated if they choose to surrender their autonomy; and so forth. These questions will be pursued in subsequent chapters in which the account of autonomy will be further developed.

These unanswered questions, however, leave untouched the agreement among liberals that all human beings have the capacity for autonomy. It is the most fundamental respect in which they are equal. It is the capacity for whose development and exercise they need freedom, the protection of their rights, and the possession of goods that distributive justice is intended to provide. It is to inspire its development and exercise and to provide it with sufficient scope that they need to have available a plurality of conceptions of a good life to endow their endeavors with meaning and purpose. And it is the fostering of the autonomous functioning of all citizens that is the ultimate purpose and justification of liberalism, its basic values, and its political programs.

The importance liberals attribute to autonomy, however, is not merely that living a good life depends on it; it is also thought to be a necessary condition of moral responsibility. For the liberal view is that people can be held responsible only for actions that are in their control: actions that reflect the agents' unforced choices, evaluations, and understanding of their significance—that is, autonomous actions. Because responsibility is an essential feature of morality, the further importance of autonomy is that morality would be impossible without it. The basic liberal values, which protect autonomy, and autonomy itself, therefore, are supposed to express not merely the essential constituents of a particular political morality but also a precondition of all morality.

The last observations will complete this interpretation of liberalism. First, the core and the basic values of liberalism cannot be treated in isolation from one another. They are interdependent in a number of ways. Pluralism requires that autonomous individuals should be able to choose freely among the many available conceptions of a good life. Human rights are defined and guaranteed by justice, and they are possessed equally by autonomous individuals. Equality derives from the capacity for autonomy that all human beings have. Justice is the distribution of goods required by autonomy, and its aim is to provide the conditions in which free and equal citizens can autonomously choose among conceptions of a good life.

The interdependence of autonomy and the basic liberal values at once reinforces liberalism and makes it more vulnerable to fundamental criticism. The reinforcement occurs because if one of these essential constituents is successfully defended, then logic compels that the others entailed by it must also be accepted. But the contrary also holds: successful criticism of any of the essential constituents tends to call into question those other essential constituents that depend on it. Liberalism should be viewed, therefore, as a coherent outlook whose justification or criticism is unlikely to be piecemeal, for the reasons successfully adduced for or against some part will tend to reverberate throughout the whole of it.

The second observation is that liberalism is a general outlook that fits its adherents no more closely than conservatism, socialism, Christianity, democracy, feminism, or rationalism fit theirs. Adherence to one of these general outlooks indicates a frame of mind, a flow of sympathy, a disposition to view matters in a certain light. To be sure, these attitudes are governed by the essential constituents of the general outlook. But these are themselves complex, open to various interpretations, and people committed to them routinely disagree about their interpretations and relative importance. It is not to be expected therefore that the interpretation of liberalism just completed will perfectly fit everyone who may be identified as a liberal. The loose fit is a consequence of the nature of the subject, not a fault of the interpretation.

This, then, is the interpretation of liberalism that will be the target of criticisms advanced throughout the book.

CHAPTER 2

The Prevalence of Evil

"Evil" is not a term that has been prominent in contemporary
philosophical ethics. . . . The notion of evil is the idea of a force
. . . not merely contrary to all that is praiseworthy and admirable
and desirable in human life, but a force which is actively working
against all that is praiseworthy and admirable. . . . If one follows
the liberal tradition of Mill, Sidgwick, G. E. Moore, and John
Rawls, one is liable to think of great public evils as a falling away
from the pursuit of justice or of the good. . . . The known suc-
cesses of the Nazi movement . . . ought to have destroyed forever
a previous innocence in moral philosophy: an innocence which
[led them to write] . . . as if it was sufficient to establish some
truth about the great goods for mankind, and then deduce from
these truths the necessary human virtues . . . and the necessary
social policies. It is not sufficient.

—STUART HAMPSHIRE, *Innocence and Experience*

It is a remarkable feature of liberal thought that it pays almost
no attention to the prevalence of evil. The topic is ignored or barely
touched on by the authors of the many books and articles surveyed in the
preceding chapter. There *are* some rare attempts by liberals to grapple
with the problem, but they are either inadequate or lead in a direction
that is incompatible with liberalism.[1] For the most part, however, liberals
labor mightily to explain why it is reasonable to increase autonomy by
realizing their basic values and political programs, but they take no account of the fact that evil is prevalent even in liberal societies. This omission would be justifiable only on the assumption that the attractions of
liberalism are sufficient to incline people to conduct themselves according to its prescriptions. But the assumption is false: much human conduct
is evil even though its agents understand what liberals tell them. It needs

23

to be explained, therefore, why people who understand liberalism often cause evil in violation of its prescriptions.

The most obvious explanation is that in human beings, morally good dispositions coexist with morally evil dispositions. If autonomy is fostered, then both good and evil dispositions are encouraged. Liberalism must therefore have two equally important aims: the positive one of pursuing the good and the negative one of avoiding evil. Each is glaringly deficient without the other. A theory of political morality must attend to both aims: it must say yes, and it must say no. Liberal thinkers, however, concentrate on saying yes and have very little to say about no. Evil is conspicuously absent from the articulated thought of liberals.

There *is* a liberal view of evil, but it is not explicit. The first task of its critic must be to make it so. This will be done by drawing out some implications of centrally important liberal beliefs, implications that consistency requires liberals to accept. This implied view will then be attributed to liberals, but it should not be supposed that liberals must consciously hold it. They are nevertheless committed to it because they hold other beliefs from which this view of evil follows. The problem for liberals is that their positive aim, as defined by their political programs, basic values, and autonomy, is inconsistent with their negative aim, which is to avoid evil.

2.1 THE PREVALENCE OF EVIL

There are some realistic treatments of evil in the history of Western political and moral thought: those of Thucydides, Aristotle, Augustine, Hobbes, Machiavelli, and Nietzsche come readily to mind. They disagree about many things, but they would have been unanimous in lambasting, each in his own fashion, but naïveté of liberalism. They would have focused on the assumption that informs liberal thought that autonomy makes the struggle for pluralism, freedom, rights, equality, and distributive justice worthwhile. They would have found absurd the liberal supposition that if the conditions were created in which individuals could act autonomously, then these individuals would cooperate with one another in a reasonable manner, as each is engaged in pursuing some conception of a good life. They would have said that alongside reason and their conceptions of the good, human beings are also motivated by unreason and evil; that reason does not always dictate right actions; and that aggression, hatred, prejudice, selfishness, cruelty, resentment, envy, greed, fear, and dogmatism are also among human motives. They would have insisted that whether autonomy is good or evil depends on the use that specific individuals in specific contexts make of it. And they would have been right.

A moment of reflection on the morality and politics of our age brings to mind mass murder, unjust wars, vicious dictatorships, concentration camps, large-scale preventable starvation and disease, oppression, rampant crime, systematic torture, and an easily expandable list of further evils. How could it be supposed by liberals that if the conditions for autonomy were made more favorable than they have been historically, then these evils would diminish rather than multiply manifold?

One answer that liberals may give is that they suppose no such thing. They will then readily acknowledge that evil is prevalent and that much of it is due to misused autonomy, and they will repudiate the charge that they are naïve about evil. This answer, however, is belied by liberal practice. If liberals did indeed accept the prevalence of evil and if they did think that much of it is caused by autonomous actions, then they could not advocate political programs and basic values that are designed to foster autonomy and yet claim to be other than naïve about the predictable increase in evil that will be the outcome of the programs they favor.

Liberals may respond in one of two ways. First, they may hold to their political programs and basic values and continue to regard autonomy as the core of liberalism but go on to claim that appropriate safeguards must be put into effect as protection against the evil consequences that result from the misuse of autonomy. Whatever these safeguards are, however, they must curtail autonomy, for how else could its misuse be avoided? But curtailing autonomy means curtailing pluralism, freedom, rights, equality, and the supposedly just distribution of goods that protect actual and potential evildoers. It also means supporting political programs required for the avoidance of evil, such as strengthening law and order, enforcing morality, and insisting on the moral education of citizens, especially young ones. And these programs, of course, go against the liberal grain. It does not help the liberal case to argue that the need for such programs is small, and so the core of liberalism and the basic liberal values are not seriously compromised by these programs. For this argument relies on denying the prevalence of evil, which alone could render small the need for the political programs that liberals find unacceptable. If liberals were to respond in this way, they would strengthen the charge of naïveté, which their response was meant to weaken.

The second way liberals may respond is by denying that the prevalence of evil is due to autonomous actions. They acknowledge then its prevalence but attribute it to nonautonomous actions, which involve compulsion, forced choices, and failures in evaluation or understanding. They concede that some evil is caused by people who autonomously do what they know is evil, but they argue that such people are rare. Liberals can then argue that the political programs motivated by the basic liberal values—ones designed to make people more autonomous—represent the best hope of decreasing the influence of nonautonomous actions, to which so much evil is due.

The second liberal response is stronger than the first, and a great deal will be said about it as the argument develops. But two problems with it should be noted immediately. If a theory of political morality is concerned with decreasing evil, as it surely must be, and if much evil is due to nonautonomous actions, then liberals cannot be right in identifying the domain of moral responsibility with the domain of autonomy. It cannot be regarded as a morally neutral or indifferent or irrelevant fact that many people habitually and predictably cause evil, albeit nonautonomously. To suppose, however, that people may be held morally responsible for their nonautonomous actions is inconsistent with the liberal understanding of both moral responsibility and autonomy. Discussion of this problem will be the topic of the next chapter.

The other problem with the second response is that if the prevalence of evil were correctly attributed to nonautonomous actions, the question would still remain, Why are autonomous actions supposed to be less likely to cause evil than are nonautonomous ones? Why should vices be less likely to flourish under conditions in which autonomy is fostered by pluralism, freedom, rights, equality, and distributive justice than they would be under conditions in which virtues are encouraged and vices suppressed by political programs that liberals would find unacceptable? Why suppose that if actual or potential evildoers were provided with the opportunity and resources to act as they please, they would then go against their evil dispositions and start acting benignly?

These questions are the topic of this chapter. The significance of the prevalence of evil in the present context is that liberalism appears to be driven to respond to it either in ways that are inconsistent with its positive aim or by denying the undeniable fact of its prevalence.

2.2 UNDERSTANDING THE PREVALENCE OF EVIL

Evil is the most severe condemnation contemporary moral vocabulary allows. Murder, torture, enslavement, prolonged humiliation, and preventable starvation are some examples of it. Evil must involve harm, which must be serious enough to damage its victims' capacity to function normally. Furthermore, the harm must be unjustified, because not even serious harm is in itself necessarily evil, as it may be just punishment for crimes committed or the means of preventing even greater harm. What harm can be justifiably inflicted is one of the fundamental questions of moral philosophy, but one that need not be considered here.

Evil may be the product of human or nonhuman agency. Inclement weather that causes crop failure and widespread starvation is an example of the latter, and it is usually described as natural evil. Evil caused by human beings, such as torture of an innocent person, is moral evil. This traditional distinction between natural and moral evil is useful but should not be drawn too sharply, because human beings may be agents of natural evil, as carriers of a disease, for instance, and evil caused by nonhuman agency may warrant moral opprobrium, if it was preventable and those responsible for doing so were negligent. Moral and political thinking nevertheless tends to focus on moral evil, since it is much more likely to be within human control than is natural evil.

The primary subjects to which moral evil ("evil" from now on, unless otherwise indicated) may be ascribed are human actions. Mental states, choices, agents, and institutions may also be evil, but only in a derivative sense. For mental states and choices are evil if they are likely to lead to evil actions; agents are evil if most of their actions are evil; and institutions are evil if they regularly prompt agents representing them to perform evil actions. In its primary sense, therefore, evil is essentially connected with human actions that cause serious, unjustified harm to human beings.

The evil actions of human agents may be rare episodes in the lives of otherwise decent people, or they may be predictable parts of a disposition that is characteristic of the agents whose actions they are. In the latter case, the disposition is a vice, such as selfishness, cruelty, dogmatism, and envy. Agents with vices may or may not be evil, for they may also have virtues, and their virtuous actions may be more numerous and significant than their vicious actions. If, however, agents are dominated by their vices, then they are wicked. Wickedness is a state of character in which the agents' vices overwhelm such virtues as they may have and result in habitual patterns of evil actions. There are extreme cases of wickedness in which agents do not merely cause evil habitually and have characters dominated by vices but also knowingly and deliberately cultivate their vices in order to perform evil actions: such agents are moral monsters.

The extent to which agents are wicked, possess vices, and perform evil actions is a matter of degree. There is no clearly definable threshold that, if crossed, would make an action evil, a character trait a vice, or an agent wicked. Clear cases of wickedness, vice, and evildoing exist, of course, but not all cases are clear. But these complications are irrelevant for present purposes because the argument is about the prevalence of indisputable cases in which actions cause serious, unjustified harm, the disposition to perform such actions is habitual, and the agents' characters are dominated by such dispositions.

That evil actions are prevalent and that they are responsible for much of human suffering is clear. To the question of why this is so, the obvious answer is that human beings are motivated by their vices, from which evil actions follow. But this is unilluminating, unless it is explained why human beings possess and act on vices.

The philosophically most influential explanation is embedded in the Socratic paradox that no one does evil knowingly (see Irwin 1977: chapter 3; and Vlastos 1991: chapter 5). The thought behind the apparently obvious falsehood of this claim is that human agents are normally guided in their actions by what seems to be good to them. The explanation of evil actions must therefore be either that the agents are ignorant of the good and perform evil actions in the mistaken belief that they are good, or that if they know what the good is and they nevertheless do evil, then it is because accident, coercion, or some incapacity interferes with their pursuit of what seems to be good to them. The Socratic view is that knowledge of the good will lead to seeking it, and if it does not, then there must be some interference with the knowledge or with the action. The explanation of specific evil actions must therefore be sought in lack of knowledge or in lack of choice.[2]

There are other explanations of evil (see Kekes 1990), but they will not be discussed here because liberals have shown no inclination to accept them. The Socratic explanation, however, is most congenial to liberalism. It attributes evil actions to ignorance and proposes as a remedy the improvement of knowledge and the protection of choice from outside interference, which, in liberal language, is but the strengthening of autonomy. Liberals nevertheless would be ill advised to accept the Socratic explanation, partly because it is driven to a metaphysical assumption about the nature of reality and its effect on human aspirations that is incompatible with liberalism and partly because of its intrinsic defects.

The metaphysical assumption that is troublesome for liberals is that since human experience of the world testifies to the falsehood of the Socratic explanation, because knowledge of the good often seems to be combined with deliberate evil actions, the disclosures of experience could only be of appearances, not reality. It must therefore be assumed, first, that underlying the human experience of the messy world that appears to belie the Socratic explanation is a suprasensible true reality in which a moral order prevails and, second, that good lives for human beings depend on knowing and living in conformity to this order rather than being led to deviate from it by deceptive appearances. Only if this two-part assumption were true would it follow that evil actions, which are contrary to the moral order, are due to lack of knowledge. Socrates explains evil, therefore, as a deviation from the good due to a human defect in knowledge, a defect that involves mistaking appearance for reality.

The explanation of evil implied by this metaphysical assumption has passed from Greek thought to Christian theology chiefly through the works of Saint Augustine and Thomas Aquinas. Christianity attributes to an all-knowing, all-powerful, all-good God the creation of the moral order that permeates reality, and it explains the prevalence of evil by the corrupting influence of original sin, which leads human beings to choose evil over the good and thereby willfully or weakly pit themselves against God's moral order. Although Christian thinking about evil has deeply influenced Western thought between the Greeks' time and the present, it nevertheless must be seen, ignoring some twists and turns of theological sophistication, as an adaptation of the metaphysical assumption and explanation of evil that was first advanced by Socrates.

This metaphysical assumption, however, cannot be reasonably maintained in the light of well-known objections to it. These objections can be stated here without elaboration, since liberals themselves tend to voice them in the course of resisting religious orthodoxy. First, any evidence that may be cited in favor of the supposed existence of a moral order in a supposed suprasensible reality beyond the world as it appears to human observers must be derived from the world as it appears to human observers. Such evidence, however, cannot reasonably be taken to point to any suprasensible order in reality because the most such evidence can imply is that human knowledge of the world as it appears is limited and fallible. It is logically impossible for evidence to support inferences about what may lie beyond available evidence.

Second, if defenders of the metaphysical assumption nevertheless pursue their speculations, then they must recognize that as the existence of a moral order in suprasensible reality is inferred from observed instances of apparent goodness, so the existence of an evil order in suprasensible reality must be analogously inferable from observed instances of evil. There is no more reason to think of evil as deviation from the good as there is to think of the good as deviation from evil.

Third, even if it were assumed for the sake of argument that the first two objections fail, the metaphysical assumption would still be indefensible, because it would account solely for moral evil, caused by human negligence, and not for natural evil, such as the scarcity of necessary resources, disasters, and disease, whose occurrence can only exceptionally be attributed to human agency.

Lastly, the metaphysical assumption fails to account for moral monsters who make it a policy for themselves to do evil knowingly and who deliberately cultivate vices in themselves. They do evil not because they mistake it for the good but precisely because it is evil. They are hostile or indifferent to the aspiration to make human life better rather than worse. Moral monsters, to be sure, are rare, but their existence is sufficient to show that the Socratic claim—no one does evil knowingly—is not only paradoxical but also false.

If the Socratic explanation of the prevalence of evil fails, then the question of why evil is prevalent stands. Liberals have a vested interest in answering it because unless they do so their positive and negative aims appear to be inconsistent. If evil is prevalent, as it is, and if liberals are committed to making it less prevalent, as they are, then how could they avoid the objection that their political programs designed to enhance pluralism, freedom, rights, equality, and distributive justice, and, through them, autonomy will make evil more rather than less prevalent by removing curbs on the conduct of evildoers? Liberals may answer this question in one of two ways.

2.3. THE PREVALENCE OF EVIL AS DUE TO AUTONOMOUS ACTIONS

The first answer attributes the prevalence of evil mainly to autonomous actions that have gone morally astray. This commits liberals to the supposition that there are many people who often make unforced choices among alternative courses of action, they perform the actions they have favorably evaluated and whose significance they have understood, and their habitual actions are evil. Such people thus knowingly, intentionally, and frequently act in evil ways. It is an implication of this answer that there must be many people of this kind, otherwise the prevalence of evil could not be due to them.

What could lead astray the agents of these autonomously evil actions? One possibility is that they are moral monsters who take satisfaction in causing serious, unjustified harm to others. They may be murderers, torturers, dictators, enforcers, thieves who doom their victims to starvation and disease, and similar wicked specimens. They make it a policy for themselves to acquire knowledge of evil and to choose to act on it. The psychological sources of this policy may be violent hatred, passionate indignation, thirst for power, self-loathing projected outward, cynicism, destructiveness, and so forth. Behind these forms of misanthropy may be real or imagined injustice, keenly felt personal shortcomings, lifelong brutalization, or extreme selfishness.

Moral monsters, however, are surely rare, probably rarer than moral saints, because monsters not only must have as clear vision, great strength of character, and exceptionally strong sense of purpose as do saints but must also hide from others their true nature, since public opinion is generally disposed to favor the good. Being a moral monster, therefore, is very difficult, so few people can be supposed to become monstrous and continue in the same state. Thus it would be implausible to attribute the prevalence of evil to these few, rare moral monsters.

Another possibility is that people do evil autonomously because they systematically subordinate moral to other commitments. These other commitments may be to personal, political, religious, or aesthetic projects. When their commitments require them to do evil, they knowingly and deliberately do it. Their justification is that living according to their commitments is more important than avoiding evil. They are self-centered and fanatical, see themselves as the instruments of their gods, or are aesthetes who have grown cruel in their indifference to humanity. In one way, they are like moral monsters because both do evil autonomously; but in another way, they are unalike because moral monsters do evil because it is evil, whereas these people do it for some other reason. They may be more or less wicked, depending on what virtues they have in addition to their vices, how their virtues and vices are balanced, and on how much evil they actually cause.

The first liberal answer, then, is that the prevalence of evil is due to such people. What must be done to make evil less prevalent is to stop them from subordinating moral to other considerations. But stopping them cannot be a matter of calling their attention to a mistake they have made, for these evildoers do not think that they have made a mistake. They know all the relevant facts, they know about the requirements of morality, and they have decided that some personal, political, religious, or aesthetic consideration justifies them in systematically violating the requirements of morality. To say to them that they should not do so is not going to alter their conduct because they have been persuaded by the personal, political, religious, or aesthetic reasons they can cite that their evil conduct is justified. Given that liberals are committed to making evil less prevalent and that the prevalence of evil is due to autonomous actions, liberals must be prepared to coerce autonomous evildoers so as to curtail their evil actions.

This curtailment, however, is not one that liberals could accept and still remain faithful to their political programs, basic values, and to increasing autonomy. For if the prevalence of evil were due to autonomous actions, then evil could be made less prevalent only by curtailing the actions that cause it. Because it is, by hypothesis, autonomous actions that do so, curtailing evil requires curtailing pluralism, freedom, equality, rights, and distributive justice, the values that make autonomously evil actions possible. The curtailment of these basic values would have to be considerable, given that the autonomous actions to which the prevalence of evil is supposed to be due must also be supposed to be numerous so as to account for its prevalence.

It is therefore a consequence of this answer that if a liberal society wishes to curtail the prevalence of evil that exists in it, then it must be committed to *decreasing*, rather than increasing, the autonomy of many people living in it, and thus decreasing, rather than increasing, the extent to which freedom, equality, rights, pluralism, and distributive justice prevail. And this decrease will be great, not small, because evil is not rare but prevalent.

Thus if this answer were accepted, the negative aim of liberalism—making evil less prevalent—and its positive aim—fostering autonomy by fostering freedom, equality, rights, pluralism, and distributive justice—would be inconsistent with each other. If the prevalence of evil were due to autonomous actions, then more autonomy would make evil more prevalent and making evil less prevalent would require less autonomy. In that case, a society committed to making evil less prevalent could not be liberal; and if it were committed to increasing autonomy by increasing freedom, equality, rights, pluralism, and distributive justice, then it would make evil more prevalent. Liberals would be well advised therefore to reject this first answer.

2.4 THE PREVALENCE OF EVIL AS DUE TO NONAUTONOMOUS ACTIONS

According to the second answer liberals may give, the prevalence of evil is due mainly to nonautonomous actions. Although they conform to the freedom component of autonomy, these actions are nonautonomous because they violate its judgment component. The thought behind this answer is that the prevalence of evil largely results from actions that their agents perform by choosing one among several alternatives that have not been forced on them, but the agents fail to evaluate or to understand the significance of the alternatives they freely choose. They do evil, but they do not see what they do *as* evil. They see their actions under some other description, and their misperceptions are due to a kind of cognitive failure.

This answer, of course, is a contemporary and attenuated version of the Socratic dictum that no one does evil knowingly. People are cruel but see themselves as just; they are dogmatic but believe themselves to be principled; they are greedy but it seems to them as taking their fair share; they are prejudiced but appear to themselves as objective about their wretched victims. They are, therefore, not moral monsters but moral idiots. They fail to see what they ought to see and what they would see if their vices did not cloud their vision. This is what led Hannah Arendt (1964) to speak about the banality of evil. There is nothing heroic about the agents of most evil actions; they do not adopt the maxim of Milton's

Satan: Evil, be thou my good. They banally mistake evil for good because they are morally deficient.

According to this answer, human motives are mixed, and human begins are complex. They are moved by both good and evil. Virtues coexist and conflict with vices. The inner life of the overwhelming majority of human beings is a struggle in which selfishness, cruelty, greed, envy, hatred, and so forth, on one side, and love, decency, pity, kindness, and so on, on the other side, are the soldiers of the ignorant armies, clashing in the dark. The sources of evil are such people: wicked in some ways and in some circumstances, virtuous in others; people like most of us. They are the agents of evil and of the good, and they act one way or another, depending on their imperfect knowledge, mixed motives, unclear aims, and on the pressures exerted on them by the historical, political, cultural, and other forces to which they are subject.

These agents do not pursue evil as a conscious and deliberate policy. They certainly do evil, but they mistake the moral standing of their actions. In a sense, they know what evil is because they can recognize it in others and may be brought to recognize it even in themselves. Moreover, they choose their evil actions, since they perform them uncoerced in circumstances where they could act otherwise. But they do not see their actions as evil because something intrudes between their general knowledge of evil and the recognition that their actions fall under it. Their own cruelty is seen by them as healthy ambition, selfishness as doing what is necessary to win in the competition of life, hatred as well-merited contempt, envy as just indignation, or fanaticism as consistency. They know that cruelty, selfishness, hatred, envy, and fanaticism are evil, but they do not know that their actions exemplify these evils. And they do not know it because early deprivation, self-deception, brutalizing experiences, fantasy, egocentrism, or a deep sense of inferiority or superiority prevents them from seeing the true nature of their actions.

Such people are like those who subordinate moral to other considerations, but they are also unlike them because they do not do so autonomously. Those who do evil autonomously know perfectly well what they are doing, but these agents do not because they have made a mistake in understanding or evaluating their own conduct. They thus cause evil nonautonomously because they have violated the judgment component of autonomy. Some people act in this way habitually and predictably, others only episodically. The former are wicked, the latter are merely prone to act wickedly in some circumstances. The second liberal answer, then, attributes the prevalence of evil to the nonautonomous wickedness of those many agents who habitually preform evil actions, although they mistake the nature of their actions. They know in general what evil is, but they do not bring that knowledge to bear on the particular actions they perform.

To make this discussion of nonautonomous wickedness more concrete, consider some familiar forms of nonautonomous wickedness. Take a particular kind of dogmatism first. People who are dogmatic in this way have a strong commitment to moral principles and act according to them, but their principles are mistaken. If they were more independent-minded and inquiring, they might discover that their principles are faulty, but, as a matter of fact, they have not developed the required critical faculty. Such dogmatists may cause great evil if they come to believe that some groups or individuals live in gross violation of their mistaken principles. For they may suppose, then, that the violators are guilty of grave offenses and deserve the serious harm these dogmatists knowingly cause them. Dogmatists may acknowledge that they are causing harm, but they believe, sincerely and yet falsely, that it is justified as punishment, corrective, self-defense, or the imposition of discipline.

An often found reason why dogmatists come to hold their mistaken principles uncritically is that they have been brought up to hold them, the same is true of everybody in their context, and such doubts as they have are allayed by the authorities whom they have been taught to respect. It often happens that people live in societies inhospitable to critical reflection on the prevailing morality. The habit of questioning need not be defensively discouraged; rather, there may be no scope for questioning, because the morality, which to outsiders may appear as pernicious, is simply taken for granted by them and by everybody who counts. Holding these mistaken principles and acting according to them is an essential part of their identity and sense of belongingness to society. The respect they give and receive, their moral status and moral judgments, and their own appraisals of themselves are all inseparably tied up with their pernicious principles. Such were the circumstances of many slave owners in the antebellum South, of just about everybody during the sixteenth-century European witch craze, of Crusaders slaughtering Muslims, of Muslims waging holy war against infidels, of the champions of the institution of judicial torture in medieval Christendom, and of numerous Nazis and Communists.

It can hardly be denied that the actions of dogmatic people may cause evil. But their dogmatism results from insufficient development of the capacity to evaluate their actions and understand their significance. Since autonomy requires conformity to the evaluation and understanding conditions, it must be concluded that such evil actions and the vices from which they sprang are nonautonomous. They conform to the freedom component of autonomy, but they violate its judgment component.

Another form of wickedness is a kind of insensitivity. Its agents are temperamentally cold and unimaginative about the suffering of others. Perhaps they are themselves stoical, ascetic, have a high pain threshold, and, not being perceptive, expect everyone to be like them. When they witness signs of pain, elicited by what they regard as insufficient cause, they treat them as signs of weakness to which people should not succumb. Their reaction to evil is thus often contempt for its victims. Imagine such people in intimate relationships in which others expect, and are entitled to expect, their sympathy, help, and understanding. They may be parents, teachers, spouses, friends, or lovers. When confronted with evil done to their intimates, they just do not see it as evil. But insensitivity can also actively cause evil because its agents do not understand that their conduct causes evil. If they understood it, they would not cause it, but they cannot understand it because they lack the sensitivity to recognize that others are vulnerable where they are not. And so they become those archetypal figures: the stern and unforgiving father, the teacher with unsatisfiable demands, or the most dangerous traitor of all, the intimate enemy who knows and condemns the vulnerabilities of his or her inmates.

Insensitivity is a vice because it regularly causes evil. But it is often nonautonomous because, like dogmatism, it does not conform to the evaluation and understanding conditions of autonomy, thus violating its judgment component. The source of this failure is the poverty of the agents' emotional lives as a result of genetic or hormonal causes or of upbringing and circumstances unconducive to the development of character traits required for sensitivity, such as being imaginative, attentive, perceptive, or objective. Yet the evil that insensitive people may cause is not diminished by their lack of autonomy.

Ruthlessness is another form of wickedness. In the normal course of events, people live their lives in accordance with some conception of what would make them good. Ruthlessness is the vice of pursuing these conceptions without regard for the evil that may result. Ruthless people are hell-bent on success. They encounter obstacles, but they do what is necessary to overcome them. As a result, they often end up causing serious, unjustified harm to those who have the misfortune to be the obstacles in their paths.

Ruthlessness is nonautonomous if its agents fail to understand the moral significance of their own conduct. They see their situation under the description of working to achieve their goals. They do not intend to exploit, humiliate, maim, or ruin people in their way, yet when their actions produce these by-products, they take as little cognizance of them as a bulldozer does of the wildlife in its way. If their attention is called to the evil they cause, their response is a shrug. If forced to explain, they talk about the importance of their goals. They do not set out to harm others, they do not enjoy doing so, but they do not care either. They just do what is necessary. Their strong commitment to their goals provides them with a rationale for conducting themselves as they do. If people did not act in this manner, they claim, nothing would ever be accomplished. Add to this that the goals they pursue may be approved by their society and that there may be a tradition of pursuing them, and then they will be the recognizable executives, politicians, soldiers, artists, and athletes who fall into this pattern.

Dogmatism, insensitivity, and ruthlessness are some forms of nonautonomous wickedness. There are many others (see Benn 1985; Kekes 1990; and Milo 1984). Their significance is that the answer they call for to the Socratic question of whether wicked agents do evil knowingly is that in a sense they do but in another sense they do not. They know what evil is and they know what they are doing, but they do not connect these two pieces of knowledge. The lack of connection is both general, affecting their knowledge of the true character of their patterns of action, and particular, concerning the moral standing of the specific actions that constitute the patterns. Socrates was right, therefore, in seeing that full knowledge is lacking in the case of nonautonomous wickedness, although he did not see that autonomously wicked agents do evil with full knowledge of what they are doing. Socrates, however, was also wrong because he supposed that to the extent to which agents possess knowledge of evil, it will motivate them to avoid it. Both autonomous and nonautonomous wickedness involve knowledge of evil, and yet the knowledge does not motivate the agents who possess it to avoid evil, for an alternative and overriding source of motivation exists, which makes them dogmatic, insensitive, ruthless, or wicked in some other way.

These forms of nonautonomous wickedness, and many others as well, develop in the same way. There are agents with reasonable and morally acceptable conceptions of a good life, to which they are strongly committed. They are also committed to observing certain moral prohibitions that rule out some ways of trying to realize their conceptions. Because of the contingencies of adverse circumstances and/or their own character defects, these two kinds of commitments come into conflict with each other. The agents must either jeopardize their pursuit of a good life or violate moral prohibitions and pursue a good life in impermissible ways. They resolve the conflict by allowing their commitment to their conceptions of a good life to override their commitment to the moral prohibitions that stand in the way. And because the contingencies that cause their conflicts persist, they violate moral prohibitions again and again. Their violations form patterns, develop into vices in accordance with which they act even in situations where the conflicts that first gave rise to them no longer persist. These agents then naturally and spontaneously act in the ways in which they were first forced by contingencies to act.

Their violations of moral prohibitions, however, are violations of some of their own moral commitments. The self-condemnations such violations warrant are painful and damaging to the agents' self-esteem. This provides them with a strong motive to present their violations to themselves in a morally acceptable light. One device they often use for doing so is the redescription of the nature of their actions. They see themselves as acting not dogmatically but in a principled way, not insensitively to the suffering of others but with disapproval of their self-indulgence, not ruthlessly but realistically. They thus become wicked, but they do not know that about themselves. Such nonautonomous wickedness is responsible for a good many of the actions that cause serious, unjustified harm and make evil prevalent.

The attractions of this explanation of the prevalence of evil are many. It is psychologically plausible; it explains how unexceptional people, such as countless Nazi and Communist functionaries, can do exceptional evil; it faces the fact that evil is prevalent; it acknowledges that it largely results from human actions; and it avoids the inconsistency between the negative and the positive aims of liberalism that is created by attributing the prevalence of evil mainly to autonomous actions.

Most pertinent for present purposes, however is what follows from this explanation about how increasing autonomy makes evil less prevalent. If the prevalence of evil is due mainly to nonautonomous actions, then, the supposition is, making actions more autonomous will makes them less evil. In particular, if much evil is caused by the agents' failure to evaluate or understand the alternatives among which they have to choose, then, it is supposed, better evaluation and understanding will improve their judgments, correct their misperceptions, and stop them from mistaking evil for good. And if this is right, then the positive liberal aim of increasing autonomy by increasing freedom, equality, rights, pluralism, and distributive justice is not inconsistent with but a necessary requirement of realizing the negative liberal aim of making evil less prevalent. Two objections render this liberal answer unacceptable, however.

2.5 THE LIBERAL PREDICAMENT

The first objection is that it does not follow from the prevalence of evil being due mainly to nonautonomous actions that if more actions were made more autonomous, then evil would be made less prevalent. After all, it is perfectly possible that even if the agents whose actions are responsible for the prevalence of evil evaluated and understood their actions accurately, and thus stopped misperceiving their true moral status, they would continue to act the same way as before. Their reaction to the realization that they are dogmatic, insensitive, and ruthless rather than principled, disciplined, and realistic may just be to embrace these vices and the actions that follow from them. They have their vices because some preexisting feeling, desire, belief, hope, or fear created receptivity to them. The newly acquired knowledge that their character traits are vices, not virtues as they previously believed, need not by itself motivate them to change their character. They may just shrug and say to themselves, That is how I am. And even if they were motivated by their new knowledge to change themselves, the force of that motive may not be sufficient to defeat the contrary forces of the preexisting motives that made them receptive to their vices in the first place; especially not, since their vices are habitual by their very nature. Making nonautonomous actions autonomous, therefore, may leave evil just as prevalent as it had been before.

To render this answer plausible, liberals must further suppose that autonomy is incompatible with evil, that autonomous actions tend to be good, and that evil actions are usually due to lack of autonomy. Only if this were so would making nonautonomous actions autonomous render evil less prevalent.

But what is the reason for the supposition that autonomous and morally good actions tend to go together and that evil actions result mainly from the lack of autonomy? The reason is the belief that if people were allowed to make choices without corrupting external influences, without having their evaluation and understanding clouded by poverty, discrimination, crime, and other social ills; if they were not brutalized, indoctrinated, or enraged by injustice; if they had the time and opportunity to think about their lives and actions, then they would do what is good and they would not do what is evil. To increase their autonomy is to decrease their openness to corrupting external influences, and it is because evil comes from these external influences that becoming more autonomous will make evil less prevalent. In other words, this answer is made plausible by the belief that people are naturally good and that they do evil because of corrupting external influences. This belief is the liberal faith, about which much will be said throughout the book. The point here is that the acceptability of the present answer depends on this faith.

That this belief is a matter of faith is shown by its being held in the face of the acknowledged fact that evil is prevalent in all known human societies. The fact is explained by there being insufficient autonomy. Its insufficiency, however, is not taken to indicate anything adverse about human nature. Evil is supposed to be prevalent because societies fail to foster the autonomy of individuals who live in them.[3] The view of human nature at the core of the liberal faith is thus that human beings are by their nature free, equal, rational, and morally good. They act autonomously when they express their nature, and when they act contrary to their nature, it must be because they are subject to nonautonomous influences.[4]

The liberal faith, however, is indefensible for several reasons. First, no evidence is taken to count against it. Manifestations of both human goodness and wickedness are taken as confirmations of it: the first for obvious reasons, and the second because wickedness is regarded as evidence that institutions corrupt naturally good agents. If human beings do good, it is because they are naturally good; and if they do evil, they are still naturally good, although they have been corrupted.

Liberals who hold this faith are in a position that in some respects is strikingly similar to that of many Christians. As many Christians believe that evil is due to human beings and not to God, so many liberals believe that evil is due to institutions and not to human beings. As many Christians base their belief on what they take to be the nature of God, so many liberals base their beliefs on what they take to be human nature. And as these Christians have to contend with the problem of evil, so these liberals have to contend with its secular version.

Second, the assumption that the prevalence of evil results from evil institutions ignores the obvious question of how institutions become evil. Whether institutions are evil depends on the human agents who create and perpetuate them. If human agents are naturally good, then how could the institutions they create and perpetuate be evil? If the moral status of human actions depends on preexisting institutions, then how could preexisting institutions be improved or better institutions be established? If human agents are as much at the mercy of institutions as these liberals suppose, then how could liberals themselves have escaped being influenced by evil institutions to an extent sufficient to diagnose their evil? If it is possible to escape the evil influences of evil institutions, then how could continued adherence to them not have something to do with the preexisting evil dispositions of the participating agents? And were *those* dispositions also the products of evil institutions? And if they were, how did *those* institutions become evil?

Third, the liberal faith is not merely unsupported by the available facts but inconsistent with them as well. The facts are that evil is prevalent in all human societies; the vices of selfishness, greed, malevolence, envy, aggression, prejudice, cruelty, and suspicion motivate people just as the contrary virtues do; and both virtues and vices may be autonomous or nonautonomous, natural and basic, or the products of external influences. It would be as implausible to claim that these facts testify to human wickedness as it is to base the faith in human goodness on them. If the facts warrant any inference, it is that human beings are morally ambivalent.

The liberal faith, however, flatters humanity by painting a rosy picture of wonderful possibilities, while neglecting the hard facts that it cannot accommodate. It is a sentimental falsification that substitutes illusion for reality. It cannot therefore provide the justification that liberals need for increasing autonomy and for regarding freedom, pluralism, rights, equality, and distributive justice as basic values.

Liberals may deny that they are committed to this faith. They may concede that some naïve liberals in the past may have been so committed, but go on to claim that liberals do not need it now and that they can be as hardheaded about the facts of evil as anyone else. In that case, however, liberals owe a reason for supposing that by increasing autonomy they will succeed in making evil less prevalent. If evil actions were mainly autonomous, then increasing autonomy would make evil more prevalent, so this explanation cannot be what liberals need to provide. If, on the other hand, evil actions were mainly nonautonomous, then liberals must still explain why increasing autonomy would make evil less prevalent. The liberal faith was the old explanation, but if liberals disavow it, if they do not believe that human beings are naturally good, if they believe that human motives are mixed and that virtues and vices may both be natural and basic, then they cannot suppose that increasing autonomy will give greater scope to virtues and smaller scope to vices. If they really do not hold the faith in human goodness, then they ought to believe that increasing autonomy will result in making evil more prevalent.

Liberals are thus left with a choice between two alternatives, both unacceptable to them: they can maintain their commitment to increasing autonomy, with or without the liberal faith, which will result in the frustration of their negative aim of making evil less prevalent; or they can acknowledge that autonomy must be curtailed to curtail evil, which will result in the frustration of their positive aim of increasing autonomy by increasing freedom, equality, rights, pluralism, and distributive justice through their political programs.

Suppose, however, that this first objection can somehow be met. Perhaps the liberal faith is not indefensible, or perhaps there is some other way of showing that the more autonomous actions are, the less evil they will be. Even if this were so, there would still be another objection to the liberal answer that the prevalence of evil is due mainly to nonautonomous actions. Assume for the sake of argument that this answer is correct. It follows from it that if nonautonomous actions were made autonomous, then evil would become less prevalent. The objection is that there is a reason, quite different from the groundlessness of the liberal faith, that vitiates this liberal supposition.

The background of this supposition is a society in which evil is prevalent because many people living in it are acting nonautonomously. The way to the moral improvement of the status quo is to make these people's actions more autonomous, which requires putting people in a position to improve their evaluation and understanding of the alternatives among which they can choose. The liberal policy that will supposedly accomplish this end is to provide more freedom, equality, rights, pluralism, and distributive justice than was available before, for the greater availability of these basic liberal values is a condition of greater autonomy. Suppose that this was done. What would happen in that society?

Before the liberal policy was put in place, evil was prevalent. Then the liberal policy is implemented and evildoers, of whom there must be many if evil is prevalent, are given more freedom, greater equality, stronger rights, a richer plurality of options, and more resources through improved distributive justice. Is it not obvious that the result would be that evil becomes more prevalent? The liberal policy involves weakening existing curbs on people's conduct. How could this not lead to giving greater scope to evil actions? Admittedly, the curbs were not particularly effective before, but weakening them further will surely not alter the vices that lead people to perform evil actions. The liberal policy will just make it easier for people to act on their vices.

Liberals will indignantly reject this criticism. They will say that no reasonable liberal ever supposed that freedom, equality, rights, pluralism, and distributive justice should be provided without qualification. They will point out that the liberal tradition has always been centrally concerned not just with increasing individual autonomy but also with protecting the potential victims of the misuse of autonomy. Increasing autonomy by increasing the freedom, equality, rights, pluralism, and distributive justice enjoyed by individuals must go hand in hand with preventing individuals from interfering with the exercise of autonomy by others. Autonomy, liberals will say, is not license to do whatever individuals please but to pursue a reasonable conception of a good life in a way that does not hinder others from doing likewise.

That this concern has been and is an abiding one of liberals is, of course, true. What has not been realized is the implication the prevalence of evil has for it. If evil is acknowledged to be prevalent and if the liberal faith is not held, then it must also be acknowledged that making nonautonomous evil actions autonomous will make evil more rather than less prevalent because it will give greater scope to evil actions. To prevent this from happening, liberals must be prepared to curb both nonautonomously and autonomously evil actions. If evil is prevalent, these curbs will have to be considerable. And their imposition, maintenance, and enforcement amount, of course, to a policy of decreasing autonomy, freedom, equality, rights, pluralism, and distributive justice for evildoers.

If evil is prevalent, evildoers must be numerous. It is to be expected, then, that in a liberal society there will be a moral minority whose actions are morally acceptable and for whom autonomy, freedom, equality, rights, pluralism, and distributive justice are guaranteed, while the remaining immoral majority, to whose actions the prevalence of evil is due, will have their evil conduct curbed. Such a society is, of course, radically at odds with what liberal rhetoric promises. But if evil is prevalent, there seems to be no reasonable alternative.

If liberals took the prevalence of evil seriously, they would have to stop advocating policies that weaken rather than strengthen existing curbs on evil conduct. In fact, however, liberals continue to advocate their policies as if evil were not prevalent. The fundamental reason for this is that they fail to see the inconsistency between their negative aim of making evil less prevalent and their positive aim of increasing autonomy by increasing freedom, equality, rights, pluralism, and distributive justice. It is true that liberals can point to their traditional and contemporary commitment to both aims. Their inconsistency, however, makes the joint realization of these aims impossible.

There are two further lines of defense that liberals may try to maintain and whose inadequacy needs to be shown. The first is to concede that autonomy cannot be defended as *the* core of liberalism, which would not mean that liberals must cease to value autonomy, only that they could no longer rely on it to provide the fundamental reason why freedom, pluralism, rights, equality, and distributive justice are to be regarded as the basic values. They may then add autonomy to these other basic values, thus demoting it from the privileged position it was previously thought to occupy. They would thereby concede that increasing autonomy need not have priority. They could then acknowledge that making evil less prevalent could on occasions require curtailing autonomy. They could argue that what has priority is to create a society in which there is as little evil and as much autonomy, freedom, pluralism, rights, equality, and distributive justice as possible. And they could consistently hold that working to realize both their negative and their positive aims may well require curtailing any one of the basic values in order to increase the chances of their joint realization.

This view is reasonable but liberals could not adopt it. If autonomy were removed from its privileged position, then liberals would need a new answer to the question that they previously answered in terms of autonomy, that is, Why regard the values that liberals favor as basic? The previous answer was that they are necessary for increasing autonomy and increasing autonomy must have priority in a liberal society. But if increasing autonomy no longer has priority, then why regard autonomy, freedom, pluralism, rights, equality, and distributive justice as basic values?

The point, of course, is not to express doubts about the importance of these values but to express doubts about these being the *only* or the *most basic* values. Why are prosperity, order, civility, peace, a healthy environment, security, happiness, and law-abidingness not as important as those thought of by liberals as basic? The answer can no longer appeal to the contribution that basic liberal values make to autonomy, but perhaps it could appeal to their contribution to good lives.

That the basic liberal values are important to good lives cannot be reasonably denied. The problem for liberals is that the same can be said of many other values that liberals do not regard as basic. In fact, thinking about values as basic commits liberals to holding that when they conflict with such other values as those listed above, then the basic liberal values should override them. But why should this be so? Why could a considerable increase in law-abidingness not justify some reduction in pluralism? Why could the preservation of peace not be worth curtailing some rights? Why could maintaining a healthy environment not be more important than some restriction of freedom? Liberals have no good answers to these questions because there are no good answers to them.

If this line of defense were adopted by liberals, they could successfully pursue their negative aim of making evil less prevalent. For this success, however, they would have to pay the unacceptable price of abandoning even their revised positive aim, which is to transform society in accordance with the basic values of autonomy, freedom, equality, rights, pluralism, and distributive justice. If they displace autonomy from the core, then they no longer have a reason for regarding these values as basic, and thus they no longer have a reason for defining their positive aim in terms of these values.

The second line of defense liberals may try to maintain is to concede that the prevalence of evil presents a serious problem for their position but to argue that all political moralities have that as an equally serious problem. They may argue that all political moralities have the negative aim of making evil less prevalent and the positive aim of transforming society to conform to whatever happen to be their basic values. And all political moralities must face the fact that their negative and positive aims may conflict, so that they could make evil less prevalent only by compromising their basic values. If this were right, it would be unfair to single out liberalism and criticize it for having a problem shared by all political moralities.

This line of defense, however, rests on a false supposition. The problem is equally serious only for political moralities whose positive aim includes the desirability of weakening the curbs on human conduct. It is only because liberalism has that as part of its positive aim that it is open to the charge that it makes evil more rather than less prevalent.

There are political moralities (such as those of Aristotle and Hobbes) that have no faith in the natural goodness of human beings, recognize that motives are naturally mixed, that human beings are no more prone to develop virtues than vices, and that human beings shape institutions just as much as institutions shape them. Such political moralities will not regard it as desirable to remove curbs from human conduct. On the contrary, they will find it advisable to strengthen the institutions that curb evil and will not commit themselves to the suicidal policy of guaranteeing the same freedom, equality, rights, pluralism, and distributive justice for agents who habitually do evil as they do for those who habitually do good. For such political moralities, the prevalence of evil will not present as serious a problem as it does for liberalism, whose defenders proceed in a contrary way. And because liberals do proceed in a contrary way, it is not unfair to blame them for their consequent inability to cope with the prevalence of evil.

The upshot of the arguments presented in this chapter is the liberal predicament: the negative liberal aim of making evil less prevalent is inconsistent with the positive liberal aim of promoting the liberal political programs, basic values, and autonomy. If liberals acknowledge the obvious facts that evil is prevalent and that much of it is caused by human actions, then they must answer the question of how evil could be made less prevalent if evildoers are encouraged by liberal political programs that increase their freedom, equality, pluralism, rights, and distributive justice and, through these, their autonomy.

The liberal attempt to attribute the prevalence of evil to autonomous actions cannot avoid the predicament because evil can then be made less prevalent only by curbing autonomous actions. If evil is prevalent, then the curbs must be correspondingly extensive. This liberal answer consequently requires decreasing rather than increasing the extent to which the basic values and autonomy are available.

If, on the other hand, liberals attribute the prevalence of evil to nonautonomous actions, then they must explain, first, why increasing autonomy would not result in nonautonomously evil actions becoming autonomously evil ones and, second, why reasonable people would adopt the suicidal policy, to which this answer commits liberals, of removing curbs on nonautonomously evil actions in order to increase autonomy. The only conceivable explanation is the faith that if people were autonomous and the basic liberal values were realized, then people's natural goodness would prevail. That faith, however, is indefensible because no evidence is allowed to count against it and the objectively viewed and readily available evidence contradicts it.

Given the failure of these answers, the liberal predicament stands. The next step in the argument, to be taken in the next chapter, is to consider whether it is possible to extract from the writings of liberal thinkers some other way of trying to avoid the liberal predicament.

CHAPTER 3

Individual Responsibility

The wrongs a man does to others correspond to the bad qualities
that he himself possesses.

—ARISTOTLE, *Rhetoric*

Consider now the position of liberals who acknowledge the
prevalence of evil, attribute it to nonautonomous actions, and believe that
the way to make evil less prevalent is by increasing autonomy through
increasing freedom, pluralism, equality, rights, and distributive justice.
The argument in the preceding chapter showed that one source of the
belief that making nonautonomous actions autonomous will make them
less evil is the indefensible liberal faith. But the belief also has another
source: that agents should be held responsible only for their autonomous
actions. Insofar as agents act nonautonomously, they do not act as responsible agents. To make nonautonomous actions autonomous is thus to
make their agents more responsible. The more responsible they are, the
more they will be open to the influence of morality and the less likely
they will be to act in evil ways.

One consequence of the identification of the domain of autonomy with
the domain of responsibility is that only autonomous actions can make
their agents wicked. On this view, the legitimate ascription of wickedness
requires that its agents be responsible for their actions. But responsible
actions must be autonomous, and according to the liberal argument, because the prevalence of evil results from nonautonomous actions, their
agents should not be called wicked and should not be held responsible.
The dogmatic, insensitive, and ruthless evildoers described in the preceding chapter certainly cause evil, but they are neither wicked nor do they
possess sufficient autonomy to be held accountable for their actions. The

46

liberal strategy is thus to deny that when evil actions are nonautonomous, then they adversely reflect on their agents. This strategy is the denial of the reflexivity of evil, and it is the topic of the present chapter.

3.1 THE LIBERAL STRATEGY

One liberal who denies the reflexivity of evil is Albert Hofstadter. He allies his position with the "Kantian image of a kingdom of ends and developments out of it," and he commits himself to the core of liberalism, autonomy: "The moral man subjects his essential individuality to the authority of what he is convinced is right. . . . He is not compelled by anything outside . . . to perform his action. The force that determines the performance is the force of his own self" (1973: 17). Against this background, he claims that in "true moral evil the actor is convinced that the norm he violates is morally right. He is convinced that he is setting himself against what he ought to do, intentionally doing what he ought not to do. Evil cannot exist . . . save in and through his active opposition to what is perceived as good and right" (5–6). He goes on to say that "this perversity of will is the essential form of evil" (8) and that this "is pure wickedness" (9). The implication is that "he who acts against the good, not realizing that it is the good he acts against, is not evil" (20) because such a person is not "an evil man acting malevolently but . . . a good man assailed by a maleficent principle that has lodged in . . . part of him" (7).

In all this, Hofstadter assumes without any supporting argument that evil is a matter of choice, understanding, and evaluation; that the less there is of them, the less there is of evil; that people cannot be wicked unless they mean to be; and thus that the essential condition of wickedness is the state of mind of the agent to whom wickedness is legitimately ascribed.

Another liberal who denies the reflexivity of evil is Stanley Benn. He says: "By 'wickedness' I mean whatever it is about someone that warrants our calling him a wicked person. It is therefore a different notion from what makes an action an evil deed, for an evil deed may be done by someone who is not wicked but only weak or misguided" (1985: 796). He distinguishes between "self-centered, conscientious, and malignant forms of wickedness" (797). Essential to the first two "is the refusal to acknowledge the moral significance of evils which one nevertheless knows or could reasonably be expected to know as evils." In these cases, the wicked agents' "responses to situations . . . are their own; theirs is the judgment, theirs the act, theirs the wickedness" (797). Wickedness presupposes autonomy because "wickedness in a person requires that he adopt an evil maxim" (803). Benn's third form of wickedness is malignity, which is what moral monsters have, so it may be ignored in the present context. What is centrally to the point, however, is why Benn thinks that "a psychopathic personality may not count as wickedness at all" (798). Such a person does evil but "he does not see it as evil, except, perhaps, in a conventional sense: This is something that I know most people do not like being done, so I had better conceal the body. But the kind of considerations that might justify and rationalize conventional disapproval can get no purchase on his understanding. . . . Such a person cannot be wicked" (799).

Like Hofstadter, Benn assumes without supporting argument that autonomy is necessary for wickedness. Benn does not think, therefore, that people who habitually and predictably cause evil, as do the previously described dogmatic, insensitive, and ruthless ones, can be called wicked if they do not "act on principles" at which they have arrived "by a process of rational reflection." Like Hofstadter, Benn does not say why this is so. Why is it mistaken to ascribe wickedness to people who regularly cause evil but have not reflected rationally on their conduct and who are unconcerned with the evil they do but are nevertheless intelligent, goal-directed agents?

A third denial of the reflexivity of evil can be found in Gary Watson's discussion of Robert Harris, a particularly callous multiple murderer. Watson provides a harrowing description of Harris' murder of two boys. He then describes, equally harrowingly, the brutalized childhood of the murderer. And then Watson agonizes: the murderer "both satisfies and violates the criteria of victimhood. His childhood abuse was a misfortune inflicted upon him against his will. But at the same time . . . he unambivalently endorses suffering, death, and destruction, and that is what (one form of) evil is. . . . [Our] ambivalence results from the fact that an overall view simultaneously demands and precludes regarding him as a victim" (1987: 275). Watson hesitates to call Harris wicked because the evil he caused was in some sense traceable to the evil that was done to him. Harris was certainly an agent of evil, but perhaps he was not an evil agent. His unfortunate personal history interrupts the progression from condemning his actions to condemning him.

But why is the evil that was done to him a reason for not condemning him as wicked? Watson eloquently and honestly answers: "The fact that [Harris's] . . . cruelty is an intelligible response to his circumstances gives a foothold not only for sympathy, but for the thought that if *I* had been subjected to such circumstances, I might have become as vile. . . . This thought induces not only an ontological shudder, but a sense of equality with the other: I too am a potential sinner. . . . Admittedly, it is hard to know what to do with this conclusion" (1987: 276).

A noteworthy feature of Watson's discussion is that almost all his attention is concentrated on what the appropriate reaction is to the murderer.
He shows great subtlety in probing our sensibility for the right response.
But he says nothing, after the murders are recounted, about the evil the
murderer caused. Two boys were brutally murdered, their future taken
away from them; their families had to endure the loss, the gory details of
the crime, and their own feelings of grief, rage, and helplessness. Such
things happen often, even in liberal societies, and they may happen to
those we love and to ourselves. In a manner consistent with liberal sensibility, Watson agonizes over the criminal and glosses over the crime.
Surely something is seriously askew here.

Just like Hofstader and Benn, Watson assumes that the legitimate ascription of wickedness depends on the autonomy of the evildoer and not
on the evil done. All three deny the reflexivity of evil, if evil actions are
nonautonomous. But why should autonomy be required for wickedness?
Why is wickedness dependent on what goes on inside the evildoers rather
than on the evil they do? Why does the absence of autonomy make it
illegitimate to condemn people as wicked if they habitually and predictably cause evil? Hofstadter, Benn, and Watson do not answer these questions. But there is an answer, and it points to an assumption about autonomy and moral responsibility that is one of the deepest sources of
liberalism.

3.2 THE REFLEXIVITY OF EVIL

Showing what is wrong with the liberal denial of the reflexivity of
evil requires a closer examination of responsibility. In uncontroversial
cases, agents autonomously perform evil actions, and they are rightly held
responsible for them. The actions meet the conditions of autonomy and
possess both the freedom and the judgment components (as described in
Section 1.5). There are also uncontroversial cases in which agents have
performed evil actions but could not rightly be held responsible because
they have acted nonautonomously. They did not choose the actions, the
choice was forced on them, or they lacked the capacity and/or the opportunity to evaluate or understand the significance of their actions.

These uncontroversial cases suggest two pairs of distinction central to
the topic of responsibility. The first is between agents and actions. Agents
are properly held responsible for their actions, but not for all their actions. One area of controversy about the ascription of responsibility concerns drawing the distinction between actions for which their agents are
responsible and actions for which they are not. The central question to
be considered in this chapter is: Is it justifiable to hold agents responsible

for the evil they habitually and predictably cause, if their actions follow from some vices constitutive of their character, but neither the vices nor the patterns of actions that follow from them are autonomous?

The reason for concentrating on this question is that (as has been argued in the preceding chapter) the strongest liberal explanation is to attribute the prevalence of evil largely to nonautonomous patterns of action. The question matters not because of a moralistic urge to find a culprit, but because the success of political programs designed to cope with evil depends on how it is answered. The liberal refusal to allow nonautonomously evil actions and vices to reflect on the moral standing of their agents makes it impossible to hold such agents responsible, thus hindering the efforts to institute political programs that would make evil less prevalent.

The second distinction is between causal and moral responsibility. Suppose that there is no doubt that a particular agent performed a particular action. There is then a sense in which the agent can be said to be responsible for the action. But this may mean simply that the agent was the pivotal link in the casual chain that has led to the action, as the recent earthquake is for the collapse of a house, or that the agent is accountable for the action, as Stalin is for the show trials in the 1930s. The first sense is "causal responsibility," and the second is "moral responsibility."[1]

Moral responsibility differs from causal responsibility in its being appropriate in its case to hold agents liable to moral judgment for their actions. What makes moral judgment appropriate in one case but not in the other is supposed to be the agents' autonomy. Autonomy is said to connect agents to their actions not only causally but morally as well. They do not merely perform their actions but also choose them without being forced, and they evaluate them and understand their significance. It is thus autonomy that distinguishes moral responsibility from causal responsibility.

This distinction may then be enlisted to defend the liberal strategy of denying that agents who cause evil habitually, predictably, but nonautonomously can be legitimately described as wicked. Such agents are only causally responsible for their actions, and so it is inappropriate to hold them liable to the moral judgment that is implied by calling them wicked. If they had caused evil autonomously, only then would it be justified to say that they are wicked.[2]

The trouble with this line of argument is that it glosses over two fundamental difficulties. The first is that moral and causal responsibility cannot be distinguished as clearly as the liberal strategy requires. If agents ought to be held liable to moral judgment only for autonomous actions, then it is important to realize that agents ultimately have no control over their possession of the capacities and opportunities on which their autonomy depends. Opportunities are provided by political, social, and economic conditions, which agents can influence, if at all, only in insignificant ways, and capacities are contingent on genetic endowments, an early environment favorable to their development, and a later life that provides contexts for their exercise. As a result, agents have ultimately only causal responsibility for their moral responsibility, and thus being an autonomous agent ultimately depends on nonautonomous factors.

The implication of this is that if liberals were right in claiming that it is illegitimate to ascribe wickedness to agents who habitually, predictably, but nonautonomously cause evil, then it would follow that it is also illegitimate to ascribe wickedness, or goodness for that matter, to agents whose actions are autonomous, since autonomous actions ultimately depend on nonautonomous factors. If the liberal argument were correct, the ascription of responsibility could never be legitimate.

It is perhaps necessary to stress that this difficulty is not due to the hoary problems raised by determinism and the ascription of moral responsibility if determinism were correct. These problems present difficulties for both liberals and their critics, so it would be unfair to tax only liberals with them. Whatever the truth about determinism, the liberal strategy is inconsistent in refusing to ascribe wickedness for nonautonomous actions, while being willing to ascribe it for autonomous actions, if autonomous actions also turn out to depend on nonautonomous factors. To avoid this difficulty, liberals must provide a further explanation of why autonomy is necessary for moral responsibility. Their attempt to do so will be discussed in the next section.

There is, however, also a second difficulty with the liberal strategy of denying the reflexivity of evil in the case of habitual patterns of nonautonomous actions. The difficulty is that their denial contradicts widely shared and strongly held moral judgments. Consider the moral standing of the dogmatic, insensitive, and ruthless agents described in the preceding chapter. Their vices lead them to cause evil habitually and predictably, but nonautonomously. They are, therefore, not to be regarded as wicked, according to the liberal strategy. Their evil actions do not reflect on them adversely because they are only causally and not morally responsible for their actions. Now consider their counterparts on the opposite end of the moral spectrum: agents who are undogmatic, sensitive, and altruistic, agents whose virtues lead them to benefit others habitually and predictably, but they too are acting nonautonomously.

The implication of the liberal strategy is that the agents of habitual evil and the agents of habitual good have exactly the same moral standing: none. Neither is liable to moral judgment because neither is acting autonomously. But what reasonable person would not think that it is morally better to be undogmatic, sensitive, and altruistic than to be dogmatic, insensitive, and ruthless? To be sure, the autonomous exercise of virtues is better than their nonautonomous exercise, but who would disagree that, autonomous or not, virtuous people are morally better than vicious people? Yet the liberal strategy commits its defenders to reject this incontestable moral judgment. What could lead reasonable and morally committed people to such absurdity? It is their acceptance of a mistaken principle. And it is this very same principle to which liberals appeal in attempting to resolve the first difficulty noted above.

3.3 THE PRINCIPLE: "OUGHT" IMPLIES "CAN"

The principle on which the liberal strategy for denying the reflexivity of evil depends is encapsulated in the formula that "ought," implies "can." It is usually interpreted as a logical principle and is criticized and defended as such. (See Gowans 1987 for seminal articles and bibliography; Gowans 1994: 77–81; and Rescher 1987: chapter 2). The criticism here proposed treats the principle as a moral one. This is a minority view of its interpretation (see, however, Brown 1977; Kekes 1986; Larmore 1987: 84–90; and White 1979). The principle derives from Kant, but it has come to be widely held by non-Kantians as well.[3]

If it is true that an agent ought to act in a certain way, the principle asserts, then it must also be true that the agent could act in that way. In other words, it is a condition of being morally responsible that the agent be able to discharge the responsibility. It follows that if it is impossible for an agent to fulfill a moral responsibility, then it is illegitimate to ascribe the responsibility to the agent. The principle thus presupposes that the agent has sufficient control over the action in question. The presence of such control is necessary for moral responsibility, whereas its absence exempts agents from it. The specifications of the required control need to be spelled out, of course, but the end product will look pretty much like the conditions of autonomy (in Section 1.5). Ought implies can, then, translates into the claim that only autonomous agents are morally responsible.

The powerful and intuitively appealing idea that lends considerable force to the principle is thus that only those agents who have the capacity and opportunity to meet their responsibility can be legitimately held to be morally responsible. This is why material objects, plants, animals, infants, and those with mental disorders are exempted from the moral responsibility to which human adults are normally subject. If this is so, then liberals can use the principal to resolve the two difficulties raised at the end of the preceding section.

The first difficulty is that liberals need to explain why autonomy is necessary for moral responsibility if autonomy ultimately derives from nonautonomous factors. The principle provides the required explanation: only autonomous agents have the capacity and opportunity to be morally responsible. The second difficulty is to explain why the ascription of moral responsibility is inappropriate for nonautonomous patterns of action. The explanation is the same: agents acting nonautonomously lack the capacity and/or the opportunity to be morally responsible. If, following the principle, it is recognized that human beings are moral agents only when they act autonomously, then the previously noted absurdity of exempting their nonautonomous actions from moral judgment disappears.

If these difficulties were removed, then the liberal strategy of denying that habitual patterns of nonautonomous evil actions warrant the ascription of wickedness to their agents would be vindicated. Liberals could then consistently acknowledge the prevalence of evil without attributing it to wickedness; the objection that autonomy, the basic values, and the political programs of liberalism foster evil would be weakened; and it could be held that the best hope of making evil less prevalent is to implement the liberal political programs, which aim to increase the scope of autonomy. The principle thus carries a heavy burden indeed in the defense of liberalism.

The principle is mistaken, however, and it cannot bear the weight liberals put on it. But the mistake is complex, not simple; it involves a misplaced emphasis. If the emphasis were not misplaced, the principle would perform a necessary and important moral task. Sound criticism of the principle, therefore, must identify its proper role by correcting its misplaced emphasis, rather than try to invalidate it. The principle is consequently mistaken only when it is used inappropriately, which means that in some contexts its use is appropriate. The initial task of criticism is thus to distinguish between contexts in which its use is appropriate and those in which it is not.

It is revealing in this connection to reflect on an assumption common to several well-known attempts to identify the precise feature whose presence justifies the ascription of moral responsibility and whose absence exempts agents from it. The obvious candidate for this feature is choice, and among others, existentialists (see, for example, Sartre 1954: especially part 4) made much of the notion of a radical choice to be a moral agent, which human beings must either accept or evade in bad faith.[4] The difficulty with this view is that radical choices may be forced, crazy, or uninformed and thus insufficient for moral responsibility.

To avoid this difficulty, it has been thought necessary to provide a finer-grained analysis of the kind of choice that is sufficient for moral responsibility. The beginning of such an analysis is the recognition that the relevant choice must involve the agents' reasoned decision to act in a particular way. This decision is among alternative courses of action that the agents believe to be open to them, and it takes the form of opting for one when the agents believe that they could have opted for another.

The problem here is that agents' beliefs may be mistaken, and the ascription of moral responsibility may still be legitimate. The reason for this is that if agents have reasonably decided to follow a particular course of action rather than what they believed were alternatives to it, they would be morally responsible even if it had been unknown to them that the alternatives they rejected were not actually available. What is supposed to matter for moral responsibility is the reasoned decision, not the availability of alternatives. Further analysis of the nature of this reasoned decision has gone roughly in three not sharply distinguishable directions.

In one, agents try to analyze the reasoned decision required for moral responsibility in terms of first- and second-order decisions. First-order decisions concern what they should do in the particular situations that confront them. Second-order decisions are about whether they should become the kind of person who makes one rather than another kind of first-order decision. First-order decisions are about what to do; second-order decisions are about what kind of person to be (see Frankfurt 1988c; Taylor 1976; and Watson 1975).

Another direction is to analyze the reasoned decision in terms of sanity, interpreted as the ability to understand and appreciate the force of reasons (Wolf 1987). Variations of this approach take moral responsibility to depend on the capacity to make and recognize judgments about the importance of reasons (Greenspan 1987) or on the responsiveness of agents to reasons for and against their actions (Fischer 1987).

Yet a further approach is to try to identify the element in reasoned decisions that creates liability for blame. To blame agents is to regard them as appropriate subjects for the reactive attitudes of others toward them. These reactive attitudes in turn are made appropriate not merely by the agents' actions but also by the agents' attitudes toward their actions, which are revealed by the nature and circumstances of their actions. Agents are thus to be blamed and are to be held morally responsible for having certain kinds of attitudes toward their actions (Bennett 1980; Scanlon 1988; and Strawson 1974c).

The assumption shared by all these attempts to identify the feature that makes the ascription of moral responsibility legitimate is that it is something *inside* the agents, something that the agents could do or have done before performing the action for which they are held morally responsible. The principle, ought implies can, is interpreted then as claiming that agents can be said to be morally responsible for doing something only if they can do whatever it is that the responsibility-warranting feature requires. The principle thus makes the ascription of moral responsibility center on psychological causes. Accordingly, it is appropriate to hold agents morally responsible for their actions only if the action was or could have been caused by the responsibility-warranting feature within themselves.

That this use of the principle is mistaken becomes obvious once it is pointed out that it leaves out of consideration an absolutely crucial moral fact. The principle ascribes moral responsibility to agents for the way in which they come to perform their actions but not for the effects their actions have on others. The principle is thus preoccupied with the causes of actions at the expense of their effects. The trouble is not that the psychological states of agents are irrelevant to their moral standing, but rather that the moral relevance of their psychological states derives from the evil these states have led the agents to cause. The principle is vitiated by this misplaced emphasis because the morally salient fact is the evil, not the manner in which it is caused. The salience of this fact is tacitly acknowledged even by this misuse of the principle, for only if evil were pivotal would it make sense to seek to assign or withhold moral responsibility for actions that cause it.

Reflection on the nature of morality will reinforce this criticism. It is common ground among those who are committed to morality and think about its nature that its ultimate purpose and justification is to prevent evil and to promote good. There are serious disagreements, of course, about what good and evil are and how they ought to be promoted or prevented, but these disagreements presuppose commitment to preventing evil and to promoting good. These moral tasks are basic, and everything else derives its moral significance from its contribution to them. It is therefore a matter of great importance to shape the character of moral agents so as to dispose them toward the good and against evil. Doing so certainly requires concentration on the psychological causes of their moral activity. What warrants that concentration, and what endows it with moral significance, however, are the good and evil effects that moral agents cause. This order of importance is lost in the principle, for it emphasizes the less important at the expense of the more important.

The principle is thus misused as a criterion for the appropriateness of moral responsibility. It mistakenly supposes that only if the psychological states of moral agents meet a certain condition if, that is, the agents are autonomous, is it legitimate to hold them morally responsible. The ascription of moral responsibility to nonautonomous agents is illegitimate. But why is autonomy important? Why should moral responsibility be made to depend on it rather than on intelligence, education, social role, experience, or whatever? Why does it matter whether agents have made unforced choices, evaluated their actions, and understood their significance?

There can be just one answer: it matters because of the evil that agents cause. (The good also matters, of course, but since the target is the liberal incapacity to deal with evil, the good is ignored.) If that is so, however, then a prior, a morally deeper, criterion exists for ascribing moral responsibility, namely, the evil effects that moral agents cause. That it is prior and morally deeper follows from it being more important to the basic tasks of morality.

The reason for holding agents morally responsible is to dispose them toward the good and against evil. Their past record and future promise in causing good and evil is what determines their moral standing. Their psychological states matter from the moral point of view because they have an effect on the moral quality of their actions. Because it focuses on psychological states, the principle leads those who accept it to lose sight of the reason why moral responsibility matters. Its defenders agonize over the extent to which agents should identify with the values on which they act, be capable of appreciating reason, and have a proper sense of the importance of what they are doing. In the course of writing specifications for the fine-tuning of agents' souls, defenders of the principle forget about reason why doing so is morally important.[5]

This theory-induced forgetfulness would not be serious if the evil that agents cause would coincide with their being in the responsibility-warranting state. But all agree that this is not so: agents cause evil both autonomously and nonautonomously, responsibly and otherwise, in particular and psychological states and out of them. So even if autonomy, responsibility, and the right psychological states were authoritatively specified, only some of the evil that agents cause could thereby be affected.

One salient fact of moral life is the prevalence of evil. Much of it is caused by human actions, but the actions are both autonomous and nonautonomous, actions over which their agents have sufficient control and those which are beyond their control. If one main task of morality is to prevent evil, then morality must be concerned with all evil-producing actions, not just with autonomous ones. The effect of the principle, however, is to place nonautonomous actions outside moral concern, thus exempting their agents from moral responsibility. Whatever restraint morality can then exercise is thereby removed from nonautonomously acting agents. This is why the principle actually fosters evil.

It has been argued in the preceding chapter that the prevalence of evil is a consequence mainly of nonautonomously acquired vices, vices that are manifested in habitual patterns of nonautonomously evil actions. When the principle makes it inappropriate to hold agents morally responsible for such wickedness, it makes morality irrelevant to much of the evil that besets humanity. Because liberals are committed to the negative aim of preventing evil, they ought not to accept this use of the principle.

3.4 TWO VERSIONS OF THE PRINCIPLE

These criticisms appear to be so obvious and damaging that the widespread acceptance of the principle cries out for an explanation. There is such an explanation, and it has two closely related aspects: the principle has a morally important use that is unaffected by the criticisms, and abandoning the principle altogether would have morally unacceptable consequences. To begin with these consequences, if the principle were abandoned, it would become legitimate to hold people morally responsible for all their nonautonomous actions. As a result, those with mental disorders or who have been brutalized would be held morally responsible for their vices and actions, even if their choices were forced, they could not evaluate their own character development and actions, and they could not understand the moral significance of their own way of being and acting.

This reversion to the barbaric practice of strict liability would be morally unacceptable (Hart 1961: chapter 7, 1968b). Surely, it will be said, it makes a difference to the moral responsibility of agents whether they could have avoided having their vices and acting on them, whether they had the capacity and opportunity to be and to act differently, and whether the evil they have admittedly caused was forced on them by circumstances they could control. If the principle were abandoned as a criterion of the ascription of moral responsibility, it would become impossible to distinguish between degrees of moral responsibility. And this would unavoidably happen if the criterion of moral responsibility were the effects of actions, rather than their psychological causes. The abandonment of the principle would make it impossible to recognize that different moral judgments may be appropriate for actions that have identical effects, depending on the choices, evaluations, and understanding of their agents.

That these consequences are undesirable must be acknowledged by all reasonable people. One measure of civilization is the extent to which strict liability is alleviated by the recognition of exempting and extenuating excuses. If the principle does indeed defend this condition of civilized life, then liberals have a very strong reason for not wanting to abandon it.

But this is not the use to which the principle is put. It is used as a criterion for ascribing moral responsibility; for determining, that is, when it is and is not legitimate to ascribe moral responsibility. The principle has another use: the one that permits recognition of exempting and extenuating excuses. When the principle is used in this other way, it determines not whether the ascription of moral responsibility is legitimate but how much moral responsibility it is legitimate to ascribe.

Two versions of the principle must therefore be distinguished. One is the legitimating version, and the other is the degree-assigning version. Both versions are sued as criteria for ascribing moral responsibility. But the legitimating version is used to determine whether the ascription of moral responsibility is at all legitimate, whereas the degree-assigning version is used to determine the degree of responsibility that is legitimate. The legitimating version is used to mark a threshold below which the ascription of moral responsibility is unjustified and above which it is justified. The degree-assigning version is used to mark gradations of moral responsibility that may justifiably be ascribed above the threshold.

To illustrate these two version of the principle, consider concrete exemplifications of the nonautonomously dogmatic, insensitive, and ruthless agents discussed in the preceding chapter. Suppose that the dogmatic agent is a sixteenth-century witch hunter whose task is to find, interrogate, prosecute, and burn witches. He is a devout Christian, convinced that witches are possessed by the devil, and sees himself as a humble servant of God in doing what he can to extirpate them. He has tortured and burned dozens of women. He has no doubts about his beliefs, he is supported in his activities by the highest authorities, and he is sincere, dedicated, and as just as he can be in following ecclesiastic law.

Suppose also that the insensitive agent is a father of many children. He has prevailed in life and achieved much by enduring great hardships and going through serious adversities that would have crushed most people. Self-denial, discipline, and unceasing application have become his second nature. His experiences have shaped his view of life. In demanding of his children to become like him, he takes himself to be acting in their best interest. He does not realize that his very achievements have made his view of life inappropriate. Nor does he see that his children are crushed by his demands; are starved for his love; find his expectations perverse, pointless, and impossible to meet; and have been maimed by him for life.

Suppose last that the ruthless agent is a self-made and highly successful businessman. He has achieved what he has through great dedication, keen competitiveness, and unwavering commitment to expediency. He is merciless to his competitors, sacrifices others when it is necessary and observes moral prohibitions only when they serve his purpose. He became like that through the example, guidance, and approval of his father, whom he has imitated throughout his life. He sees morality, friendship, love, and loyalty as sentimental foolishness when things go well but most often as obstacles to success that reasonable people will not tolerate. He believes that strong and reasonable people all act as he does, and those who question his belief are unreasonable, weak, or insincere and cunning competitors trying to prevail over him.

All three people habitually and predictably cause serious and unjustified harm to many others. Their actions are often evil and stem from their vices, and the agents are wicked. But their actions, vices, and wickedness are the understandable consequences of circumstances that affected them. They have not sought their circumstances but have been forced by them and by the potentialities inherent in their characters to respond in the ways they have. For each, the choice was between living according to a conception of a good life that they had been born to, one to which they had no acceptable alternative, and failing by the standards of that same conception. The choice was forced on them, they lacked the means for the critical evaluation of their own conduct, and they could not understand the significance of their habitual and predictable actions. They are, therefore, not autonomous agents.

Are they, however, morally responsible agents? If the legitimating version of the principle were correct, it would follow that because these agents lack autonomy, it would be unjustified to ascribe moral responsibility to them. Because of their circumstances, innate dispositions, and formative experiences, they could not have acted other than they did. If ought implies can and if they could not, then it is unjustified to say that they ought not to have done what all influences on them prompted them to do. The dogmatic witch hunter, the insensitive father, and the ruthless businessman are therefore not morally responsible for their evil actions, vices, and wickedness. And, surely, that is an unacceptable moral view.

But if they really lack autonomy, then something is also wrong with holding them morally responsible. If they really could not help being the way they are and doing what they do, then holding them morally responsible would a be reversion to the barbarism of strict liability.

It is here that the significance of the degree-assigning version of the principle emerges. The dogmatic witch hunter, the insensitive father, and the ruthless businessman habitually and predictably cause evil, and so they are wicked. This cannot be a morally indifferent matter. Those who are committed to morality must hold them morally responsible for their ways of being and acting, even if they are nonautonomous. But their responsibility is not as great as it would be if they were autonomous. Autonomous evil, vices, and wickedness are worse than their nonautonomous counterparts. The significance of the degree-assigning version of the principle is that it makes it possible to recognize both their moral responsibility and that the ascription of the appropriate degree of moral responsibility depends on, among other things, where the agents are situated on the continuum between complete lack of autonomy and full possession of it.

The criticisms of the principle discussed in the two preceding sections have been directed against its legitimating version, and they leave untouched the degree-assigning version. The misuse of the principle is the use of its legitimating version, and the right use of it is its degree-assigning version. The legitimating version of the principle could and should be abandoned without abandoning its degree-assigning version.

The sources of the differences between these two versions of the principle are the different questions they are used to ask and answer. One question is what makes particular agents liable to moral responsibility. The right answer, the one implied by criticisms of the principle, is that it is the evil effects of their actions. The wrong answer is that the autonomy of the agents makes them liable to moral responsibility. That is the liberal answer, and it is mistaken because it makes it impossible to use the resources of morality to curtail the nonautonomous wickedness from which the prevalence of evil largely results. The other question arises only after the first question has been answered. Assuming that particular agents are liable to moral responsibility for their wickedness, the question is, For how much moral responsibility are they liable? The answer is that it depends, in part, on how autonomous they are. Greater autonomy creates liability for greater moral responsibility, and lesser autonomy, for lesser moral responsibility.

By asking and answering the second question, all reasonable liberal concerns are met. It is recognized that the principle has a morally important and right use: the one that follows from its degree-assigning version. That recognition, however, is compatible with recognizing also that the principle has a morally mistaken and wrong use: the one that follows from its legitimating version. It is furthermore possible to avoid the morally unacceptable consequences of reverting to strict liability and to an unwillingness to recognize excuses that follow from abandoning the legitimating version of the principle. For the degree-assigning version can take into consideration all the exempting and extenuating excuses that make nonautonomously wicked agents liable to less moral responsibility than are their autonomous counterparts.

Suppose that the legitimating version of the principle is abandoned and its degree-assigning version is accepted. Why is this important? How does it affect liberalism? What moral difference does it make? The basic answer is that abandoning the legitimating version has the consequence of forcing the reorientation of prevailing moral sensibility in a direction that is incompatible with liberalism. The implication of the acceptance of the legitimating version is that autonomy is a central feature of morality partly because moral responsibility depends on it. The implication of abandoning the legitimating version and of accepting the degree-assigning version is that autonomy is displaced from its privileged moral position. The implication of the shift from one version to another is a revised view of what is morally important. If people become liable to moral responsibility because of their autonomy, then autonomy is the sine qua non of morality. If people become liable to moral responsibility because of their vices and corresponding patterns of action, then it is the evil effects of their conduct that occupy the central position that was previously assigned to autonomy. In this latter case, autonomy still matters, of course, but it matters much less than before. It is removed from the center of morality and relegated to the subordinate position of being one of the factors that must be considered in assigning the appropriate degree of moral responsibility.

If, however, autonomy is demoted in this manner, then liberals are left without an answer to the question of why autonomy should be placed at the core of their political morality. Their previous answer—that autonomy is the key to pursuing good and avoiding evil—is no longer acceptable. Autonomy is often put to evil uses, and the prevalence of evil is due largely to nonautonomous wickedness. If liberalism is truly committed to the basic tasks of morality—promoting good and curtailing evil—then it must drastically revise its core. The revision is not called for because liberals have mistakenly identified autonomy as the morally crucial psychological state and their position should be improved by identifying the right psychological state. The required revision is drastic because the liberal mistake is to suppose that any psychological state is crucial to morality. What is crucial to morality are the good and evil effects of human actions, not their psychological causes.

If the legitimating version of the principle is abandoned and its degree-assigning version is accepted, then the reflexivity of evil can be recognized without incurring the morally unacceptable consequences that liberals rightly warn against. If moral agents habitually and predictably cause evil because of their vices and the patterns of action that reflect these vices, then they are morally responsible quite independently of whether their wickedness is autonomous. The reason for this is that commitment to morality requires doing what one reasonably can to curtail evil, and wicked agents cause evil. Holding them morally responsible means adopting various measures to curtail their conduct. These measures include public disapproval of them and their actions; the refusal to associate with them; teaching children not to be like them; disqualifying them from responsible positions; employing persuasion, warning, and coercion to prevent them from continuing their evil conduct; warning others of the dangers involved in associating with them; and establishing and maintaining institutions to protect others from the consequences of their actions. Such measures are made legitimate by the pattern of evil these agents have caused in the past and are likely to cause in the future. It should also be remembered that the evils are habitual and predictable patterns, not rare episodes, nor are they moral peccadillos but the kind of serious and unjustified harm that dogmatic, insensitive, and ruthless agents cause. They are harms whose results are physiological and psychological damages that jeopardize their victims' continued functioning as full-fledged human beings. These measures, of course, go against the liberal grain because they curtail the autonomy of agents by curtailing the benefits they would derive from the basic liberal values of pluralism, freedom, equality, rights, and distributive justice.

The adoption of these measures is liable to abuse, and the political and moral dangers involved in them are considerable. The role of the degree-assigning version of the principle is to guard against these dangers and to prevent possible abuse by providing a principled way of deciding what measures and what severity of measures are legitimate to take in the case of different agents who have become wicked in different ways. In this context it becomes important to decide how autonomous or nonautonomous the agents and their actions are. Having a principle is, of course, no guarantee that the danger and the abuse will be avoided, but no principle has such a guarantee.

3.5 SOME IMPLICATIONS

By way of strengthening the criticism of the legitimating version of the principle, it will be useful to consider some implications that do and some that do not follow from the preceding discussion. Some may think that because the legitimating version is Kantian, both in its origin and in its insistence that moral responsibility depends on autonomy and because its criticism involves stressing the moral importance of the effects of actions, the criticism is therefore the familiar consequentialist objection to the Kantian approach to moral questions. But this conclusion is not one that follows from what has been said.

The criticism is not consequentialist, although it is compatible with consequentialism, as it is with some versions of the Kantian approach.

Consequentialism is committed to evaluating the moral standing of actions solely by reference to the consequences that follow from performing them. The objection to the legitimating version of the principle is not that it is not consequentialist but that it does not give sufficient weight to consequences. Giving them such weight need not involve giving them all the weight.

The objection is that the legitimating version concentrates on the psychological states of the agents in deciding whether they ought to be held morally responsible for their actions, and that the effects of their actions on others are ignored. By accepting the degree-assigning version, psychological states causing the action as well as the effects of the actions can be given appropriate weight. Psychological states are relevant to determining the degree of moral responsibility to which agents are liable, while the effects of their actions are relevant to answering the question of whether the agents are liable to moral responsibility. Lest it be thought that this obscures the obvious difference between evil caused by human and that caused by nonhuman agents, it should be remembered that the effects whose relevance is being stressed are habitual and predictable patterns of evil-producing actions that reflect the vices of their agents. Nonhuman agents do not perform actions that meet this specification.

Another conclusion that may be erroneously thought to follow would trivialize the distinction between the two versions of the principle. It may be thought that when a certain limit is reached, the degree-assigning version simply turns into the legitimating version. The limit in question is reached when agents are causally responsible for patterns of evil actions, but their psychological states preclude the legitimate ascription of moral responsibility to them. This may be supposed to happen, for example, if agents have mental disorders and their actions are caused by delusions; they have such low intelligence that they are incapable of making the connection between causes and effects that are separated by a short spatial or temporal interval; or they have been seriously brutalized, as feral children might have been. In such cases, both the legitimating and the degree-assigning version agree on the illegitimacy of holding the agents morally responsible. The two versions are thus shown to be not really different.

This supposition, however, is mistaken. The root of its error is the conflation of moral responsibility and punishment. Punishment is the severest reaction to moral responsibility, and naturally, numerous less severe reactions are possible, ranging from silent disapproval to social ostracism. Furthermore, punishment itself ranges from mild penalty to imprisonment or execution. It goes without saying that people with mental disorders or who have been brutalized should not be punished. But the reaction to moral responsibility need not take the form of punishment. Moral responsibility is liability to moral judgment. It remains true that these people habitually and predictably cause evil; their predictable actions cause serious, unjustified harm to others. This is not a morally neutral fact. One cannot be committed to morality and not think that such people are tainted by the evil they habitually and predictably cause, even if they cannot help causing it.

It can justifiably be said about such people that their ways of being and acting are morally deplorable; that it would be a morally better world if there were no people like them; that others should be protected from them; that the details of their actions horrify and disgust us; and so forth. To what else do such opinions come than a moral judgment that implies some degree of moral responsibility. It would be barbaric to punish such benighted agents, but it remains true that their lives and conduct are morally repugnant.

The limiting case of moral responsibility, therefore, is not one from which human agents are exempted. Human agents cannot be exempted from moral responsibility for their vices and patterns of actions. What makes moral responsibility inseparable from being human is the vulnerability of others to the evil that human agents can cause them. What human agents can and should be exempted from is punishment, if they cause the evil they do because of such lack of autonomy as is true of the individuals in the examples given above.

A further implication of the preceding discussion relates to the point just made about the moral responsibility of people who through no fault of their own lack autonomy. What is at stake in the disagreement between the liberal tendency to exempt such agents from moral responsibility altogether and the opposing tendency to regard them as liable to it, but not to punishment, is the question of who is a moral agent. In the liberal view, the legitimating version of the principle can be employed as a criterion for its answer: moral agents are those who can act autonomously.[6] On the liberal view, therefore, moral agency is a low-level moral achievement. This view is, of course, intimately connected with the previously criticized one that makes liability to moral responsibility depend on the psychological states of the agents. The connection is that autonomy is the criterion of both moral agency and moral responsibility, and all and only moral agents are liable to moral responsibility. But if the legitimating version of the principle and this view of autonomy and moral responsibility are rejected, as the reasons adduced against them compel that they must be, then the conception of moral agency that is intimately connected with them cannot escape being affected.

The assumption underlying autonomy as a criterion of moral agency is the familiar dictum of Kant about actions: "Their worth consists, not in the effects which result from them . . . but in the attitudes of mind . . . which are ready in this way to manifest themselves in action" (Kant 1964: 102–3). But why does moral agency depend on "attitudes of mind" and not on "the effects which result from them"? How could it not be said of people who fail to possess the accrediting attitudes of mind but who habitually cause evil that they are moral agents? Do their victims not bleed? How could one be committed to the basic moral task of preventing evil and not be willing to recognize that "attitudes of mind" matter from the moral point of view because of "the effects which result from them"?

The answer which these rhetorical questions are meant to elicit is that it is a mistake to suppose that moral agency depends on autonomy. Moral agency is not an achievement but a condition—the human condition. Human beings are moral agents because their actions affect other human beings—what they do has unavoidable moral significance. That is what makes them moral agents and liable to moral responsibility. Autonomy has a bearing on what kind of moral agents they are, what sort of moral judgment is appropriate to make of them, and what degree of moral responsibility can be legitimately ascribed to them.

If this is so, then, it will be asked, why are the virus that causes AIDS, man-eating beasts, and inconveniently situated active volcanos not moral agents and liable to moral responsibility? The answer is that they are not because they are not human. Morality is an attempt to avoid evil and to pursue good caused by human agency. Its vocabulary, its praise and blame, its rules, ideals, values, principles, and theories are intended to influence human conduct. And even if some human beings will not be influenced by them, the influence is still worth exerting because it will shape the responses of others to those who are not or cannot be affected by morality. It is, of course, very much in the human interest to do something about disease, predators, and natural disasters, but that is not what morality is supposed to do. The reason why human agents are within the domain of morality and nonhuman agent are outside it is not that human agents are autonomous and nonhuman ones are not but that human conduct can, directly or indirectly, be affected by morality, whereas nonhuman activities cannot be.

The last implication to be considered that emerges from the criticism of the legitimating version of the principle is an absurdly counterintuitive view of moral improvement to which defenders of this version are committed. If moral agency and moral responsibility depend on autonomy, then moral improvement is from less to more autonomy; it consists in increasing control over one's action through subjecting one's choices and actions more and more to the sort of evaluation and understanding that autonomy requires.

Consider now the dogmatic, insensitive, and ruthless agents used to illustrate nonautonomous wickedness. They habitually cause evil partly because choices were forced on them, making it impossible for them to subject their choices to reasonable evaluation and to understand their significance. Given the view of moral improvement that follows from the legitimating version of the principle, what these agents ought to do to become morally better is to increase their autonomy by improving their evaluation and understanding. The more they can do this, the greater will their moral improvement be. Suppose that they succeed and actually become much less dogmatic, insensitive, and ruthless, and cause less evil than before. They revert to their old ways only when there is great pressure on them or when circumstances force them to act immediately and they have no time for moral reflection.

Now contrast these people with undogmatic, sensitive, and altruistic agents who are just as nonautonomous as their wicked counterparts used to be. These benign agents have their virtues because they have been born and raised in some tight benevolent orthodoxy, they live utterly conventional lives, they have not been seriously tried or challenged, such questions as may occur to them are readily answered by the resident moral authorities, and they habitually and predictably act in a morally good way, at least as far as being undogmatic, sensitive, or altruistic is concerned.

The absurdly counterintuitive conclusion that follows from the legitimating version of the principle is that the dogmatic, insensitive, and ruthless agents who have made themselves more autonomous and thus improved are morally better than the undogmatic, sensitive, and altruistic agents who have not improved at all because they have remained in their nonautonomous state; a state in which, it should be remembered, according to this version of the principle, it is illegitimate either to praise or to blame them. If moral improvement depends on increasing one's autonomy, then the moral standing of agents who are increasing their autonomy is bound to be higher than the moral standing of those who continue in a nonautonomous state.

This unacceptable view of moral improvement overlooks several crucial facts. One is that some moral agents have not improved because there was no need for it, since they were already doing morally well in some particular respect. Another is that the undoubted improvement of some agents may merely make them less wicked than they were, and their improvement may still leave them in a morally worse state than those who have remained unimproved. And yet another is that although increased autonomy may lead to moral improvement, it is clearly not sufficient for it, because the control that is gained may be put to evil uses. People who have increased their autonomy may thus once again, although for a reason different from that noted before, be morally worse than those who have persisted in their nonautonomous benignity.

If this is an unacceptable view of moral improvement, then what is an acceptable one? The unexciting answer is the commonsensical one: moral improvement consists in causing less evil and more good. An increase in autonomy is not irrelevant to this process, but it is neither necessary nor sufficient for it. It is one way in which moral improvement may be effected, but there are others, and it may lead to moral deterioration. Moreover, moral improvement is not a reliable indicator of moral standing, for the moral improvement of some people may merely bring them to the lower rungs of decency, a position that others occupy without needing to improve.

It may be concluded then that the criticisms of the legitimating version of the principle is not committed to consequentialism, does not involve strict liability or the punishment of people who cannot help being wicked, and rejects the untenable identification of moral agency with the capacity for autonomy, as well as the supposition that moral improvement depends on becoming more autonomous.

The implication of these criticisms, as indeed of the argument in this and the preceding chapter, is that liberalism cannot be consistently committed to its negative aim of making evil less prevalent and to its positive aim of increasing autonomy by implementing the basic values and political programs of liberalism. If liberals attempt to remove this inconsistency by abandoning autonomy as the core of liberalism, then they must face the question of why pluralism, freedom, rights, equality, and distributive justice are to be regarded as the basic values, because the previous answer, that they are essential to autonomy, no longer holds. Why should not peace, order, law-abidingness, prosperity, a healthy environment, security, and happiness be as basically valuable? If, on the other hand, autonomy continues to be held as the core of liberalism, then the question is how liberalism can prevent the prevalence of evil. Working for greater autonomy cannot be the answer, for it will give greater scope to both autonomous and nonautonomous evil. It will do the former because greater autonomy gives freer reign to autonomous wickedness. And it will do the latter because it involves the denial of the reflexivity of evil for nonautonomous wickedness, which places its agents beyond moral responsibility and thus removes a most important curb on their conduct. The only way of avoiding these morally unacceptable consequences is to impose restrictions that systematically run counter to the liberal political programs, the basic liberal values, and to autonomy itself. Wickedness and the prevalence of evil therefore present a most serious problem for liberalism.

It is not, of course, that liberals cannot or do not recognize that evil is prevalent and that wickedness is widespread. The trouble is rather that their recognition of them is inconsistent with the central moral importance they attribute to the possession of autonomy. The sphere of morality cannot be restricted to the sphere of autonomy because individual agents are morally responsible for much nonautonomous evil. As liberals struggle with this inconsistency, they are forced to adopt such a desperate measure as denying that habitual and predictable patterns of nonautonomous evil actions reflect on the moral standing of their agents.

The liberal strategy of denying the reflexivity of evil isolates individual agents from the evil that exists in the world: it aims to prevent the evil consequences of their morally deplorable actions from redounding to their detriment. Evil actions are allowed to reflect on their agents only if agents cause them autonomously. Because much evil is caused nonautonomously, the result of these stratagems is to deprive liberals of much-needed moral resources to face evil and to cope with it. The inference is hard to avoid that what motivates this denial of the obvious is the groundless faith that human beings are better than the historical record indicates that they are. Tempting as this is, it should not be believed, and the hope based on it is false.[7]

CHAPTER 4

Collective Responsibility

Modern philosophers have often followed a course in their en-
quiries . . . different from that of the anscients. In later times . . .
philosophers . . . were necessarily led to [regarding] . . . *voluntary*
and *involuntary* the foundation of their whole theory. . . . [B]ut
this, in the mean time, must be allowed, that *sentiments* are every
day experienced of blame and praise, which have objects beyond
the dominion of will and choice, and of which it behoves us . . .
to give some satisfactory theory and explication.

—DAVID HUME, *An Enquiry concerning the Principles of Morals*

Collective responsibility is ascribed to people for actions they
have neither performed nor had control over. The supposed justification
for its ascription is that individuals are liable for actions performed by
other members of a group to which they belong. One would expect liberals to regard collective responsibility as anathema, but this is by no means
the case. Many liberals positively clamor to hold themselves and others
collectively responsible for actions they could not have performed or controlled because they took place long before they were born. Such is the
attitude of American liberals toward past discrimination against blacks
and women, to name one example among many. Many liberal policies,
among them antipoverty and equal opportunity programs, quotas for academic admission and business contracts, foreign aid to some countries,
the redistribution of wealth, and the preferential treatment of blacks and
women, are motivated by the tacit acceptance of collective responsibility.

The ascription of collective responsibility, however, is inconsistent with
the central liberal belief that people should be held responsible for only
their own autonomous actions. The actions for which members of a
group are supposed to share collective responsibility fail the freedom

component of autonomy (see Section 1.5) because they were not performed by the agents who are held responsible for them. Here then is
another clash between the negative and the positive aims of liberalism.
Increasing autonomy, in accordance with the positive aim, is inconsistent
with decreasing the prevalence of evil, dictated by the negative aim, because evil will be made less prevalent by the acknowledgment of collective
responsibility, which depends on extending the sphere of responsibility
beyond the sphere of autonomy.

This inconsistency can be removed either by abandoning autonomy as
the core of liberalism or by rejecting collective responsibility and with it
the justification of many characteristically liberal political programs. The
argument in this chapter will be that liberals are right in their view that
collective responsibility may be legitimately ascribed. Consistency therefore requires the displacement of autonomy from the core of liberalism,
which in turn removes the justification for privileging liberal over nonliberal values. It will also be argued that if collective responsibility is properly
understood, it fails to justify the political programs that liberals base on
it.

4.1 THE INTUITIVE CASE

Collective responsibility can be legitimately ascribed to individuals for the actions of other members of the groups to which the individuals belong (Feinberg 1970b and May and Hoffman 1991). Such groups
may be nations, cultures, religions, institutions, professions, and so forth.
The first step in the argument for the legitimacy of collective responsibility is to consider some putative examples. This will be followed by a more
analytical discussion of the conditions for its legitimate ascription, which
may or may not validate the previous examples. It is a ubiquitous experience among American liberals to feel responsible for racial and sexual
discrimination. Numerous Catholics feel likewise about the Church's attitude toward contraception and abortion. A Russian psychiatrist may feel
it about his colleagues' having colluded in the incarceration of political
dissidents in psychiatric hospitals. Indians may have the same feeling
about the recurrent religious massacres in their country. American physicians may feel it about the rampant commercialism of their profession.
And the obverse also holds. People often take pride in the achievements
of their country, the high standards of their profession, the reputation of
the corporation for which they work, the willingness of their political
party to defend justice, or the number of Nobel Prize winners at their
university.

Such experiences are common and share the feature that the agents who acknowledge their responsibility do so on account of actions they have not performed or controlled. In many cases, these agents could have done nothing to make the actions happen or to stop them from happening. Yet they feel that the actions somehow reflect on their moral standing, and so they accept some measure of blame or praise and thus moral responsibility for them. This should not happen if the liberal assumption were true that responsibility could be legitimately ascribed only for autonomous actions that the agents have performed and had some control over.

Consider another aspect of these familiar experiences. Take people who are committed and feel allegiance to a culture, a religion, an institution, a profession, and so forth and who take pride in its achievements. They feel that their participation makes them morally better. Being an American, a Christian, an officer of the law, or a physician has become part of their moral identity. They feel inspired by American ideals, the life and teachings of Jesus, the evenhandedness of the law, or the ideal of using technical expertise for alleviating illness. Now suppose that they come to believe something that they cannot reconcile with the values that inspire them, for example, that American ideals led to racial and sexual discrimination, Christianity encouraged the persecution of non-Christians, the law has been corrupted for political purposes, and the practice of medicine has become mercenary. If the people in question are genuinely committed, if their allegiance is real and not just window dressing, then they are bound to feel responsible for such violations of their values. As Americans, Christians, officers of the law, or physicians, they have a stake in the moral standing of their group because their own moral standing is connected with it. They have an obligation to accept not only the good but also the bad. If they can be ennobled by their membership in a group, then they can also be demeaned by it, even if they have not caused evil and have no control over the evil that others have caused. Those who refuse to accept this obligation either betray their commitments or demonstrate their weakness.

There is a suggestive analogy here with the laws governing inheritance. Just as recipients of a bequest inherit both property and the claims against it, so the present members of a group inherit the moral credits and debits accrued to the group. They cannot belong to the group and reject its moral record. To have committed themselves entails that they feel responsible for the group's realization of its values. This responsibility, however, is wider than their own actions; it includes responsibility for the actions of others over which they have no control.

This line of thought leads to a dilemma for liberals: either they must abandon their call to the present generation to accept responsibility for supposed past evils, such as racial and sexual discrimination, or they must abandon the belief that responsibility attaches only to autonomous actions, that is, to actions that the agents have themselves performed and had at least some control over. The former would deprive many liberal political programs of their justifications, whereas the latter would invalidate one of the pivotal assumptions on which the programs rest.

4.2 THE ANALYTICAL CASE

The intuitive case for collective responsibility raises many questions: Do all groups confer collective responsibility on their members? How strong and how lasting an allegiance is required for collective responsibility? What does the acceptance of collective responsibility oblige agents to do? What is the liability that collective responsibility creates? How can legitimate and illegitimate ascriptions of collective responsibility be distinguished? The time has come to consider these questions.

The conditions for the ascription of collective responsibility that have so far emerged are: first, *agents are held morally responsible for actions, thus deserving of moral praise or blame;* second, *the agents neither performed nor had control over the performance of the actions for which they are held responsible;* third, *the actions were performed by other agents who belonged or belong to the same group as the agents who are held responsible;* and fourth, *the agents' moral responsibility for the actions of others derives from their joint membership in the same group.*

It may be objected that even if the ascription of collective responsibility has some intuitive plausibility if the group is a nation, culture, religion, institution, or profession, it rapidly diminishes if the group is a chess club, the participants in a Charlie Chaplin look-alike contest, or the retired people who work part-time at McDonald's. The clue to the difference between these two sets of groups is to be found in collective responsibility being moral. It is responsibility for actions on account of their being good or evil. The existence of some groups is essentially connected with morally significant activities, whereas the activities of other groups acquire moral significance only incidentally, if at all. The first group will be called "moral," and the second, "nonmoral." How important the moral dimension is for the identity of a group depends on how closely the activities of the group are connected with human welfare: treating illness is obviously connected, imitating Chaplin is not. How central the moral dimension is to the activities of a group is often controversial. The ascription of collective responsibility is then also controversial. But such controversies presuppose that its ascription is legitimate in principle and focus on its legitimacy in a particular case. This suggests the fifth condition, namely, that *the group to which the agents belong is moral.*

Even moral groups, however, are engaged in a wide variety of disparate activities. Some of them are characteristic of the group, and engagement in them is part of the reason for the group's existence. Nevertheless, these characteristic activities can be carried on only if numerous enabling activities are also conducted. New members must be initiated, achievements must be honored, procedural rules must be formulated and maintained, disputes must be settled, and so on. Thus within the activities of a group, it is necessary to distinguish between characteristic, enabling, and incidental activities. Treating illness is a characteristic activity of the moral group of physicians, training future physicians is an enabling activity, and driving expensive cars is an incidental one. From this follows the sixth condition for the legitimate ascription of collective responsibility: *the actions for which agents are held morally responsible are part of the characteristic activities of the moral group.* The reason for this condition is that it is through its characteristic activities that a group primarily influences human welfare and thus elicits moral attention. The moral influence of enabling activities is exerted only indirectly, through the effects they have on the characteristic activities of the moral group, and so they have less moral significance. And the moral standing of incidental activities is even more remotely connected with the moral standing of the group.

The two preceding conditions help to specify more precisely the identity of the groups and the activities relevant to collective responsibility. But it is also necessary to specify further the nature of the participation of individual agents in such groups and activities. Individual agents are members of many groups. Family, schooling, ethnic origin, friendship, work, hobbies, politics, religion, citizenship, neighborhood, and so forth are some of the more or less natural groups to which most people belong. Membership in a group often just happens to people. They have not chosen it, they simply find themselves having it. Membership in these groups may be trivial or important. It is important if it has a formative influence on the character of participating individuals. Many of the values of the group then become the values of its members. These values influence their conceptions of a good life, define some of their possibilities and limits, supply criteria for some of their moral judgments, shape their aspirations, and provide grounds for developing solidarity, fellow feeling, comradeship, or just simple goodwill based on mutual understanding with other participants in the same group., Thus individuals may be said to have "identified" with the moral group, which is what makes membership in it important. A seventh condition for the legitimate ascription of collective responsibility is therefore that *the agents have identified with the moral group.* Such identification may or may not be conscious, articulate, or reflective. The sign of identification is not what people say or think but what they do. They have identified with the group if participation in many of its characteristic activities has become an important part of their lives; if they evaluate their own and other people's relevant activities by appealing to the values of the group; and if they come to share part of the moral dimension of their lives with their fellow participants. Citizens, colleagues, worshipers, comrades, artists, political activists, or members of the same profession may develop such fellowship with one another.

Identification with a moral group is rarely total. Most groups are not monolithic; they allow some disagreements within themselves. And people who identify with the same group may have serious disputes with one another over the values of the group. What is important for identification is continued participation in at least some of the characteristic activities of the group. If agents decline the opportunity to participate, then their identification is weakened. Identification is usually a matter of degree, and it is often difficult to say how strong it must be for agents to remain members of a group.

Even if this identification is achieved, however, it may not last. People can repudiate their culture and country, lose their faith, change professions, and give up politics. Membership in a moral group must be lasting and continuous for the legitimate ascription of collective responsibility. Thus the eighth condition is that *the agents' identification with the moral group is enduring.* Given enduring identification with a moral group, when one member performs a particular characteristic action in a particular situation and the action conforms to the shared values of the group, then it is true of members outside that situation that they too would have done what the agent on the spot did. In other words, one agent did what the values prescribe that any agent should do, and enduring identification with the group leads to general agreement about right actions. The ninth and final condition for collective responsibility is therefore that *if the agents had been in the place of the actual agent, they would have done what the actual agent did.*

If these conditions are met, it is legitimate to hold individual agents morally responsible for actions they have not performed and could not control. Their responsibility derives from their enduring identification with a moral group whose values have become their own. Membership in the group forms their character, constitutes part of their moral identity, makes them participate in the characteristic activities of the group, and provides some of the values in accordance with which they feel they ought to act. Thus members of the group share a general consensus about how they should act in many of those contexts in which the characteristic activities of the group are appropriate. And when one member acts as others feel they themselves should, then it is true to say of them that they too would have acted the same way as did the one who actually acted. Such agents sustain the group. It is their shared, enduring identification, their dedication to the values and characteristic activities that keeps the group going. America is sustained if Americans act according to the Constitution and the Bill of Rights, Christianity endures if Christians follow the teachings of Jesus, medicine flourishes if physicians abide by the Hippocratic oath, and the law prevails if its officers administer it impartially.

Members of a moral group are therefore collectively responsible for the characteristic activities of the group with which they have identified. Their responsibility is on account of the good or evil effects of the characteristic activities of the group. And the source of their responsibility is that they and agents like themselves constitute the group whose characteristic activities cause these good or evil effects. Thus they are liable to moral praise or blame.

These are the reasons, then, that make the intuitive case for collective responsibility plausible. It is for these reasons that Americans, Christians, physicians, and officers of the law may be legitimately praised or blamed on account of particular characteristic actions performed by other members of their moral group, even if they themselves had no control over them. If these reasons hold, however, then the liberal view, which regards the connection between autonomy and responsibility as necessary, cannot be right. Before possible liberal responses to this case are discussed, a further implication of collective responsibility needs to be considered.

The discussion has proceeded so far on the assumption that the ascription of collective responsibility for good and evil actions is symmetrical. According to this assumption, collective responsibility may result in legitimate praise or blame. But this assumption is not obviously true. It sounds distinctly odd to say that people are held responsible for having done something good. The tendency in common discourse is to raise the question of moral responsibility only when there is a question of evildoing. In the normal course of events, moral responsibility is taken to indicate moral failure. Usage is not unequivocal in this respect, but it does tend in the direction just noted.

As often happens, thinking about usage leads to something important. Collective responsibility is grounded on identification with the characteristic actions of a moral group. But there is a presumption, at least among its members, that the actions are good. After all, the actions are characteristic because they represent the values of the group. Members of a group will act in characteristic ways, otherwise the group would disintegrate or they would cease to be its members. It is not noteworthy when members of a group do what members of that group are supposed to do. The usual context in which questions arise about responsibility, then, is when a norm is violated. This can happen in two ways: one banal, the other morally significant.

Members of a group may simply violate the values of the group and do what is evil. If they indeed have an enduring identification with the group, then they recognize or can be brought to recognize that their actions were evil. It is proper to hold them responsible, but there is no question here of collective responsibility. The individual evildoers should be blamed for what they have done.

The usual context of collective responsibility is another kind of evildoing. Members of a group may do what is evil not because they violate the values of their group but because they act according to them. This could happen if some or all the values of the group are evil. Agents do what they believe is good, but they are mistaken in their belief. They follow the values with which they have identified, the values that have come to inform their character; they act in characteristic ways; and they end up causing evil. They may or may not realize that this has happened. But the legitimate ascription of collective moral responsibility does not depend on their realization but on meeting the following conditions: other members of the moral group with which the agents have an enduring identification have performed a characteristic action that correctly represents some central values of the group, and it is true of the agents that if they had been in the other agents' position, they too would have done what the other agents did. Given these conditions, agents can legitimately be held responsible for actions they have neither performed nor had control over. And then the liberal assumption that autonomy and responsibility go hand in hand is mistaken. How might liberals respond to this argument?

4.3 LIBERAL RESPONSES

Perhaps the first liberal response will be to reject the case for collective responsibility. It will be said that it is barbaric to hold people responsible for what they have not done. People ought to be treated as autonomous individuals, not as members of groups. They should answer for their autonomous actions, not for the actions of others. If they are members of groups, then they should be held responsible for their membership, and only for that.

Juxtaposed to this response is the previous case for collective responsibility. If people are autonomous, they should certainly be treated accordingly. But autonomy is inseparable from membership in various groups.

Autonomy is not developed through a series of stark existential choices between fundamental options. People are born into various groups, whose values they imbibe. The development of autonomy consists in learning to use the moral vocabulary of their groups to identify and articulate their needs, wants, desires, ambitions, and hopes and to find some non-Procrustean fit between them and the available conventional avenues for their satisfaction. And even if they reject their native groups and their values, they do so in the name of other groups and their values.

Autonomy is not valued higher in the first way of thinking than in the second. Both are ways of interpreting autonomy. The first liberal response presupposes one interpretation: the case for collective responsibility presupposes another. So there is a clash of intuitions. Appeals to intuition, however, cannot prove or disprove anything. They merely create receptivity to particular interpretations of particular cases. Whether an interpretation is correct depends on the arguments for and against it. The liberal response requires more than intuitive appeal. It requires giving the sorts of arguments that have been given here for collective responsibility, and it requires showing why the opposing arguments are defective.

These requirements are especially pressing because the liberal response presupposes a dubious interpretation of autonomy. That this interpretation is dubious is the point of the communitarian criticisms of it (see Section 1.4). These criticisms force a choice between two options on liberals who give this response. They must either find a way of defending the extremely implausible view that individuals become autonomous as they succeed in isolating themselves from the values that prevail in their social context, or if these liberals reject this implausible view, then they must accept liability to collective responsibility. In other words, if liberals accept that membership in a group has a formative influence on the autonomy of individuals, then they cannot consistently reply to the point that such membership may make individuals liable to collective responsibility by insisting on evaluating the moral standing of individuals independently of the moral standing of the group that profoundly affects their autonomy.

Another response liberals may offer is to concede that there are occasions on which the ascription of collective responsibility is legitimate but to claim that these occasions occur so rarely and exceptionally as to justify relegating collective responsibility to the margins of morality. In most cases, it is individual responsibility that matters. Liberals may claim, therefore, that the case for collective responsibility requires no more than minor revision of their position.

The trouble with this response is that it underestimates the significance of collective responsibility. Collective responsibility is legitimately ascribed when the characteristic activities of a moral group are governed by the wrong values. It is admittedly rare to have a moral group most of whose values are wrong and the group is totally corrupt. But it is not at all rare, in fact, it is what happens most of the time, that the moral credentials of the values of a group are mixed. Some values are right, some are wrong, and some are partly right and partly wrong. Nations, religions, institutions, professions, and so on rarely have anything but a mixed record. Their members are therefore liable to collective responsibility. And since this happens frequently, collective responsibility cannot be reasonably relegated to the margins of morality. The temptation to do so comes from the misguided liberal tendency, noted above, to underestimate the moral importance of membership in groups to the development of autonomy.

Another liberal response may be to deny that collective responsibility is incompatible with autonomy. Autonomy involves choice, and it will be said, individuals can normally choose whether to be members of a group. It is true that birth, infancy, and childhood make it impossible to choose whether to become members of many groups, but when people reach the age of reason, they can choose whether to remain members. It will be said that one of the conditions of collective responsibility is enduring identification with a group, which is but another name for autonomous choice of membership.

This response fails for two reasons. First, while it is no doubt true that continuing membership in a group, especially in a moral group, is sometimes a matter of choice, it is also true that the possibility of choice is simply unavailable for many people. Part of the reason for this is that membership in some groups prior to the age of reason may influence many people's character so deeply as to require exceptionally strong countervailing influences to overcome it. In the absence of great upheavals, serious personal crises, and such social changes as wars and revolutions, people just take for granted their citizenship, ethnicity, race, sexual orientation, family ties, and, to a lesser extent, religion and class as well. This is not to deny that exceptional individuals can repudiate the groups to which they start out belonging, but it is to deny that for very many people doing so is a live option.

A substantial portion of the population of any stable society die as members of many of the same groups into which they were born, and not many of them maintain the continuity by choice. This is not because they are coerced by threats; it is rather that choice requires options, and the early training they have received as members of various groups so influences their characters as to make them unable to see alternative possibilities as options for themselves. Depending on one's ideological predilections, this may be seen as indoctrination or as moral education. But however it is labeled, the fact remains that for most people, enduring identification with several groups is not a matter of choice. This liberal response is mistaken, therefore, in supposing that enduring identification must involve the exercise of autonomy.

Suppose, however, that this reading of the social facts if mistaken and enduring identification always involves the exercise of autonomy. Even if this were so, the case for collective responsibility would remain unaffected. For collective responsibility is not ascribed to people for their enduring identification but for specific, characteristic evil actions that other members of their group have performed. It is true that collective responsibility could not be legitimately ascribed in the absence of enduring identification. Nevertheless, the object (namely, an evil action) and one of the conditions (namely, enduring identification) of collective responsibility must be distinguished from each other, even if they occur together.

By way of analogy, compare this with legal responsibility for, say, murder. The object of legal responsibility is the murder; one condition of the legitimate assignment of legal responsibility is being of sound mind. But the two are different, and it is a grotesque error to suppose that what is involved in possessing a sound mind is the same as what is involved in murder. The same goes for the enduring identification and the evil action for which collective responsibility is ascribed. There is no collective responsibility without enduring identification (and, let us continue to suppose, without the exercise of autonomy). Individuals, however, are not held collectively responsible for their enduring identification but for the evil actions of other members of their group. Their autonomy could not be a requirement of those actions because spatial and temporal distance make their involvement often impossible. Collective responsibility therefore need not involve the exercise of autonomy.

The last liberal response to be considered centers on the question of the practical implication of holding people collectively responsible. Suppose for the sake of argument that collective responsibility is actually ascribed to individual agents. What does the responsibility require them, their critics, or their judges to do? Should these agents be punished for what they have not done? What kind of punishment would be appropriate? And what is moral punishment anyway? Is it anything more than having disapproving cluckings directed at oneself? Punishment with teeth in it, like imprisonment, seems to be inappropriate, and mere moral disapproval would be ineffectual name-calling. Liberals may therefore argue that it is hard to see how the ascription of collective responsibility would serve any practical end beyond perhaps allowing critics to vent their disapproval.

The reply is that the practical significance of moral responsibility—both individual and collective—derives from what the agents who are held responsible themselves do, not in what is done to them. Moral responsibility is an inward matter and, in this respect, it differs from legal or official responsibility, for which external sanctions are readily available. What individual agents ought to do if collective responsibility legitimately befalls them, is to acknowledge it.

4.4 THE ACKNOWLEDGMENT OF COLLECTIVE RESPONSIBILITY

The acknowledgment of collective responsibility is no easy matter because it usually results in a serious moral crisis. It leads agents to see both themselves and the group that has had a formative influence on their moral identity as being guided by the wrong moral values. To acknowledge this is to stand condemned in their own eyes, and not just for this or that action, but for part of what they are (see Buruma 1994).

One might think that such acknowledgments would not occur because the agents who maintain an enduring identification with a group derive their values from the group. They thus have no other values on the basis of which they could condemn the values of their group. But this is not so for two reasons. First, agents are members of many groups—one and the same person may be an American, a Christian, a physician, and an officer of the law—and they may criticize the values of one of the groups to which they belong from the point of view of the values of another group to which they belong. Second, because moral groups are seldom monolithic, the questioning may involve criticizing a central value of the group by appealing to other central values of the same group.

The fact remains, however, that although the acknowledgment could occur, powerful defensive forces stand in its way. Coming to question one's moral identity opens the door to self-condemnation, which is a dangerous act with potentially destructive consequences. This may be one source of the reluctance to acknowledge the legitimacy of collective responsibility. Be that as it may, the acknowledgment of collective responsibility forces the question liberals are likely to ask about its practical significance.

The answer to it is that the acknowledgment of collective responsibility involves public disclosure, the feeling of regret and its appropriate expression, the offer of such compensation as is possible, and the endeavor to reform the group (Jedlicki 1990). Each of these has considerable practical significance. The discussion of these facets of acknowledgment requires concrete examples, which are bound to be controversial. The general point, however, does not depend on any particular example. Those that follow should be treated as illustrations rather than as moral claims. If one of them sticks in the craw, others are readily available. But the examples also serve to strengthen the case for collective responsibility by showing situations in which its acknowledgment is the right thing to do.

Public disclosure is a more or less formal statement by some authoritative representative of a group that the group is responsible for the evil that has been caused. Such is the statement, for instance, of the Russian government that the massacre of several thousand Polish officers at Katyn was done by the Red Army, rather than by the Nazis, as has been falsely maintained by a succession of Soviet officials. Or, to illustrate the same point by the morally offensive lack of public disclosure, consider the inexcusable refusal of the Turkish government to admit the Turkish massacre of Armenians. Nothing can undo the past evil, but public disclosure indicates acceptance of responsibility for it and thus represents the first step toward making amends. The action of the Russian government is a moral promise, whereas the inaction of the Turkish government exacerbates the moral outrage already committed.

Public disclosure should be accompanied with the feeling of regret and its expression. Members of a group should mind that the values of the group have led to the evil that has been done, and they should say so publicly. If members of the American Medical Association genuinely care that countless Americans are without adequate medical care, even though such care is available, then they should express their regret for participating in a price-fixing monopoly, motivated partly by greed, which is a major contributing factor to the wrong that is being done. The feeling and expression of regret establish a personal connection between individual agents and the evil actions that have been characteristic expressions of the wrong values of their group. The connection rests on individual agents who come to understand that they have identified with the wrong values and that they too would have been lead to cause evil had they been in the appropriate situation. The expression of regret is thus on behalf of their own moral identity. And the suitable expression of it is toward the people, or their descendants, who have suffered evil as a result.

A further facet of the acknowledgment of collective responsibility is the offer of compensation to the victims of the group's wrong actions. This is a complicated matter for several reasons. It is often impossible to find compensation that would be commensurate with the undeserved harm that has been done. The sufferings of the victims of massacres, of innocent people who spent the best years of their lives in concentration camps or the Gulag, or of those who have been thwarted and humiliated throughout their lives because they fell afoul of some irrational prejudice cannot be redeemed by a sum of money, especially not if it is given to their descendants. Nor will such compensation as is offered always be accepted, because the victims or their descendants may be reluctant to ease their persecutors' responsibility at such a cheap price. There are good reasons to think, therefore, that the compensation should be symbolic. Any appearance of being paid off, bargaining about conscience money, or contributing to the forgetting of the evil that has been done would thereby be avoided. Such symbolic compensation may be the creation of a national holiday, the erection of a monument, or regularly scheduled meetings commemorating the victims. Or it may be the steady political and moral support of the group to which the victims belonged by the group of the evildoers. Neither symbolic nor actual compensation can, of course, relieve collective responsibility. But it can acknowledge its burden, and doing so is a moral debt that the group of evildoers owes to the group of its victims.

The most direct practical implication of the acknowledgment of collective responsibility, however, is the endeavor to reform the group. This requires identifying the wrong values that motivated the evil actions. Reasonable reform is extremely difficult because the values of a group are rarely independent of one another. Values normally form an interconnected whole, and alteration of a part tends to reverberate throughout the whole. Wrong values, therefore, cannot be simply ejected or exchanged for right ones. Changing the values of the group usually involves changing the group. And the question is always whether there would be enough left of the group after the changes have been made to continue to support the moral identity of its members. Whether traditional Japanese culture can survive without the samurai ethic, whether Catholicism is viable without the claim that it is the only road to salvation, whether an effective army can be maintained without the male camaraderie that excludes women and gay men are difficult questions. Serious reform, however, requires struggling with them, and the struggle is likely to be particularly taxing because it often involves individual agents in struggling with themselves as they pit against each other the right and wrong values that constitute their moral identity.

Partly because reform is so hard, the acknowledgment of collective responsibility is much rarer than it should be. Instead of public disclosure, there is a conspiracy of silence; instead of genuine regret and its appropriate expression, there is a phony pretense of an impartial view of the evil in which the evildoers' predicaments receive sympathetic understanding and the victims' sufferings are glossed over; instead of symbolic or actual compensation, there is talk of healing, which often means that the subject should not be discussed; instead of reform, life goes on as before, in the doomed hope that the lessons of the past are sufficient to change future conduct.

To sum up, the practical implication of the acknowledgment of collective responsibility is that it calls for public disclosure, the feeling and suitable expression of regret, the offer of compensation, and attempted reform. Or, to put it the other way around, the practical implication is opposition to denial, falsification, dissociation, and reversion to the old ways that the reluctance to acknowledge collective responsibility is all too likely to produce.

4.5 COLLECTIVE RESPONSIBILITY AND LIBERAL POLITICAL PROGRAMS

The argument just concluded for the defense of collective responsibility and for the moral requirement of its acknowledgment may be found surprising coming, as it does, from a critic of liberalism. For, as it has been noted at the beginning, many liberal political programs are motivated by collective responsibility for past discrimination, a responsibility whose acknowledgment liberals urge. It may be supposed that the present argument constitutes an endorsement of these political programs. This supposition, however, is mistaken, and making it rests on a failure to appreciate the implications of the argument. To show that this is so, it is necessary to concentrate on a specific political program, and the preferential treatment of blacks and women is as good an example as any.

The program in question is not affirmative action, which aims to guarantee that no qualified person is excluded from the pool of candidates for some position. The program is to discriminate in favor of some candidates on the ground that they or other members of the group to which they belong have been discriminated against in the past. One justification that is often given by liberals for such preferential treatment is the collective responsibility of the present generations of Americans for the evil caused to blacks and women by the discrimination against them of past generations of Americans. Similar arguments are used to justify antipoverty and equal opportunity programs, setting quotas for academic admission and business contracts, foreign aid to some countries, the redistribution of wealth, and so forth. But let us stay with preferential treatment and acknowledge that many blacks and women have suffered serious, unjustified harm because of discrimination against them.

The question is whether it is justified to hold present generations of Americans collectively responsible for past discrimination. And the answer is that it is not because doing so fails to meet several of the conditions required for the justified ascription of collective responsibility. The first condition that it fails to meet is that the actions for which agents are held responsible must be part of the characteristic activities of the moral group with which they have identified (the sixth condition described in Section 4.2). An activity of a moral group is characteristic if it expresses some central values of the group and it directly influences the welfare of the people who are affected by it. Now it is certainly true that past discrimination had a direct influence on the welfare of its victims, but it is not true that discrimination has expressed the central values of American society. Discrimination against blacks and women has been widespread, but so has been oppositions to it. Such opposition has resulted, among other things, in the Civil War, the Nineteenth Amendment to the Constitution, and the Civil Rights Act, none of which would have been possible without extensive popular support. Moreover, the most powerful argument used by opponents of discrimination has always been that it violates the central values of American society as expressed by the Constitution and the Bill of Rights.

Suppose, however, that this point is mistaken. Suppose that discrimination has expressed central values of American society. Suppose that those perfervid voices who accuse American society as a whole of having been racist and sexist actually speak the truth. The ascription of collective responsibility for past discrimination would still be unjustified because it violates the condition that the agents who are held responsible have identified with the moral group whose members discriminated (the seventh condition described in Section 4.2). Even if Americans in the past have identified with discrimination, very large numbers of them certainly do not do so in the present. These large numbers are made up of not only blacks and women but also numerous members of that much maligned group: white males. Not least among them are white male liberals, but contrary to malign rhetoric, of course, plenty of white male nonliberals condemn discrimination against blacks and women as firmly as anyone else. So even if discrimination expressed the central values of American society in the past and even if Americans in the past have identified with the group whose values they were, these values are no longer central in the moral group that Americans form in the present. Nor do numerous Americans in the present identify with the moral group whose members discriminated in the past. It would be unjustified, therefore, to hold these Americans collectively responsible for past discrimination.

It must be stressed, however, that it is not true that discrimination has ever expressed central American values or that all or most Americans have identified with the moral group whose members characteristically discriminated against blacks and women. To deny this does grave injustice to the memory of those countless Americans, mostly white males, who publicly condemned both discrimination and its practitioners; who, in their private lives, quietly, decently, and spontaneously treated blacks and women on their merits; and who brought about the political and moral changes that have made discrimination unacceptable.

The ascription of collective responsibility to the present generations of Americans for past discrimination also violates the condition that if the agents who are held collectively responsible had been in the place of the agents who discriminated in the past, then they would have done what past agents did (the ninth condition given in Section 4.2). This condition embodies a counterfactual claim, and such claims are easily misunderstood. The right understanding of this condition is to suppose that if present-day Americans, with their present-day values, commitments, and identifications with various moral groups, were in the place of Americans in the past, with their values, commitments, and identifications, then present-day Americans would have discriminated against blacks and women just as much as past Americans did. Once again, this is obviously false. No reasonable person can deny that there is much less discrimination against blacks and women now than there was in the past. That means that there must be much fewer Americans now who would have discriminated in the past. The ascription of collective responsibility to the moral group of Americans for past discrimination against blacks and women is therefore unjustified for yet a third reason.

It is reasonable to conclude that the defense of collective responsibility is perfectly consistent with the rejection of liberal political programs that are motivated by the acknowledgment of collective responsibility. For the acknowledgment of collective responsibility may be mistaken in that the activities for which people are held collectively responsible fail to meet one or more of the nine conditions on which its justified ascription depends. The policy of the preferential treatment of blacks and women is a case in point, but similar cases could be made against numerous other liberal programs, insofar as their justifications rest on collective responsibility.

To avoid the misunderstanding of present argument, it should be emphasized that the argument grants that discrimination has occurred, that it is an evil, and that Americans have been responsible for it. What the argument denies is that the sources of this evil have been central values with which members of the moral group of Americans have identified. Its sources have been precisely the actions of Americans that have violated some of the central values. Those who are guilty of their violations have caused evil and should be held responsible for it. But their responsibility does not carry over to those past and present Americans who have opposed discrimination and who neither have nor would have practiced it. In general, therefore, it may be said that liberals are right to condemn those Americans who have caused past and present evils but are wrong in cultivating an atmosphere of guilt, which, according to them, all Americans ought to feel. The liberal error is not to suppose that it may be justified to hold people collectively responsible but to ascribe collective responsibility without the necessary justification.

The argument in this chapter further strengthens the case for the inconsistency of liberalism. It does so directly by showing that the liberal political programs that are mistakenly supposed to be justified by collective responsibility are inconsistent with the liberal conception of autonomy that excludes collective responsibility. If the liberal conception of autonomy is correct, then responsibility can be ascribed to individual agents only for their autonomous actions, but collective responsibility is ascribed for actions that are not even the agents' own, so they cannot possibly be autonomous. If the liberal political programs directed at alleviating the evil effects of discrimination are justified by collective responsibility, then the sphere of responsibility must be much wider than the sphere of autonomy. In that case, however, it is the good and evil that have been caused and experienced that must be regarded as having central moral importance, and in violation of liberalism, they must displace autonomy from the core of an acceptable political morality.

The argument has also shown the inconsistency of liberalism in a less direct way. The positive aim of liberalism is to create conditions in which people can make good lives for themselves. Liberals pursue this aim by providing more freedom, equality, rights, distributive justice, and pluralism. The negative aim of liberalism is to make evil less prevalent.

It was argued in Chapter 2 that these two aims are inconsistent because increasing autonomy will make evil more, not less, prevalent, regardless of whether the prevalence of evil is due mainly to autonomous or to nonautonomous actions. It was argued further in Chapter 3 that the liberal strategy of attributing the prevalence of evil to nonautonomous actions but refusing to hold their agents responsible for them also leads, contrary to the negative liberal aim, to making evil more prevalent. For the refusal to hold agents responsible for their habitual, predictable, but nonautonomously evil actions weakens the curbs on their conduct, thus making it easier for them to cause evil.

The argument in the present chapter has added yet another reason for regarding the positive and the negative aims of liberalism as inconsistent. One way of pursuing the negative aim of making evil less prevalent is to hold people collectively responsible for the evil actions performed by other members of the moral group with whose central values they have identified and according to which they tend to act, and to urge them and their group to acknowledge their collective responsibility for such actions. Doing so, however, decreases their autonomy, and thus violates the positive aim, because it holds them responsible for actions over which they could have had no control. Once again, therefore, making evil less prevalent is inconsistent with making people more autonomous. Liberals must opt for one or the other, and whichever aim they choose, they themselves must see their political morality as seriously defective on account of its neglect of the other aim.

CHAPTER 5

The Errors of Egalitarianism

Democratic nations are at all times fond of equality, but there are certain epochs at which the passion they entertain for it swells to the height of fury. . . . The passion . . . penetrates on every side into men's hearts, expands there, and fills them entirely. Tell them not that by this blind surrender of themselves to an exclusive passion, they risk their dearest interests: they are deaf. Show them not freedom escaping from their grasp, whilst they are looking another way: they are blind—or rather, they can discern but one sole object to be desired in the universe.

—ALEXIS DE TOCQUEVILLE, *Democracy in America*

The purpose of Chapters 2–4 was to argue for the inconsistency of liberalism on account of the incompatibility of its negative and positive aims. These two aims cannot be pursued together because increasing autonomy, thought by liberals to be necessary for good lives, will make evil more prevalent, and making evil less prevalent requires decreasing autonomy.

The purpose of Chapters 5–9 is to argue for the inconsistency of liberalism in another respect. The positive aim of liberalism cannot be approximated, let alone achieved, by trying to realize three of the basic values of liberalism. The reason being that if equality, distributive justice, and pluralism are conceived as liberals conceive them, then they are incompatible with good lives.

The criticism of equality proceeds by accepting the liberal conception of it but arguing that equality so understood is detrimental, rather than conducive, to good lives. The criticism of justice, by contrast, begins by denying that the liberal conception of it is correct but showing that, given the correct conception, justice is indeed a requirement of good lives. The criticism of pluralism starts off by accepting both the liberal conception of it and it's being a requirement of good lives but denying that liberals can be pluralists and regard autonomy and the other basic liberal values as necessary for good lives.

5.1 THE NATURE OF EGALITARIANISM

Egalitarianism is the belief that equality is a basic value of political morality and that its claims take precedence over the claims of many other values that may conflict with it. Egalitarians need not think that equality is the most important value of political morality, but they must be committed to regarding it as at least one among a handful of the most important values. Nor need opponents of egalitarianism reject equality as a value; they must only deny that it is a basic one.

Liberalism is egalitarian because it regards equality as a basic value. But this does not mean that liberals agree with one another about equality. They disagree about its interpretation, about the contexts in which it is rightly valued, and about the reasonable resolution of conflicts between it and other basic values of liberalism. As a result, all liberals are egalitarians, but they may be more or less so. The more egalitarian they are, the closer they move to socialism on their left, and the less egalitarian they are, the more they move in the direction of conservatism on their right. Although egalitarians need not be liberals, egalitarianism will be understood here to mean only its liberal version.[1]

The acceptability of egalitarianism ultimately depends on whether it is right to regard equality as a basic value. That question however can be answered only if equality is first understood. A step to that end is to distinguish between formal and substantive equality. Formal equality is expressed by the Aristotelian formula: equals should be treated equally, and unequals should be treated unequally (Aristotle 1984b: Book 5). The force of the formula is that *if* two or more things are equal, then it is unjustified to treat them in different ways, and *if* they are unequal, then it is unjustified to treat them in the same way. The formula is formal, however, because it does not specify how to convert the conditional claim into a categorical one. Religious or racial discrimination, for instance, may be made consistent with formal equality by the simple expedient of pointing to differences among any two religions or races. Formal equality thus expresses no more than the logical requirement of consistency, namely, like cases ought to be treated alike and different cases differently. Substantive equality is needed to specify what makes things equal or unequal and what gives equality a moral content that goes beyond mere consistency. The substance of equality is the claim that the good of every human being matters and matters equally.[2]

This claim, however, may be factual or moral. If it is factual, it is supposed to rest on some actual characteristic that all human beings share, and substantive equality holds because of it. If, on the other hand, the claim is moral, then it rests on the conviction that morality itself, independently of what characteristics human beings have, prescribes that the good of every human being ought to matter and matter equally.

Neither interpretation is persuasive when it stands alone. Suppose that there actually is some common human characteristic. Why should its possession warrant equal treatment? Say that human beings have ten toes. Why should that have any moral force? Whatever the common characteristic is, it must be one that has demonstrable moral relevance. But the moral interpretation by itself is similarly unpersuasive. If it is true that there are differences among human beings, is it then not inconsistent with equality to treat different human beings alike? The moral interpretation of equality therefore requires both that equality should be grounded on some universal human characteristic and that this characteristic should have sufficient moral weight to warrant the good of everyone possessing it to matter, and matter equally. The claim expressing the force of substantive equality is therefore both factual and moral, both descriptive and prescriptive. All human beings ought to be recognized as mattering equally because of some universally shared and morally significant human characteristic.

The favored liberal candidate for this characteristic is, of course, autonomy, understood as the capacity to act on the basis of unforced choices that involve the agents' favorable evaluation and understanding of the significance of their chosen actions. It is crucial to this claim that autonomy, as the universal and morally significant characteristic in virtue of which the good of all human beings matters and matters equally, is a capacity. It is something all human beings can exercise, not something that they must exercise; it is a potentiality, not an actual performance.

Many bad arguments have been directed at egalitarianism on the ground that human beings obviously differ in the extent to which they live autonomously. Egalitarians not only acknowledge such differences but appeal to them in support of many of their political programs. The universal and morally significant respect in which human beings are alike is their capacity for autonomy. One of the ways in which they are different is the extent to which they realize this capacity. Such differences exist because genetic and environmental factors cause variations in temperament, talent, intelligence, education, upbringing, wealth, health, opportunity, and so forth. Egalitarians can acknowledge these differences because their position is not based on the absurd claim that people matter equally because there are no differences between them. People matter equally because they have a capacity for autonomy, even though they differ in their realization of that capacity.

Egalitarianism involves the insistence on the moral significance of both this similarity and this difference. The moral significance of the similarity is that the good of everyone matters equally, and the moral significance of the difference is that it is an evil that people are prevented by it from living autonomously. Egalitarianism therefore combines the valuing of this particular similarity with an attempt to minimize this particular difference. Many of the egalitarian political programs are therefore designed to minimize differences in the extent to which people live autonomously. Even though people are equal in their capacity for autonomy, it is justified to treat them unequally if by doing so differences in the realization of their equal capacity are minimized.

The egalitarian moral vision is thus of a world in which all human beings live as autonomously as possible. To have such a world, it is necessary to protect conditions in which people can realize their capacity to live that way. Some egalitarian political programs are designed to encourage people in this endeavor, others are designed to remove obstacles from their way. Substantive equality, understood as the claim that the good of everyone matters and matters equally, does not mean, therefore, that everyone ought to be treated alike. It means that everyone ought to be treated so as to have an equal opportunity to realize his or her capacity to live autonomously. Owing to human differences, this is going to require political programs that respond to these differences. Egalitarianism thus routinely involves treating people unequally.

The egalitarian insistence on the concept of equality thus understood must be further elaborated in terms of conceptions of equality. These conceptions spell out the nature of particular political programs that are required for promoting equality and removing obstacles from its way. There is general agreement among egalitarians and between egalitarians and their critics that these political programs concern the fostering of equality in respect to political power, legal impartiality, social status, and economic condition. There is no serious disagreement about the desirability of political and legal equality, although one need not be committed to egalitarianism to believe that. Universal adult suffrage and representative government are intended to give everyone equal initial political power and assure that delegation is the only legitimate means of acquiring greater power. And the rule of law is generally recognized to mean that its jurisdiction ought to apply to all citizens equally, regardless of their economic, social, or political status.

The desirability of social and economic equality, however, is a hotly contested issue. For reasons that are more historical and sociological than philosophical, contemporary debates focus on economic rather than social equality. The crucial question is whether political programs designed to lessen economic inequality foster or hinder the autonomous functioning of people in a particular context. Economic egalitarians think that they do foster it; some of their critics disagree because they have doubts about that particular conception of equality. This is a noisy debate, with passions running high on both sides. But from a philosophical point of view, it is a side issue, which has to do with translating equality into practical terms. The deeper question is whether equality should be regarded as a basic value. It is in their answers to this question that egalitarians and their critics disagree most fundamentally.

A further step toward the clarification of the egalitarian claim is to understand just how strong it is meant to be. There are three possible interpretations, all of which stress the importance of equality as a basic value but differ over how to resolve conflicts between equality and other values. One interpretation is that equality is an absolute value that allows no exceptions: in any particular situation in which the fostering of equality conflicts with some other value, equality should prevail. This is the Kantian view of the matter. All human beings are equal and ought to be treated equally as ends in themselves because they are all equally capable of autonomy. The difficulties of this extreme view are well known. Claims of equality may conflict with each other; the moral cost of equality may be prohibitively high because a great deal might be gained in pluralism, freedom, rights, and distributive justice by surrendering a small amount of equality; and equality in general may best be served by sacrificing some equality in particular cases.

A more plausible interpretation is that equality is an overriding value, not an absolute one. It is the most important of all the basic liberal values, but it allows for exceptions in certain specific cases. These are cases in which the claims of equality conflict or in which the surrender of a small amount of equality strengthens the cause of equality in general. Equality still overrides other values, but it allows for legitimate exceptions— namely, those warranted by equality itself.[3]

This interpretation is more defensible than the previous one, but it shares the difficulty with the Kantian view that equality, being only one of the basic values of liberalism, may conflict with the other basic values. Egalitarianism is a liberal position only if the importance attributed to equality is consistent with attributing similar importance to pluralism, freedom, rights, and distributive justice. Liberals will not favor equality at the cost of other basic liberal values of the same importance.

For these reasons, liberals are likely to find most congenial a third interpretation, which holds that equality is neither an absolute nor an overriding but a prima facie value. There is always an initial presumption in favor of equality, but it can be defeated by sufficiently strong countervailing considerations. This interpretation is similar to the preceding one in regarding equality as defeasible, but it differs from it by widening the range of considerations that can legitimately defeat equality. The wider range makes it possible to accommodate the claims of other basic values of liberalism by acknowledging that the importance of all the basic values of liberalism derives from their contribution to autonomy. Autonomy is what ultimately matters, and the basic values, including equality, matter because they are important for it. The prima facie case for equality may be justifiably defeated, then, by some other basic liberal value if thereby the whole system of basic values is better served than otherwise. And the whole system matters more than equality when, and only when, preferring it is the best way of increasing autonomy. Egalitarians believe that most often it is by promoting equality that autonomy is increased. This is the egalitarianism of such liberals as Ronald Dworkin.[4]

This conception of equality takes it then to be the substantive, not the merely formal, claim that the good of all human beings matters equally. The substance of the claim is that human beings are alike in possessing a capacity to live autonomously. Possession of such a capacity is taken to be a morally significant fact about human beings. Equality expresses the moral requirement that each and every human being should have the same opportunity to live a good life by exercising and realizing this capacity. Egalitarians generally agree that equality is best secured in the present Western context by political programs that favor economic equality.

5.2 THE JUSTIFICATION OF EGALITARIANISM

One would expect that a great deal has been written on the justification of egalitarianism, but one would be disappointed. Most liberal arguments concentrate on clarifying the nature of equality, working out the details of favored conceptions of it, and championing one conception against its competitors. The literature is reminiscent of scholastic debates about the nature of the Trinity. Everything is considered in minute detail except the tenability of the basic assumption. The liberal attitudes responsible for this state of affairs range from disclaiming the need for justification to offering ones so cursory that they carry only the believers' conviction. The deeper reason underlying these attitudes is the supposition that no decent person who understands what is at stake could fail to be committed to egalitarianism in one form or another. This too brings to mind a scholastic attitude: the one toward atheists.

By way of illustration, consider some examples. Isaiah Berlin tells us: "Equality is one of the oldest and deepest elements in liberal thought, and is neither more nor less 'natural' or 'rational' than any other constituent in them [*sic*]. Like all human ends it cannot be defended or justified, for it is itself which justifies other acts" (1978b: 102). Equality is thus an article of faith that is not rationally defensible.

Joel Feinberg declares: "In attributing human worth to everyone we [are] . . . expressing an attitude—an attitude of respect—toward humanity in each man's person. That attitude . . . is not grounded on anything more ultimate than itself, and it is not demonstrably justifiable. It can be argued further against skeptics that a world with equal human rights is a *more just* world . . . a *less dangerous* world . . . and one with a *more elevated and civilized* tone. If none of this convinces the skeptic, we should turn our back on him and examine more important problems" (1973: 94). One wonders whether liberals would be satisfied with such a treatment when they occupy the position of skeptic regarding conservative or religious attitudes.

Will Kymlicka writes: "I want to explore a suggestion, advanced by Ronald Dworkin, that . . . every plausible political theory has the same ultimate source, which is equality. . . . A theory is egalitarian . . . if it accepts that the interests of each member of the community matter, and matter equally. . . . [I]f a theory claimed that some people were not entitled to equal consideration from the government, if it claimed that certain kinds of people just do not matter as much as others, then most people in the modern world would reject that theory immediately. . . . [T]he fundamental argument is not whether to accept equality, but how to interpret it" (1990: 4–5). But he does not give reasons for these breathtaking claims: they are his initial assumptions.

Thomas Nagel says that he is going to explore the individualistic argument "because that is the type of argument that I think is likely to succeed. It would provide a moral basis for the kind of liberal egalitarianism that seems to me plausible. I do not have such an argument" (1979b: 108). This does not stop him, however, from saying that "moral equality, [the] attempt to give equal weight, in essential respects, to each persons' point of view . . . might even be described as the mark of an enlightened ethic" (1979b: 112). Years later he says, "My claim is that the problem of designing institutions that do justice to the equal importance of all persons, without unacceptable demands on individuals, has not been solved" (1991: 5), but he nevertheless endeavors to "present a case for wishing to extend the reach of equality beyond what is customary in modern welfare states" (1991: 63).

Larry Temkin characterizes his book as offering "a coherent, systematic, non-ad hoc method for accommodating, explaining, and ultimately guiding our egalitarian judgments. . . . [A]lthough I think most of the arguments that have been offered against equality can be refuted, let me emphasize that this book is neither a defense, nor an attack on, the ideal of equality. I do not address the question of whether one *should* care about inequality" (1993: 5–6). Apparently "our egalitarian judgments" may be taken for granted—all we need is a method for guiding them.

Not far below the surface of this flaunted indifference to making a reasoned case for egalitarianism and its political programs, which, it should be remembered, involve taking from people what they have legitimately acquired and giving it to people who are thought to need it more, is the widely shared sentiment that the rejection of equality as a basic value is morally unacceptable. The labels of Nazi, racist, proapartheid, proslavery, Social Darwinist, egoist, and so forth spring readily to the lips of many egalitarians by way of maligning their opponents and making the justification of the liberal case unnecessary. As Kymlicka remarks: "Some theories, like Nazism, deny that each person matters equally. But such theories do not merit serious consideration" (1989: 40). If their opponents avowed analogous sentiments instead of defending their positions, liberals would rightly charge them with substituting righteous moralizing for reasoned arguments.

Not all egalitarians proceed in this manner. One strategy for actually trying to defend equality as a basic value that is prima facie preferable both to the other basic values of liberalism and to less basic ones is to argue that there is a strong intuitive case for it and that arguments against the intuitive case fail. The intuitive case is: "Every nation of the world is divided into haves and have-nots. . . . The gap between the life prospects of the best-off and the worst-off individuals, in terms of wealth, income, education, access to medical care, employment or leisure-time options, and any other index of well-being one might care to name, is enormous. . . . Confronting these disparities, the egalitarian holds that it would be a morally better state of affairs if everyone enjoyed the same level of social and economic benefits" (Arneson 1993: 489).

If someone, beholding the miseries of the worst-off and the badly-off people throughout the world, as well as close to home, did not think of their miseries as evil, then doubts about such person's commitment to morality would indeed be justified. It may then be regarded as common ground between egalitarians and at least some of their critics that there is widespread, unequally distributed suffering in the world, that there are great differences in the social and economic well-being of people, and that morality requires some response to this state of affairs. The question is whether egalitarianism is the right response.

As a beginning toward answering it, it should be noted that there are many people who are not Nazis, who have given thought to the egalitarian case, and who have rejected it.[5] It is, therefore, false to claim that the "fundamental argument is not whether to accept equality, but how to interpret it" (Kymlicka 1990: 5). The significance of these criticisms is that the intuitive case dose not create a presumption in favor of egalitarianism, for the case can be accepted and egalitarianism can still be rejected without irrationality or immorality. There are four independent criticisms of egalitarianism, which will be discussed in the next four sections.

5.3 FIRST CRITICISM: MISDIAGNOSIS

The argument in support of egalitarianism is then to point out that great inequalities exist, that as a result of them people's chances of living a good life are vastly different, and that this is morally objectionable. The next step is to ask what follows from this intuitive judgment.

Dworkin's answer sets out what he calls "the abstract egalitarian thesis": "From the standpoint of politics, the interests of the members of the community matter, and matter equally" (R. Dworkin 1983: 24). These interests are "in having as a good a life as possible, a life that has in it much of what a life should have. Almost everyone acts as if he or she had that interest, and it is necessary to assume it in order to make sense of the kind of deliberation and judgment we exercise at important moments in our lives" (26). This, of course, is the familiar notion of autonomy, and it is with respect to their autonomous functioning that individuals "matter, and matter equally." But autonomy must be genuine: "We must not propose, as a fixed social goal for any person, some goal that he himself could not endorse as a . . . goal for himself" (29). This would be "unduly, deeply paternalistic" (28), with "totalitarian consequences" (29). What is needed for autonomy in Kymlicka's gloss on Dworkin's position "is that we lead our life from the inside, in accordance with our beliefs about what gives value to life . . . and that we be free to question these beliefs" (1989: 13).

It follows that "politics should aim that people have better lives, on the whole, and to aim at this in some way that treats the highest-order interest as equally important for each person" (R. Dworkin 1983: 26). Thus "according to liberalism, since our most essential interest is in getting these beliefs right and acting on them, government treats people as equals, with equal concern and respect, by providing for each individual the liberty and resources needed to examine and act on these beliefs" (Kymlicka 1989: 13).

The consensus in intuitive judgments about inequality being morally deplorable reflects the condemnation of political arrangements that fail to treat people with equal concern and respect. It is morally wrong if a "citizen has less than an equal share of the community's resources just in order that others may have more of what he lacks" (R. Dworkin 1985c: 206). To put this wrong right is the purpose of "an egalitarian priority system . . . [that] counts improvements to the welfare of the worst off as more urgent than improvements to the welfare of the better off. . . . [W]hat makes a system egalitarian is the priority it gives to the claims of those . . . at the bottom. . . . Each individual with a more urgent claim has priority . . . over each individual with a less urgent claim" (Nagel 1979b: 117–18). Such a priority system follows Rawls's "lexical difference principle," which is "first maximize the welfare of the worst . . . second . . . the welfare of the second worst-off and so on until the last case which is . . . maximize the welfare of the best off" (Rawls 1971: 83).

The trouble with this argument is that it misdiagnoses what it is that intuitive judgments find morally wrong. It is true that there are great differences in the resources people need and have to live autonomously. It is also true that most people find this deplorable. What is deplorable, however, is not inequality but that some people do not have enough. This point and the argument for it are Frankfurt's (1988b). He uses them to criticize economic egalitarianism, but they will be adapted to present purposes and generalized to apply to all resources.

That the intuitive case does not support egalitarianism becomes obvious if instead of thinking about inequalities between those who are well-off and those who are badly-off, the inequalities between the rich and the superrich are considered. It is certainly not intuitively deplorable that billionaires have more money than millionaires. Those who find even this deplorable are not thinking of differences among those who possess great wealth but of other inequalities that supposedly harm those who are poor and benefit those who are rich and superrich. Thus what is deplorable is not inequality as such but inequality that results in some people not having sufficient resources for living autonomously. It is poverty that matters, not inequalities of income; disenfranchisement, not politicians' having more power than professors; racial prejudice, not the recognition of different levels of achievement; inadequate medical care, not the ability of a few to buy cosmetic surgery.

The alternative to recognizing that it is not inequality but insufficient resources for autonomous living that is an affront to morality is to object to the unavoidable consequences of there being human differences. Genetic endowments and social conditions vary, and they influence how successful people are in exercising their autonomy. To begrudge the success of others when one had a fair chance of achieving it oneself is the vice of envy. But if the resources for living autonomously are available, it is not envy to find it morally repugnant that some people are deprived of them for no good reason. The question is whether the egalitarian policy of trying to improve the condition of those who are worst off by redistributing resources is the right answer. There are several reasons for thinking otherwise.

In order to give these reasons, it is necessary to refer to what will be called "the autonomy level." Above this level, people have the resources they need to live autonomously; below it, they do not. These resources are understood to include money, as well as education, health, physical security, respect, and so forth, as necessary for autonomous living. Inequalities above the autonomy level are not morally objectionable, assuming that they are the consequences of legitimate activities. Inequalities below the autonomy level are morally objectionable, unless good reasons can be given to justify them. Some good reasons are scarcity of resources, irrational conduct that led someone to move from above the autonomy level to below it, and punishment for serious illegal or immoral acts that endangered the capacity of others to live autonomously.

The first reason to doubt the egalitarian policy of redistributing resources to improve the condition of those who are worst off is that it makes all the difference whether they are below or above the autonomy level. If they are above it, they have sufficient resources for living autonomously. In that case, however, not only is there no good reason to institute government policies to help them but there are good reasons not to pursue such policies. These reasons are the familiar ones against paternalistic meddling with people's lives for their supposed good, especially in circumstances, which ex hypothesi are these people's, where they do not need the additional resources foisted on them. Of course, few societies are so fortunate as to have their worst off citizens above the autonomy level.

Take another case: the resources available in a society are scarce and most people are somewhere just above the subsistence level but below, often substantially below, the autonomy level. The redistribution of resources from the better off to the worst off in this context will do nothing toward achieving the egalitarian goal of making it possible for people to live autonomous lives, because even those who are better off lack the necessary resources. If the resources are taken from those very few who live above the autonomy level, given widespread poverty, the result will be to deprive even them of the resources needed for autonomous life without putting anyone above the autonomy level. The net misery will increase.

Actually, however, societies typically fall between the extremes of having most people either above or below the autonomy level. Consider therefore a society in which a third of the people live below the autonomy level, while the rest live above it, some far above. The egalitarian redistribution will then take resources from those above the autonomy level and transfer these resources to those below it, thereby raising them from below to above, without putting anyone below. This is the ideal case for the egalitarian policy of redistribution, and it is important to see that it does not obtain in the real world.

The reason is the chronic scarcity of resources, which is common ground between egalitarians and their critics. The disagreement is about how scarce resources should be distributed. The egalitarian policy of redistributing them from those above the autonomy level to the worst-off below it is bound to result in fewer and fewer people having the resources to live autonomously.

The available and scarce resources of a society are put to two basic types of uses: consumption and production. The significance of scarcity is that there are not sufficient resources to place everyone above the autonomy level simply by reducing the consumption of some people and increasing that of others. This being so, the only way of obtaining additional resources for consumption, and thereby improving the condition of the worst-off, is to use fewer resources for production. But that of course will inevitably lead to greater scarcity of resources in the future. That is why the egalitarian policy of redistribution will result, under the condition of scarcity, in ever fewer people having the means to live autonomously.

These doubts about egalitarianism operate on two levels. One is practical, and the relevant doubts concern the efficacy of the policy of redistribution. This level eventually involves complicated issues in economic theory that have been glossed over above. Although the doubts that have been expressed on this score rest on apparently forceful arguments that are independent of the intricacies of economic theory, appearances can be deceptive, and the force of the arguments may dissipate in the mist of the uncertainties of economic theorizing. If this were indeed the case, then the uncertainties would affect both the egalitarian case and this objection to it. The possible uncertainties should consequently not be interpreted as providing license to pursue the policy of redistribution; rather, they would provide a reason for suspending it.

The other level on which the doubts operate is that of justification. The egalitarian justification for the policy of redistribution to improve the condition of those who are worst off was supposed to rest on the basic liberal value of equality, which renders inequality prima facie morally objectionable. The argument has shown, however, that this justification fails. Inequality per se is not morally objectionable. What is morally objectionable is that some people, for no good reason, are deprived of the available and sufficient resources to live autonomously. The intuitive case on which egalitarians attempt to base their justification of equality as a basic value does not, therefore, provide what is needed. This conclusion, of course, is compatible with recognizing equality as a nonbasic value.

5.4 SECOND CRITICISM: ABSURD CONSEQUENCES

It is a basic egalitarian belief that serious, unjustified inequalities are morally objectionable and that the measure of a just society is the extent to which it eliminates or at least reduces them. Inequalities are serious if they affect primary goods, which are goods necessary for living a good life, such as adequate income, health care, education, physical security, housing, and so forth. There are several egalitarian views about what serious inequalities are unjustified, but only one of them will be considered here. According to this view, all serious inequalities are unjustified unless they benefit everyone in one's society, especially those who are worst off. The best-known defenders of this view are probably John Rawls (1971, 1993) and Thomas Nagel (1991).

One obvious implication of egalitarianism is that overcoming serious, unjustified inequalities requires the redistribution of primary goods, which involves taking them from those who are better off and giving them to those who are worse off. The effect of such redistribution is to make the worst off better off, thus gradually reducing the unjustified inequalities. This is one aim of and justification for many policies intimately connected with the welfare state, namely, graduated taxation, affirmative action and equal opportunity programs, the preferential treatment of various minorities and women, and a whole panoply of antipoverty policies inaugurated by the Great Society legislations.

Consider now the table on page 101, which is extracted from the *Statistical Abstract of the United States*. These figures make it obvious that American men born between 1970 and 2010 have an actual or projected life expectancy that is significantly lower than American women born in the same years. Because the difference in the life expectancy of men and women is roughly between seven and eight years and life expectancy ranges from 67 to just over 81 years, it may be said that the life expectancy of American men born in the relevant years is about one-tenth lower than that of women born in the same years.

Expectations of Life at Birth, 1970–1992, and Projections, 1995–2010

Year	Men	Women
1970	67.1	74.7
1975	68.8	76.6
1980	70.0	77.4
1981	70.4	77.8
1982	70.8	78.1
1983	71.0	78.1
1984	71.1	78.2
1985	71.1	78.2
1986	71.2	78.2
1987	71.4	78.3
1988	71.4	78.3
1989	71.7	78.5
1990	71.8	78.8
1991	72.0	78.9
1992	72.3	79.0
1995, Projections	72.8	79.7
2000	73.2	80.2
2005	73.8	80.7
2010	74.5	81.3

Source: U.S. Bureau of the Census 1994: 87, table no. 114.

There is thus an inequality in respect to the life expectancy of men and women. (The qualification that it holds for Americans born between 1970 and 2010 will from now on be omitted but should be understood to hold.) This inequality is serious because life expectancy has at least as strong a claim to being a primary good as any other candidate. Generally, it is better to live longer. But men tend to have lives about one-tenth shorter than women. With regard to the primary good of life expectancy, men form a group whose members tend to be worse off than the group whose members are women. Because there are only two groups, men in this respect are not only worse off but also the worst off.

But is this inequality unjustified? It may be justified, but only if it could be shown that it is in everybody's interest, and especially in the interest of men, who in this case are the worst off. It is obvious, however, that this is not so. In the first place, it is not in the interest of men to live shorter lives. In the second place, it is not in the interest of women either, because the lives of men and women are intertwined in countless relationships, such as love, friendship, parenthood, and so on, and men provide knowledge, skill, and services on which women rely. Women, of course, do the same for men, but that is beside the point in the present context. The shorter life expectancy of men thus constitutes a loss not just for men but for women as well to the extent to which women wish for the continuation of these valued relationships and rely on men.

Egalitarians have said that "the gap between the life prospects of the best-off and the worst-off individuals, in terms of wealth, income, education, access to medical care, employment or leisure-time options, and any other index of well-being one might care to name, is enormous. . . . Confronting these disparities, the egalitarian holds that it would be a better state of affairs if everyone enjoyed the same level of social and economic benefits" (Arneson 1993: 489); that "how could it not be an evil that some people's prospects at birth are radically inferior to others?" (Nagel 1991: 28); and that "undeserved inequalities call for redress; and since inequalities of birth and natural endowments are undeserved, these inequalities are to be somehow compensated for. . . . The idea is to redress the bias of contingencies in the direction of equality" (Rawls 1971: 100–101). If egalitarians mean what they have said, then they must find the serious and unjustified inequality between the life expectancy of men and women morally objectionable.

If this inequality *is* morally objectionable, then the question arises of what ought to be done about it. Egalitarians give a clear answer: "What makes a system egalitarian is the priority it gives to the claims of those . . . at the bottom. . . . Each individual with a more urgent claim has priority . . . over each individual with a less urgent claim" (Nagel 1979: 117–18). Such a priority system follows the "lexical difference principle," which is: "first maximize the welfare of the worst off . . . second . . . the welfare of the second worst-off and so on until the last case" (Rawls 1971: 83). This answer is guided by the belief that "those who have been favored by nature . . . may gain from their good fortune only in terms that improve the situation of those who have lost out" (Rawls 1971: 101).

These egalitarian policies cannot be applied directly to unequal life expectancy, for life expectancy is not a good, like money, that can be taken from one and given to another. But it is easy to see how the policies could be applied indirectly. Available resources that tend to lengthen life expectancy ought to be redistributed from women to men and "undeserved inequalities . . . somehow compensated for" (Rawls 1971: 100). Redistribution and compensation will not eliminate this unjustified inequality, but they will reduce the morally objectionable gap between the well off and the worst off.

What policies would bring about the appropriate redistribution? The most obvious one affects health care: men ought to have more and better health care than women. How much more and how much better are difficult questions of fine-tuning. The general answer, however, is that redistribution ought to aim to equalize the life expectancy of men and women by making men have longer and women shorter lives. But life expectancy is also affected by stressful, demeaning, soul-destroying, and hazardous jobs. So what obviously ought to be done is to employ fewer men and more women in these undesirable jobs. Another factor affecting life expectancy is leisure. Men therefore ought to have shorter working days and longer vacations than women. This will not lead to diminished productivity if loss in man-hours is counterbalanced by gain in woman-hours.

Yet a further policy follows from the realization that because men have shorter lives than women, they are less likely to benefit after retirement from social security payments and medicare treatments. As things are, in their present inegalitarian state, men and women are required to contribute an equal percentage of their earnings to the social security and medicare funds. This is clearly unjust from the egalitarian point of view: why should men be required to subsidize the health and wealth of women in their declining years? The policy this suggests is to decrease the levy on men, or to increase it on women, or possibly do both at once. There is thus much that egalitarians could do by way of redistribution to reduce the unjustified inequality in the life expectancy of men and women.

However much that is, it will affect only future generations. There remains the question of how to compensate men born between 1970 and 2010 for the unjustified inequality of having lives one-tenth shorter than women. No compensation can undo the damage, but it may make it easier to bear. The obvious policy is to set up preferential treatment programs designed to provide for men at least some of the goods that they would have enjoyed had their life expectancy been equal to women's. Much pleasure could be had in those years that men are not going to have. And because those years would have come at the end of their lives, when they are more likely to know their minds, their loss affects not only the quantity but also the quality of their not-to-be-had pleasures. One efficient way of compensating them for their loss is to set up government-sponsored pleasure centers in which men may spend the hours and days gained from having shorter working days and longer vacations.

Having dwelt on the absurd policies that follow from egalitarianism, the time has come to ask: What is wrong with these policies? Let it be said immediately that this question will not be answered here. Indeed, the very point of the argument is to raise the question and then leave it to egalitarians to try to answer. They *should* try because the absurd policies follow from basic egalitarian beliefs, and their absurdity casts doubt on the beliefs from which they follow. That of course means that the justification customarily given for the policies that are more usually associated with egalitarianism—namely, antipoverty programs, various welfare legislations, the preferential treatment of minorities and women, and so forth—is called into question as well.

Egalitarians should try to answer this question for another reason as well. The very absurdity of the policies discussed above will create the suspicion in some minds not completely set in the ideological mold of egalitarianism that the policies more usually associated with egalitarianism suffer from analogous absurdity. Such uncommitted people may suspect that the reason why the familiar egalitarian policies do not appear absurd has more to do with familiarity produced by repetition than with the justification available for them. Egalitarians should try to answer the question to dispel that suspicion.

It is a safe bet, however, that if egalitarians do not ignore the question altogether, then they will claim that it has an obvious answer. It is impossible to tell what all the yet-to-be-given answers may be, but there are three predictable ones, and it needs to be discussed why each fails.

The first is to claim that there is a significant disanalogy between men being worst off in respect to life expectancy and the poor, minorities, and women being worst off in respect to some other primary goods. The disanalogy, egalitarians may say, is that members of these other groups are worst off because preventable injustice has been done to them, such as exploitation, discrimination, prejudice, and so forth, while this is not true of men.

A moment of thought shows, however, that this answer is untenable. In the first place, the group of men includes minorities and the poor, who, according to egalitarians, have suffered from injustice. And the groups of minorities and women include high achievers, middle- and upper-class people, people with considerable wealth, as well as recent immigrants who came to this country voluntarily and could not have suffered from injustice here. It is but the crudest prejudice to think of men as Archie Bunkers, of women as great talents sentenced to housewifery, and of blacks and Hispanics as ghetto dwellers doomed by injustice to a life of poverty, crime, and addiction. Many men have been victims of injustice, and many women and minorities have not been.

It will be said against this that there is still a disanalogy, for the poor, minorities, and women are more likely to have been victims of injustice than have men. Suppose that this is so. What justice requires then, according to egalitarians, is the redistribution of the relevant primary goods and compensation for their loss. But these policies will be just only if they benefit victims of injustice, and the victims cannot be identified simply as poor, minorities, or women, who, as individuals, may not have suffered any injustice. Moreover, those members of these groups who do lack primary goods may do so not because of injustice but because of bad luck, poor choices, or having taken risks and lost. Overcoming injustice requires, therefore, a much more precise identification of the victims than merely membership in such amorphous groups as those of women, minorities, or the poor. This more precise identification requires asking and answering the question of why people who lack primary goods lack them.

Answering this question must include consideration of the possibility that people may cause or contribute to their own misfortune and that it is their lack of merit, effort, or responsibility, not injustice, that explains why they lack primary goods. The consideration of this possibility, however, is regarded as misguided by egalitarians. According to them, the mere fact of being worst off is sufficient to warrant redistribution and compensation.

It need not be considered here whether egalitarians are right about this, for, right or wrong, they face a dilemma. If the policies of redistribution and compensation do take into account the degree to which people are responsible for being among those who are worst off, then the justification of these policies must go beyond what egalitarians have been willing to provide. For the justification must then involve consideration of merit, desert, effort, and so forth. To the extent to which this is done, the justification ceases to be egalitarian.

If, on the other hand, the policies of redistribution and compensation do not take into account the degree of responsibility that people have for being among the worst off, then there is no disanalogy between men, who are worst off in respect to life expectancy, and women, minorities, or the poor, who are worst off in other respects. Consistent egalitarian policies would then have to aim to overcome all inequalities, which is just what produces the absurd policies noted above.

Egalitarians may try in a second way to show that the absurd policies do not follow from their position. They may say that these policies are based on an assumption that they do not hold. The policies do cast doubt on this assumption, but they leave the basic egalitarian beliefs intact. The argument that has been given against egalitarianism thus rests on a misunderstanding.

The assumption from which the absurd policies follow is that inequalities ought to be overcome in respect to *specific* primary goods, such as life expectancy. The egalitarian position, by contrast, is that the inequalities that should be overcome hold in respect to primary goods *taken together* in a complete life.[6] It may be, egalitarians will say, that there is inequality between men and women in their life expectancy, but if inequalities of education, income, a decent job, and so forth are also considered, then they counterbalance the inequality of life expectancy. Overall inequalities clearly favor men over women. It is, according to this egalitarian answer, the overall inequality of primary goods taken together that is morally objectionable.

This answer, however, is no better than the preceding one. The first problem with it is the specification of primary goods. If the inequalities that matter are of primary goods collectively, then there must be an account of what all the primary goods included in the collection are. But no such account exists. Egalitarians say that primary goods "are things which it is supposed a rational man wants whatever else he wants" (Rawls 1971: 92), and they proceed to give a more or less impressionistic list of some obvious candidates. The following list is typical: "The chief primary goods at the disposition of society are rights and liberties, powers and opportunities, income and wealth. . . . The primary good of self-respect [also] has a central place. . . . These are the social primary goods. Other primary goods such as health and vigor, intelligence and imagination, are natural goods" (Rawls 1971: 62). That this list is incomplete is obvious, since "a rational man" will want a lot of other things in addition to these primary goods, such as a satisfying sex life, an interesting job, success, no physical and psychological pain, a meaningful life, not to die prematurely, not to be bored or ridiculed, and so on. How could it possibly be established who is worst off in respect to the primary goods taken together, if it is left unspecified what the goods are that are to be taken together?

Suppose, however, that this problem has been solved and there is an authoritative list of primary goods. Suppose further that only those goods are included in this list that are directly or indirectly open to social control. The question remains, How could it be established that some people are the worst off in respect to these goods regarded collectively?

Taken the simplest of cases: two lives, in one of which all the primary goods are present except an interesting job and another in which the one missing primary good is free expression. What compelling reason is there for holding that one of these people is bound to be worse off than the other? And which one is that? In the usual course of events, of course, nothing is as simple as this. Primary goods are weighted differently by different people, they are possessed in different degrees, and people differ in their capacity to enjoy what they have or to compensate for what they lack. If the inequalities that matter concern the primary goods taken together, then these impossible comparisons must be made possible. That has not been done, however, and it is most unlikely that it could be done, especially because the comparisons must support policies that are bound to disregard individual circumstances and apply impersonally to members of some group.

It is perhaps for this reason that actual egalitarian policies are never derived from the identification of the worst off group on the basis of the overall possession of primary goods. When women or minorities are treated preferentially, no one asks about their income. When the poor are made beneficiaries of antipoverty programs, no one asks what powers and opportunities they actually have. When welfare legislation denominates a large number of people as its clients, no one asks about the extent to which they feel self-respect. Actual egalitarian policies are thus at systematic variance with the attempt to repudiate the assumption that inequalities hold and are responded to in respect to specific primary goods rather than in respect to primary goods taken together.

Egalitarians may reply by acknowledging the difficulties inherent in applying their general position to the complex situations that confront those who make and implement policies. Such people are no more exempt from intellectual and moral error, no less subject to constraints of time, resources, and personnel, than is anyone else. Their failings and constraints, however, are *theirs*. They should not be taken to reflect adversely on the general position that they are trying to apply. The application of all general positions to complex situations encounters difficulties. It would be unfair to single out egalitarianism for having a difficulty that its competitors also have.

This reply, however, misses the nub of the objection. The difficulty egalitarians have is not just one of practical implementation, but a defect in the general position that is being implemented. The defect is that the implementation of egalitarian policies requires an authoritative list of primary goods, but there is no such list, and even if there were one, no reasonable basis has been found for comparing people with regard to their enjoyment or frustration on account of the primary goods on the list.

The third way in which egalitarians may try to avoid the absurd implications of their position is not so much an argument as a moral appeal. It takes the form of a restatement of the basic egalitarian beliefs in the conviction that reasonable and morally committed people share these beliefs, that disagreements among such people about these beliefs are due to some misunderstanding that can be cleared up, and that the sort of difficulties which have been raised here are mere questions of detail that have no bearing on the rational and moral credentials of the basic egalitarian beliefs.

Nagel provides one compact expression of these basic egalitarian beliefs: "How could it not be an evil that some people's prospects at birth are radically inferior to others?" (1991: 28). The expectation is that the question will be regarded as rhetorical because the answer is obvious, at least to right-minded people. The large body of critical responses to egalitarianism shows, however, that this expectation is mistaken.

That some people's prospects at birth are radically inferior to those of others is a statistical necessity. Being a necessity, it holds in all societies, even in perfectly just ones. Given any population and any basis of ranking the prospects of individuals in the population, some will rank higher, and others will rank lower. Those who rank lowest will have prospects radically inferior to those who rank highest. Inveighing against this unavoidable fact of life is as reasonable as lamenting differences in height or weight. To call this statistical necessity a moral evil is a sentimental cheapening of the most serious condemnation that morality affords. And the refusal to call it moral evil shows respect for fact, not moral insensitivity.

What makes it a moral evil that some people's prospects at birth are radically inferior to those of others is a combination of three factors. First, those who are worst off in this respect must lack the primary goods they need for a good life. In other words, the inequalities must be serious if they are to count as morally evil. It is not a moral evil if children born into comfortable, middle-class families are worse off than children born into families of billionaires.

Second, not even serious inequalities that make people the worst off and foreclose their chances of having a good life are in themselves morally evil, for the inequalities may not be preventable. Famine, epidemics, natural disasters, and the scarcity of necessary resources often produce serious inequalities for which no one can be blamed and which no one can undo. Serious inequalities are morally evil if they stand in the way of a good life and if, although they are preventable, they are allowed or caused to occur.

Third, even if preventable inequalities that make living a good life very hard are morally evil, it does not follow that morality requires a just society to do anything about them. If these inequalities are due to discrimination, exploitation, prejudice, and similar acts of social injustice, then a just society will do what it reasonably can to prevent them. But many inequalities do not result from social injustice but from personal short-comings and misfortune. Egalitarians need to provide compelling reasons to support their view that redistribution and compensation are morally required in such cases, especially because they involve depriving people of what they have acquired by legitimate means.

Morality requires a society to do what it reasonably can to prevent the injustice that occurs because of its institutional arrangements. But not all serious inequalities are unjust, preventable, or result from institutional arrangements. One basic egalitarian belief is that all serious inequalities are instances of social injustice. Egalitarian policies are then designed to overcome these inequalities. When the policies are challenged, egalitarians appeal to the moral requirement of opposing social injustice. That appeal, however, rests on the subsumption of all serious inequalities under social injustice. The point of the second criticism of egalitarianism that has just been completed is to show that this is a mistake and that making it has absurd implications.

5.5 THIRD CRITICISM: INCONSISTENCY

Readers of these lines are likely to be familiar with David Hume's famous complaint against moral philosophers who begin by talking about what is and then by imperceptible steps and without appropriate justification end up with claims about what ought to be (Hume 1960: 469). The third criticism of egalitarianism is that its defenders are guilty of a similar unwarranted slide, which reveals a serious inconsistency at the heart of their position. The slide begins with the universal claim of equality that is said to hold for all human beings and proceeds by imperceptible steps and without appropriate justification to particular political programs that affect only citizens of prosperous, Western, pluralistic, and industrialized liberal democracies.

As one among many possible illustrations of this unwarranted slide, consider Richard Arneson's distinction between two ideals of equality. One is "equality of condition," which applies to everyone: "The egalitarian holds that it would be a morally better state of affairs if everyone enjoyed the same level of social and economic benefits." The other is "equality of democratic citizenship," which "demands that each member of a society should be assured basic rights" (1993: 489). But he does not explain how an egalitarian can be consistently committed to the universal ideal of equality of condition and then restrict its application to equality among the citizens of a particular liberal democracy. Other egalitarians proceed in the same manner.[7] Does the value of equality not hold outside of that context? If it does, as it is obviously meant to do, why is his discussion restricted to a particular context?

Equality is a political value. As such, it is, or it ought to be, the value of some particular political unit, which for convenience is assumed to be a state. Egalitarianism is the view that equality ought to be a basic value of the state and perhaps of all states, although that is not absolutely clear because many states do not meet the requirement of forming a "reasonably harmonious and stable pluralist society" (Rawls 1993: xxv). There is no doubt, however, that egalitarians think that in a liberal state there is a prima facie case for the value of equality guiding the relevant political programs. It is also clear that these egalitarian programs are thought to be the responsibility, not of individuals, but of the governments of the appropriate states. Individuals *qua* individuals can favor egalitarian programs, but they cannot be responsible for them because family ties, special obligations, love, and friendship make it psychologically impossible and morally undesirable that they should act on the assumption that the interests of everyone matter equally. But governments can try to act on that assumption, they can try to sustain the required impartiality and impersonality, and egalitarians believe that the governments of liberal states ought to act in that way. The question is, for what reason?

Egalitarians base their reply on the formula that the interest of everyone matters, and matters equally. But no government acts according to this formula, and if one did, it would thereby betray its most basic responsibility: to promote the interests of the citizens who elected it—not everyone's interests but only those of its citizens. It would be absurd to demand of a government that it should be equally concerned with prosperity in the state it represents and elsewhere; with the welfare of poor citizens and poor foreigners; with the education of children born in the state and of those living elsewhere; and with security, epidemics, natural disasters, taxation, solidarity, and public spiritedness at home and in other states. If everyone's interests matter, and matter equally, then all governments always have acted, always will act, and always ought to act in gross violation of this egalitarian interpretation of equality.

It is in order to avoid placing absurd requirements on the government that egalitarians make the unwarranted slide from the universal to the particular interpretation of equality. Let their claim therefore be that a government should pursue only political programs which recognize that the interests of its citizens matter, and matter equally, and never mind about foreigners. The question of why governments ought to do this, then, arises once again. This time, however, the answer cannot appeal to a universal interpretation of the equality of all human beings, because the government, by representing the interests of only its citizens, acts against it.

If there is an answer, it must be based on some characteristic shared by all and only the citizens of a particular state. This characteristic cannot be the capacity for autonomy because foreigners also have it. For the same reason, it cannot be rationality, moral agency, self-consciousness, having a soul, or any other supposedly universal human characteristic. If there is a characteristic that fits the requirement, it must be something like citizenship acquired by birth or naturalization, having the right to vote, being subject to taxation, or sharing a culture composed of such elements as language, religion, history, common customs, and so forth. But whatever the characteristic, it, and not equality, is what makes it appropriate for the government to recognize that the interests of its citizens matter, and matter equally, whereas the interests of foreigners do not.

Equality plays no substantive role here; it is a rhetorical shorthand that refers to whatever characteristic distinguishes citizens from noncitizens. It is not a value that gets added to that which the relevant characteristic is already supposed to have; the value resides in the characteristic and in the prevailing attitude toward it. To say that the interests of citizens matter equally because they share the same culture, because they have the right to vote, because they are all taxpayers, or just because they are citizens is to make a substantive claim. But to say that they matter equally because they are equals is to convert an adverb into a noun that refers either to nothing or to an actual characteristic that would be less misleadingly identified by naming it rather than by disguising it under the label of equality.

Given the substantive claim, it would, of course, still have to be justified, but at least it would then be clear precisely what needs to be justified. And that is the supposition that the actual characteristic in respect to which all and only citizens are to be treated equally is a morally relevant one. Why does or should it make a difference to how much people's interests matter where they are born; in which, if any, elections they are entitled to vote; to whom they pay taxes; or what their cultural allegiances are? If such considerations make a moral difference to how much their interests matter, then the egalitarian claim that the interests of everyone matter equally is inconsistent with moral differences. If such considerations do not make a moral difference, then egalitarians are inconsistent in restricting their claim to a particular political context. They must opt for one or the other; whichever it is, inconsistency follows; and that is the third criticism of egalitarianism.

Egalitarians may try to respond to this criticism by claiming that restricting the universal claim of equality to a particular context is a necessary evil. It is a fact of politics that the state is the basic unit of organization. Realistic political programs must take this into account, and doing so requires working for equality in a particular state (much as Stalin said to Trotsky about socialism). But this is a poor response. The state is indeed the natural context of political programs. But maintaining the state so that the favored political programs can be implemented requires proceeding on the assumption that the interests of citizens matter more than the interests of noncitizens, and that the concern, respect, and resources a government owes to its citizens are much greater than what it owes to noncitizens. Restricting equality to a particular context, therefore, is not merely a temporary expedient forced on egalitarians until enlightenment spreads and universal equality becomes universally recognized. Particular equality requires political programs that are incompatible with universal equality. Restricting equality to a "reasonably harmonious and stable pluralist society" (Rawls 1993: xxv) will unavoidably increase inequality between the citizens of that society and others.

Egalitarians may take this as a reason for rejecting particular in favor of universal equality (see, for example, Beitz 1979: part 3; Pogge 1989: part 3; and Sterba 1980: chapter 6). But then they have to face the question that the scarcity of resources poses: Why would rational and at least partly self-interested agents forgo the resources they need for living autonomously in order to provide resources, probably insufficient, to make autonomy possible for strangers about whom they know very little, except that they are needy?

Suppose that the question is answered by consequentialists in terms of a universalized notion of benevolence, by contractarians in terms of human rights, or by Kantians in terms of the moral necessity of establishing a kingdom of ends. All such answers require the abandonment of the liberal state, as it now exists, and the establishment of something like a world government. The idea that existing states, both liberal and not, including states that have achieved independence only recently, would freely surrender their sovereignty is, to put it mildly, utopian. Moreover, if a world government were established, freely or by force, the idea that it would then have sufficient resources to redistribute so as to bring a significant number of people above the autonomy level requires evidence that has not been supplied. Finally, the idea that such a world government would promote the basic liberal values of freedom, equality, rights, pluralism, and distributive justice so that everyone could live autonomously is rendered chimerical by observation of existing states, among which only a small minority are liberal.

5.6 FOURTH CRITICISM: MORAL INEQUALITY

If one looks past the rhetoric in which egalitarianism is couched and asks what its claim actually means in practice, it is impossible not to be struck by its implausibility. The claim, as Ronald Dworkin puts it, is that there is "a natural right of men and women to equality of concern and respect, a right they possess not by virtue of birth or characteristic or merit or excellence but simply as human beings" (1977b: 182). Or, in Gregory Vlastos's words, "The human worth of all persons is equal, however unequal may be their merit" (1962: 43). The claim, therefore, is that all human beings, regardless of the balance of good and evil they have caused, have equal worth, that they have a right to equal concern and respect because of it, and that they are equally entitled to the resources needed for living autonomously.

The practical implication of this claim is that the just and the unjust, the kind and the vicious, the benevolent and the cruel, the benefactors of humanity and its scourges have an equal right to the resources they need for their continued functioning. And this is so regardless of how scarce the resources are and how recipients are likely to use them. Life-long patterns of good or evil conduct are supposed to be irrelevant to the respective worth of the people whose conduct form these patterns. No reasonable person could accept this. The problem for egalitarians, however, is that their position has this implication.

Egalitarians will naturally deny this. The first line of their defense will be that the claim of equal human worth is prima facie. There is a presumption in favor of treating people accordingly, but the presumption can be defeated by sufficiently strong reasons. In the case of wickedness, it will be said, the presumption is defeated.

One difficulty with this is that the reasons which can justifiably lead to the defeat of the prima facie case for human worth being both equal and independent of moral merit are nothing but appeals to unequal moral merit. The reason for condemning, imprisoning, shunning, and being suspicious of and outraged by wicked people whose conduct causes a long and predictable pattern of evil is that they have accumulated a great deal of moral demerit. And the reason for praising, trusting, and seeking the company of and admiring people who habitually benefit others is their considerable moral merit. When the prima facie case for equal human worth holds, therefore, it holds because of moral merit; and when it fails to hold, it fails because of moral demerit. Commitment to morality is inseparable from concern with the good and evil actions of people, actions that benefit or harm others. The ascription of human worth, especially comparative human worth, cannot therefore be independent of the moral merit of the agents and of their conduct.

One possible response to this objection may be to concede that moral merit affects human worth, but to argue that there is nevertheless a minimum level of concern, respect, and entitlement to resources, of which no amount of wickedness can legitimately deprive people. This minimum level may then be equated with what has been called the autonomy level (see Section 5.3). The idea then is that there is a deep sense in which commitment to morality brings with it the recognition that it is good if people can develop their potentialities. Morality is inseparable from wishing well for humanity. The insistence on the equal worth of all human beings is meant to capture this commitment people have, or ought to have, to the welfare of humanity collectively. The presumption of the equal worth of individual human beings is a distributive consequence of the general idea.

The obvious difficulty is that human potentialities are mixed; they are benign and aggressive, altruistic and selfish, generous and envious, gentle and cruel. If the commitment to human welfare calls for the development of morally good human potentialities, it also calls for the suppression of morally evil potentialities. If the idea of equal human worth licensed the indiscriminate fostering of human potentialities, it would not support human welfare. The importance of moral merit is that it serves as a basis on which morally good and evil potentialities can be distinguished, and that it provides a ground for encouraging the first and discouraging the second. Human welfare is better served by fostering or suppressing human potentialities according to their moral merit than by the egalitarian indiscriminateness that follows from the presumption of equal human worth.

The only way to resist this argument is by assuming that morally good and evil human potentialities do not have an equal status in human nature. This defense of egalitarianism rests on the already discredited faith in human nature being basically good (see Section 2.5). If this were so, there would indeed be a reason for fostering the development of human potentialities. The usual strategy for making the liberal faith support the egalitarian belief is to contrast people who have greater and lesser moral merit. It is then argued that the ones with less moral merit do not get written out of morality; they are still moral agents and have a claim to moral consideration, for although they have misused their potentialities, they still possess them. There is, therefore, hope for reform and improvement. Human worth attaches to potentialities that cannot be lost, only misused. Because potentialities are prior to their use or misuse, human worth is prior to moral merit.

There goes with the liberal faith a particular metaphor for morality. Morality is like language, and becoming a moral agent is like learning one's mother tongue. Both are skills; both are possessed by just about everybody; both are acquired as a matter of course, and it is not their possession but their lack that requires explanation; both allow for ranking agents according to their performance; both are necessary for the well-being of individuals as well as of society; both require conformity to rules; both can tolerate some deviations; and the rules of both can be changed either deliberately or by gradual evolution.

The suggestion implicit in this metaphor, and the significant one for the present purposes, is that vis-à-vis the skill, all human beings start, as it were, at zero and go on from there. As they become more or less good at its exercise, their performances have various merit, but it cannot happen, no matter how poor their performances are, that they fall below zero. In this realm, there cannot be negative merit. As with the learning of language so with moral development: it is impossible to deteriorate in the opposite direction. The zero that is the starting point is absolute zero. The important implication is that wickedness is not the opposite of goodness, but being a poor moral performer. Wickedness is due to the inadequate development of moral potentialities; it is not the development of another countervailing potentiality. The worst that can happen to people is that they fail to develop their potentialities at all. And the corollary is that what needs explanation is why they fail to develop them, or, if they do develop them, why they perform poorly. Because everybody has the potentialities, the explanation must be some interference with their development. This explanation underlies the egalitarian idea that equal human worth supports inalienable rights to the conditions in which the potentialities can be developed without interference.

The trouble with the language metaphor is that it cannot accommodate central features of morality. It is true that one form of wickedness is to fail to do good, but another form is to do evil. And, often, to do evil is not to fail to act on morally good potentialities but to act on morally evil potentialities. Wickedness is not just a form of omission but also a form of active malevolence. Cruelty, selfishness, aggression, greed, hostility, and malice are also human potentialities; they are regular performers in the repertoire of human motivation.

The significance of this understanding of wickedness is that it shows the inadequacy of the metaphor suggested by the liberal faith. For people whose actions form a lifelong pattern of evil conduct do not merely have unrealized good potentialities: they have realized evil potentialities. They do not just lack moral merit, they have moral demerit. It is not that they have risen only a very little above the absolute zero point at which morality, according to the egalitarian metaphor, starts. Rather, they have sunk more than a little in the opposite direction, in the direction of wickedness. The existence of wickedness shows that it is a mistake to think of morality as a skill, like speaking a language, in whose acquisition it is possible only to improve.

If there must be a metaphor for morality, it should be one that allows for both improvement and deterioration, gain and loss, perfectibility and corruptibility. One metaphor that suggests itself is that morality is like health, whereas immorality is like sickness. Although this metaphor also has its misleading implications, it at least allows noting the analogy that human beings are born with potentialities of both sickness and health and wickedness and goodness. As they live their lives, so they may develop one or the other and often a mixture of both: just as they can be healthy or sick, so they can be good or wicked. Human life is a continuum between the extremes of perfect health and fatal illness, and different people are situated at different points on it. Moral life is similarly a continuum between total corruption and saintly perfection.

If goodness and wickedness are thought about in this way, then the inappropriateness of regarding the worth of human beings as equal becomes apparent. Human worth can be lost, because people may accumulate so much moral demerit as to come to occupy a position on the moral continuum well below the point at which goodness and wickedness are equally balanced or at which the potentialities to go in one or the other of these opposite directions are equally unrealized. Kant, to whom egalitarians often turn for support, is quite clear about this. Human worth, according to him, can be lost through moral demerit: "Lying is the . . . obliteration of one's dignity as a human being. A man who does not himself believe what he says to another . . . has even less worth than if he were a mere thing" (Kant 1983: 90–91).

Critics of egalitarianism need not peg their case on Kant being right about the seriousness of lying. But Kant's general point is correct. Human worth is proportional to moral merit, partly because the egalitarian attempt does not succeed in tying universal and necessary human worth to morally good potentialities that can never be lost. The problem is not that morally good potentialities can be lost but that they can be overwhelmed by morally evil potentialities. As morally evil potentialities may dominate morally good ones, so human worth may be replaced by its opposite. And its opposite is not less worth but the virulent growth of wickedness.

The argument has been that egalitarians do not provide an acceptable reason for rejecting the obvious and commonsensical conviction that human worth is proportional to moral merit. It is rationally and morally justified to recognize the inequality between people who habitually harm and those who habitually benefit others. It is likewise justified to take moral merit into account in the distribution of scarce resources. The practical implication of the rejection of egalitarianism is not that open season should be declared on wicked people. Of course, no one should be harmed without good reasons. But it does seem to be reasonable and morally right that people who are habitual and predictable evildoers should receive less of scarce resources to support their way of life than those who habitually and predictably benefit others.

Egalitarians perhaps will not disagree with this position. The point is, however, that they cannot both agree and hold that human worth is independent of moral merit. For the moral demerit of wicked people undermines the claim that they have the same human worth as benefactors of

humanity. Because egalitarians are committed to such absurd consequences of their position as, for instance, that the sheer human worth of
Stalin or Hitler is equal to that of Einstein or Hume, they should give up
their position. Furthermore, it also seems reasonable and morally right
that in prevailing circumstances people with lifelong patterns of wickedness should be discriminated against in respect to the distribution of
scarce resources. How could it be other than right that mafiosi should not
get the same police protection as do the district attorneys who prosecute
them, that school lunches should be more nutritious than prison lunches,
or that the welfare of criminals matters less than the welfare of their victims?

The argument has been that egalitarians cannot give the obvious answers to these questions and hold, as Ronald Dworkin does, that there is
"a natural right of men and women to equality of concern and respect, a
right they possess not by virtue of birth or characteristic or merit or excellence but simply as human beings" (1977b: 182), as Rawls does that it is
wrong for "common sense to suppose that . . . the good things in life . . .
should be distributed according to moral desert" (1971: 310), or as Vlastos does that "the human worth of all persons is equal, however unequal
may be their merit" (1962: 43). It is rationally and morally justified that
common sense should prevail against the ill-advised political programs of
egalitarianism.

It should be emphasized in order to avoid misunderstanding that the
merit on which human worth has been argued to depend is moral, not
merit based on birth, talents, membership in some social group, or inheritance. Nor has it been suggested that equality is not valuable. On the
contrary, interpreted as legal or political equality, it is morally important,
although not as much as egalitarians think. But its proper interpretation
excludes the claim that morality requires treating human beings as if they
had equal human worth and consequently equal claim to scarce resources.

It should also be emphasized that arguments based on moral merit are
prone to abuse. History is full of horrible things that have been perpe-
trated in the name of moral merit and demerit. But all moral and political
arguments face this danger. The way to avoid it is not to deny such rational and moral credentials as the arguments may have but to prevent their
abuse.

The argument in this chapter was meant to show that the liberal conception of equality is incompatible with good lives and, consequently, that
liberalism is inconsistent. The fundamental reason for this position is that
the liberal conception of equality requires taking resources from people

who acquired them legitimately and redistributing them to those who are worst off, regardless of why they are worst off or how badly off they are. The implementation of egalitarian political programs ignores the moral merits of both the people from whom resources are taken and to whom resources are given. It results in making good lives worse and wicked lives better. The justification that egalitarians offer for these misguided political programs fails for four independent reasons.

First, egalitarianism appeals to the intuitive judgment that it is morally wrong for some people to have more resources than they need for their autonomy, while other people are prevented from living autonomously by lack of resources. This intuitive judgment, however, shows at best that what is morally wrong is not inequality but that some people do not have enough. But it is doubtful that it shows even that because not having enough is often due to the scarcity of resources, for which no one can be held morally responsible.

Second, if the egalitarian case were consistently applied, it would lead to absurd consequences. These consequences are absurd because the alleviation of many serious inequalities is neither morally required nor morally desirable. It is therefore necessary to distinguish between inequalities that are morally objectionable and those that are not. The only way of doing so, however, is to admit the relevance of the question that egalitarians refuse to ask: Why do specific inequalities hold? If egalitarians did ask it, they could no longer maintain that inequalities in themselves are morally objectionable. For inequalities may be deserved or they may fall outside the jurisdiction of morality.

Third, the egalitarian case unwarrantedly slides from a universal to a particular claim of equality. If all human beings have equal worth, if they are all entitled to equal concern, respect, and resources for their autonomy, then it is morally unjustified to restrict equality to the citizens of a particular state, as egalitarian political programs always do. If, on the other hand, the universal claim of equality is taken seriously, then egalitarians must explain why it would be reasonable for people to jeopardize the resources they need for their own autonomy by redistributing such resources to those who lack them.

Finally, the assumption of equal human worth, and the resulting entitlement to equal concern, respect, and resources for autonomy, rests on the liberal faith, which is vitiated by the wickedness of many people. It is absurd to make it a basic value of political morality that scarce resources should be used to further morally good and evil activities alike.

All four criticisms of egalitarianism point to the relevance of the question that egalitarians will not raise: Why is it that people lack the resources they need for autonomy? In some cases, the answer will no doubt be that they lack them because they are undeservedly deprived of them. In some other cases, however, as in the case of wickedness, people may lack resources because they do not deserve them and have been justly deprived of them. This leads to the topic of the next chapter.

CHAPTER 6

Justice and Desert

the brave new world begins
When all men are paid for existing
and no man must pay for his sins.
—RUDYARD KIPLING, "The Gods of the Copybook Headings"

The topic of this chapter and the next is justice, another basic value of liberalism. The central argument is that while liberals are right in regarding justice as a basic value of political morality, they are wrong in their conception of it. If the concept of justice is rightly understood, desert must be recognized as an essential component of it. In that case, however, any conception of justice that interprets the concept of justice without acknowledging the centrality of desert to it is mistaken.

The most widely accepted account of justice as liberals understand it is that of John Rawls (see Rawls 1971, 1993). Since Rawls's conception of justice is egalitarian, he regards desert as irrelevant to justice, so his interpretation of the concept of justice cannot be acceptable. On the other hand, if the centrality of desert to justice is acknowledged, then justice cannot be a basic liberal value because it is inconsistent with many liberal political programs, with other basic values of liberalism, with the interpretation of autonomy as the core of liberalism, and with good lives.

Underlying the liberal conception of justice and this criticism of it is a clash of intuitions. The liberal intuition is that justice requires the recognition of the equal rights of human beings to the resources they need for living autonomously. The contrary intuition is that justice makes the right to such resources contingent on what their recipients deserve. The liberal intuition is motivated by the egalitarian belief that at a fundamental level all human beings have equal worth. The contrary intuition is motivated by the antiegalitarian belief that the worth of human beings varies with their moral merits. Rawls's conception of justice is an attempt to exhibit

120

the rational basis on which the liberal intuition rests and to show that the contrary intuition lacks such a basis. It will be argued that Rawls's conception fails on both accounts and that this has damaging consequences for liberalism.

The assumption that humans have equal worth has been the target of the third criticism of egalitarianism (see Section 5.5). The criticism was that differences in moral merit invalidate that assumption. One might reply that the evaluation of the moral merits of agents and their actions, on which the ascription of desert depends, becomes possible only after appropriate institutions have been established. According to Rawls, "Desert presupposes the existence of . . . [a] cooperative scheme" (1971: 103). Institutions are these cooperative schemes, and they are needed to provide the laws, principles, rules, criteria, or whatever that can be used as standards for ascribing desert. Justice is basic because it governs how such institutions ought to be shaped.[1] If this were so, the legitimate ascription of desert could occur only after just institutions have been established. Justice would have to be recognized then as more basic than desert, and a conception of justice would have to be independent of desert. The exclusion of desert from a conception of justice would not then be a fault but a consequence of understanding how basic a value justice is.

This rejoinder leads to the question of whether desert is bound to be contingent on institutional arrangements. The answer that will be defended here is that it is not. But consideration of the question and the argument for the negative answer raise some of the deepest questions of morality and politics. It is proper to acknowledge that part of the great virtue of Rawls's conception of justice is that it forces these questions on its critics. The criticisms that follow are meant to call into question the defensibility of Rawls's conception, while paying tribute to its importance.

6.1 THE CONCEPT OF JUSTICE

Socrates of *The Republic* was the first philosopher to see and insist on the deep connection between justice and a good life. He believed that a life is good only if it is virtuous and the agent is, all things considered, satisfied with it. The distinguishing mark of the Socratic belief is the further assumption that these two components are inseparable. A virtuous life cannot fail to be satisfying, and satisfaction with one's life must be derived from its virtue because they have the same source: the endeavor to approximate the good. The appearance that a virtuous life may lack overall satisfaction or that overall satisfaction may be derived from a wicked life deceives only those who are ignorant of the good. Those who know the good will be satisfied with their life in proportion to their virtue.

Contemporary Western sensibility rejects this Socratic ideal because there are good reasons to doubt the assumption that underlies it: the two components of good lives may diverge. Socrates was right to value both, but he was wrong to believe that virtuous lives are bound to be satisfying or that overall satisfaction can be derived only from a virtuous life. The truth is that a virtuous life may be full of dissatisfaction and a wicked life may be very satisfying, even in the long run, even when all things are considered. The fundamental reason for the contemporary Western rejection of the Socratic ideal is disbelief in cosmic justice, understood as a moral order in nature, which guarantees that virtuous lives will be satisfying and that wicked lives will not be. In the absence of cosmic justice, injustice is an incorrigible feature of the human condition. This is a deplorable fact, but Socrates notwithstanding, it is now widely believed to be a fact. As Nietzsche put it, "God is dead . . . we have killed him" (1974: 125).

Justice should thus be thought of as a substitute for cosmic justice. It is bound to be a poor substitute because circumstances beyond human control impose ineliminable limits on its realization. Justice nevertheless calls for doing what is possible to ameliorate obstacles to living a good life by making the coincidence of virtuous and satisfying lives more likely. Justice is thus a basic value because it is an essential condition of good lives.

As a beginning toward understanding what the pursuit of justice involves, it should be acknowledged that, like equality, it may be an essentially contested concept, one that is open enough to allow numerous evaluatively charged and incompatible interpretations (Gallie 1964: chapter 8). The concept must nevertheless possess some core of uncontested meaning, for without it there would be no reason to suppose that the numerous interpretations are of the same thing. Controversies about justice thus presuppose some, at least minimal, agreement regarding the subject about which the participants disagree.

This point may be expressed in terms of Rawls's distinction between the concept and various conceptions of justice: "It seems natural to think of the concept of justice as distinct from various conceptions of justice and as being specified by the role which these different . . . conceptions have in common" (1971: 5). As a start toward identifying this common element, it will be useful to begin at the same point as the discussion of equality did, with Aristotle's general formula for justice: treat equals equally and unequals unequally.

This general formula, however, is much too vague because nothing connects it specifically with justice. It is a condition of the consistent application of any rule in any context that like cases that come under its jurisdiction should be treated alike and different cases differently. This is as true of classifying fauna, diagnosing illness, appraising antiques, and so forth as it is of justice. The Aristotelian formula, therefore, is insufficiently informative about why some rules are rules of justice. It needs to be supplemented with an account that goes beyond simple consistency and explains what permits the identification of particular rules as those of justice.

Considerable care must be exercised, however, about the content of this additional account. It would be unreasonable, for instance, to add to consistency the requirement of equal treatment in respect to economic distribution. For this would make economic equality just by definition, which would, of course, beg questions. This way of proceeding would arbitrarily identify the concept of justice with a particular conception of it. The unacceptable result would be that conceptions that allowed for economic inequality could be challenged not merely on moral or political grounds but also for being self-contradictory. Whatever is added to consistency, therefore, must be specific enough to identify some rules as rules of justice and yet remain sufficiently general to allow for conflicting conceptions of justice.

The clue to the missing core of justice may be found in the expectation of cosmic justice that guarantees that a virtuous life will be satisfying and that a satisfying life will be virtuous. A belief that is implicit in this expectation and lends much strength to it is that living virtuously is not merely necessary but also ought to be sufficient for living satisfyingly. This belief is compatible with acknowledging that the Socratic ideal is mistaken in its claim that virtue *is* sufficient for a satisfying life, for the belief is not that it is sufficient but that it *ought to be.* Justice is thought to be violated if the connection between virtue and overall satisfaction is severed. If the divergence between them is too great, if a virtuous life is full of suffering or a wicked life is filled with enjoyment, then justice is not merely violated but outraged. The expectation of justice thus routinely survives the disappointment that reality will conform to it because justice is not a description of any human society but an ideal motivating the improvement of existing societies.

This ideal is the expression of the basic moral belief that people ought to get what they deserve.[2] It is the key to what was earlier called cosmic justice. The concept of justice should then be analyzed in terms of consistency and desert: equals should be treated equally and unequals unequally in respect to the allocation of desert. The next step is to try to understand better the nature of desert. (The following account is indebted to Feinberg 1963; Galston 1980; Miller 1976; Sandel 1982; and especially Sher 1987.)

6.2 THE NATURE OF DESERT

If agents deserve some benefit or harm, it is because of some fact about them. This fact is the *basis* of desert, and that the agents merit some benefit or harm on that basis creates a *claim* of desert. Desert is thus relative to agents because its basis is a fact about the agents, and the claim is for some benefits or harms that the agents ought to have (Feinberg 1963: 69–72).

The fact about the agents that forms the basis of desert may be a character trait, such as a virtue or a vice, an excellence or a fault, a skill or a deficiency; it may be a relation in which the agent stands, for instance, being a taxpayer, a competitor, or an employee; it may be an explicit or implicit agreement into which the agent has entered, like having made a promise, gotten married, or enrolled as a student; or it may be a way in which the agent has acted, for example, kindly or cruelly, thoughtfully or unthinkingly, fairly or unfairly. The basis of desert, then, is some characteristic, relation, agreement, or conduct of some agent. Each basis allows for considerable variety within it. Desert, therefore, does not have a unitary basis; it is a pluralistic notion (Sher 1987: especially chapter 1).

The claim of desert is that the agent ought to enjoy some benefit or suffer some harm on the relevant basis. The claim need not be one that the agent makes; indeed, it is not often that agents lay claim to some deserved harm. Nor need any particular person or institution make the claim on behalf of the agent. The claim should be understood in the very general sense that the agent has a certain benefit or harm coming and that it would be good, right, proper, in a word, fitting if the agent received it. The claim sometimes could and should be enforced, but it need not be. It need not even be enforceable, because there are perfectly legitimate claims of desert that are not directed toward any person or institution, such as that wicked people do not deserve to live happily until they die of old age or that good people do not deserve the misfortune that befalls them.

The ascription of desert is partly backward- and partly forward-looking. It looks backward toward its basis, and it looks forward from there to lay claim to the appropriate benefit or harm. The ascription of desert thus always requires a particular type of reason, and the claim it creates always requires a particular type of justification. Both requirements are met by the basis of desert. It may therefore be said that hard work deserves success, employees deserve wages from their employers, and acts of kindness deserve gratitude from their recipients, just as hypocrites deserve to be exposed, incompetent physicians deserve to lose their licenses, and criminals deserve punishment. The justification of these claims is to point at the relevant characteristic, relation, agreement, or conduct, which provides the basis for claiming that their agents deserve the appropriate benefits or harms.

The basis for justified claims of desert, however, has a further requirement because not just any characteristic, relation, agreement, or conduct provides the required reason. To serve as a reason, the basis must be something that merits the benefits or harms consequent on it. There must be an explanation of what it is about the basis that makes it fitting that the agent should receive some benefit or harm. Why does hard work deserve success or kindness gratitude? The appropriate explanation then strengthens the reason that can be derived from the basis of desert by pointing at the feature that makes the characteristic, relation, agreement, or conduct in question a fitting basis for the appropriate benefits or harms. The required explanation therefore must point at some excellence or fault, achievement or failure, compliance or noncompliance, or commission or omission that provides the basis for claiming that the agent in question deserves the corresponding benefits or harms.

It has been said at the end of the preceding chapter that the basis of desert is some moral merit or demerit of the agents. The sense in which this is meant, however, needs to be explained. Both "moral" and "merit or demerit" can be interpreted in a broad and in a narrow sense. In the broad sense, "moral" may be taken to mean the evaluative dimension of the effort to live a good life. Lives are morally good in this sense if they are virtuous and the agents are satisfied with them overall. In the narrow sense, "moral" may be used to refer only to the virtue component of good lives. Lives are morally good in this sense if they are virtuous, and they are good even if the agents lack overall satisfaction with them. The broad sense includes, whereas the narrow sense excludes, the agents' satisfaction. If the distinction is kept in mind, it makes no substantive difference in what sense "moral" is used. It will be used in the broad sense here. The *moral* merit or demerit of agents that is said to form the basis of their desert therefore calls for benefits or harms that are fitting responses to the extent to which the agents' lives have been virtuous and satisfying. What makes responses fitting is that the benefits and harms they provide are aimed to make commensurate the virtue and satisfaction, as well as the wickedness and dissatisfaction, in particular lives.

"Merit" and "demerit" have an analogous ambiguity. In the broad sense, to say that agents have a particular merit or demerit is to refer to the characteristic, relation, agreement, or conduct that forms the basis of the claim that they deserve some particular benefit or harm. In this sense, "merit" or "demerit" is synonymous with "the basis of desert." What makes "merit" and "demerit" moral in the broad sense is that the benefits and harms nontrivially affect the goodness of the agents' life. In the narrow sense, "merit" and "demerit" refer to the bearing that the characteristic, relation, agreement, or conduct has on the agents' living virtuously. This sense is thus connected with the narrow sense of "moral," and the agents' moral merit or demerit depends on what the agent has done or is doing to live virtuously. Just as "moral" will be used here in the broad sense, so also will be "merit" and "demerit."

To say then that moral merit or demerit is the basis of desert is to say that a certain characteristic, relation, agreement, or conduct of a certain agent is a fitting basis for that agent's receiving some particular benefit or harm that nontrivially affects the goodness of the agent's life.

The foregoing account suggests several ways in which the ascription of desert may be mistaken. The first is a factual mistake about the basis of desert. The person who was thought to be a burglar really was not, so punishment is inappropriate. The second is a mistake in thinking that the basis of desert merits the benefits or harms that it is thought to do. This may involve a mistaken evaluation of the basis, such as thinking of chastity as a virtue. Or it may involve a correct evaluation that is mistakenly applied, for instance, thinking correctly that modesty is a virtue but mistaking humility for modesty. The third is a mistake in proportion. The agents in question do indeed deserve benefits or harms on the basis that is rightly supposed to exist and merit benefit or harm, but the benefits or harms received exceed what is appropriate. The burglar deserves imprisonment, but not for life; the novelist deserves good reviews, but not a Nobel Prize. The fourth is the logical mistake of ascribing desert without regard for its basis. The mistake is not that there is thought to be a basis when there is none; rather, the ascription of desert occurs in disregard of whether it has an appropriate basis. In this way, benefits or harms may be distributed not on the basis of some properly evaluated characteristic, relation, agreement, or conduct but for some other reason.

The significance of this fourth kind of mistake about the ascription of desert is considerable. The mistake, it needs to emphasized, is logical. Just as a person cannot be held to a promise if none has been made or be guilty of a crime if none has been committed, so desert cannot be ascribed unless it has a basis. The reason for this is that without a basis, the benefits and harms received cannot—logically cannot—be deserved. Benefits and harms may be received for reasons of need, want, love, prudence, generosity, paternalism, religious belief, political expediency, and so forth. But they can be deserved only if there is a specific reason for receiving them. And the reason must be that their recipients merit them in virtue of some characteristic, relation, agreement, or conduct of theirs which makes it fitting that they should enjoy or suffer those particular benefits or harms.

It is just this element of fittingness that egalitarian distribution schemes lack. To say that everybody deserves the same benefits is to ignore the fact that people differ in respect to their characteristics, relations, agreements, or conduct and thus in respect to the bases on which desert can reasonably be ascribed to them. The charge Rawls famously leveled against utilitarianism also applies (as Nozick [1974: 228] points out) to egalitarianism: it "does not take seriously the distinction between persons" (1971: 3).

To reply to this by saying that there may be some respects in which all persons are alike, such as their capacity for autonomy, and that is why they all deserve the same benefits is to make a logical mistake about the basis on which desert can be reasonably ascribed. For it is not enough for the ascription of desert that people be alike in some way, it must also be explained why that likeness creates a basis for desert. The basis of desert must be something that has moral merit or demerit, broadly understood; it must nontrivially contribute to or detract from the agents' living a good life; and if it is to be a basis of a claim for some benefit or harm, it must be ascertained what its actual positive or negative effect is. The capacity for autonomy, or indeed any respect in which human beings are alike, fails these conditions because there are obvious differences among people in how their shared characteristics, relations, agreements, and conduct affect the goodness of their lives. For instance, the capacity for autonomy may be used or not; if used, it may be for good or for evil; if used for good, it will contribute to good lives in various degrees—and all these affect whether it provides a basis for desert, whether the basis is of moral merit or demerit, and whether the moral merit or demerit is great, small, or somewhere in between.

This is the reason why the ascription of desert is essentially antiegalitarian and why consistent egalitarians will repudiate distributive schemes based on desert. But if desert is an essential component of justice, then egalitarians cannot base the distribution scheme they favor on justice either, because justice, involving desert, will not be egalitarian. Egalitarians must deny, therefore, that desert is an essential component of justice. And, of course, they do deny it; it remains to be seen, however, with what success.

6.3 JUSTICE AND DESERT

Suppose that the ascription of desert is reasonable because it is free of the mistakes in fact, evaluation, proportion, and logic that have been discussed above. The claim it creates, then, is that deserving agents ought to receive some benefit or harm. How strong is this claim?

Since it may be impossible to provide the desert that is reasonably claimed, the claim cannot be unconditional. One obstacle may be the unavailability of the deserved benefits or harms as a result of nonculpable scarcity of resources. Another obstacle may be that the available resources cannot be distributed proportionally to what is deserved. How could people who have been negligently blinded or maimed by prolonged torture be fittingly compensated? What benefit could be provided for those who nobly died in the line of duty or chose a life devoid of most satisfactions in order to make others less miserable? Underlying these obstacles is the fact that the human control over the distribution of deserved benefits and harms is insufficient. People are often unavoidably prevented from having what they deserve and ought to have.

Two of the numerous consequences of this limitation of justice are apposite in the present context. The first makes it superficial to claim, as Rawls does, that "justice is the first virtue of social institutions" (1971: 3). Surely, a prior virtue of social institutions must be to generate ample resources to increase the likelihood that justice could be done in their distribution. If social institutions were to have a first virtue, which is a highly dubious belief for a liberal to hold, as it will argued in Chapter 9, prosperity would be a much stronger candidate than justice.

The second consequence strengthens the previous objection to the principle: "ought" implies "can" (see Chapter 3) by presenting yet a further counterexample to it. If the principle were correct, it would be a logical error to claim that people ought to have what they deserve even though the unavoidable lack of resources or proportionality makes it impossible. But there is nothing logically faulty about this claim; it is one of the most important sources of the motivation to extend justice by increasing human control over the resources needed for it.

If reasonably based claims of desert are not unconditional because conditions beyond human control may make it impossible to meet them, can they then be said to be overriding claims? They could perhaps be expressed as claiming that insofar as it is possible to arrange that people get what they deserve, it ought to be done. But this is still too strong an interpretation of these claims. Desert is a basis for distributing benefits and harms, and it calls for distributing them proportionally to the moral merit or demerit of their recipients. There are, however, other bases of distribution, and they may support a moral case for giving people more or less than what they deserve.

Love, friendship, family ties, special relationships, and so forth may place an obligation on people to be generous rather than punctilious in benefiting others with whom they stand in such a relationships. Since relationships of this sort are essential to most conceptions of a good life, there may often be good reasons to provide benefits greater than what their intended recipients deserve. A similar case can be made for making people suffer less than they deserve. Mercy, forgiveness, hope of reform, remorse of the wrongdoer, the uncharacteristic nature of the wrong that has been done, and the like may provide reasonable bases for not inflicting harm proportional to the moral demerit of some people. The claim that people ought to have what they deserve may be overridden, therefore, by a stronger case that rests on some alternative basis of distributing benefits and harms.

These alternative bases, to be sure, require fairly close familiarity with the people who are provided with more benefits or harms than they deserve. Such familiarity cannot be made a condition of workable institutions, political programs, and numerous personal decisions. So it would be impracticable to suggest that it should compete with desert as a basis of distribution. But it is not impracticable to recognize that when such familiarity does exist, then it can be appealed to as a reasonable basis for overriding claims of desert. Those who are willing to accept that justice essentially involves desert and who join Rawls in regarding justice, in one sense or another, as a first virtue of social institutions may still disagree with Rawls's further claim that "laws and institutions . . . must be reformed or abolished if they are unjust (1971: 3). It may often be right that the claims of love, mercy, and so on should prevail over the claims of justice.

The most reasonable interpretation of the strength of the claim that people should have what they deserve is that it is prima facie. It should be assumed to hold, unless some stronger consideration overrides it. It would be neat if a general account could be given of what consideration would be stronger than desert, but no such account is to be had. Just as there is a plurality of bases of desert, so there is a plurality of ways in which the claims of desert can be reasonably defeated. Desert may be a basic value, but there are also other basic values, and their claims may conflict with and override the claims of desert. The best that can be done a priori is to indicate the logic of a claim that would reasonably defeat the claim of desert.

The context of the competing claims of desert and whatever conflicts with them is people's aspiration to live a good life, understood as one in which virtue and satisfaction coincide as closely as possible. The prima facie case for desert derives its strength from the importance of desert to this aspiration. What a claim that reasonably overrides that of desert would have to show is that in a particular case some consideration other than desert, such as love or mercy, is more important to living a good life. But what such considerations may be cannot be specified a priori because there is a plurality of conceptions of a good life, and what is important to one may not be important to another. In this context a reasonable case must be particular, and a general case can only be prima facie.

In summary, justice should be understood as the combination of consistency and desert. Consistency requires that like cases be treated alike and different cases differently. Desert provides the basis on which the likenesses and differences should be evaluated. That basis is to distribute benefits and harms in proportion to the moral merit or demerit of their recipients. Moral merit and demerit, in turn, are to be understood in terms of people's characteristics, relations, agreements, or conduct that make it fitting that they should receive the appropriate benefits or harms. And the evaluative force of fittingness derives from justice being an ideal that serves as a substitute for cosmic justice; an ideal that requires social institutions, political programs, and individual efforts to be directed toward making lives good by making their virtue and satisfaction proportional to each other. The claim of justice is neither unconditional nor overriding but prima facie.

This understanding of justice is, of course, unacceptable to egalitarians because they reject the idea that benefits and harms should be distributed according to desert. The time has come to consider Rawls's conception of justice, which is the strongest liberal attempt to support egalitarianism.

6.4 RAWLS'S CONCEPTION OF JUSTICE

Rawls's conception of justice is well known and extensively discussed (see, for example, Barry 1973; Daniels 1975; Korsgaard 1992; and Kymlicka 1990: chapter 3), so there is no need to provide a detailed exposition of it here. But it is important to have the logic of his argument clearly in view so that the soundness of the reasons about to be given for rejecting it can be readily judged. Its logic will be exhibited backward, beginning with Rawls's rejection of desert as a basis for justice and then going deeper by bringing out the more and more fundamental reasons Rawls gives in support of his egalitarian conception of justice.

Rawls writes: "There is a tendency for common sense to suppose that income and wealth, and the good things in life generally, should be distributed according to moral desert. Justice is happiness according to virtue. While it is recognized that this ideal can never be fully carried out, it is the appropriate conception of distributive justice, at least as a prima facie principle, and society should try to realize it as circumstances permit. Now justice as fairness [Rawls's theory] rejects this conception" (1971: 310). In claiming this, Rawls does not deny that people are entitled to various benefits, although he says nothing about harms. "A just scheme . . . answers to what men are entitled to; it satisfies their legitimate expectations as founded upon social institutions. But what they are entitled to is not proportional to nor dependent upon their intrinsic worth. The principles of justice . . . do not mention moral desert, and there is no tendency for distributive shares to correspond to it" (311). What people are entitled to thus depends on social institutions, and just institutions recognize no connection between entitlement and desert, regardless of what common sense says.

The reason Rawls gives for these strong and counterintuitive claims is that the "essential point is that the concept of moral worth [and desert] does not provide a first principle of distributive justice . . . because it cannot be introduced until after the first principles of justice have been acknowledged. Once the principles are on hand, moral worth [and desert] can be defined as having a sense of justice. . . . Thus the concept of moral worth [and desert] is secondary to those of . . . justice, and it plays no role in the substantive definition of distributive shares" (312–13). It follows that "it is incorrect to say that just distributive shares reward individuals according to their moral worth [and desert]. But what we can say is that . . . a just scheme give each person his due: that is, it allots to each what he is entitled to as defined by the scheme itself" (313). According to this suggestion, people get their due, but that has nothing to do with what they deserve on the basis of their moral worth.

It may be thought that a way of alleviating doubts about this suggestion is to allow that whatever the first principles of justice turn out to be, they should connect what is due to people with what they deserve. But Rawls rejects this on the ground that benefits should not be based on desert "since the initial endowment of natural assets and the contingencies of their growth and nurture in early life are arbitrary from a moral point of view. The precept which seems intuitively to come closest to rewarding moral desert is that of distribution according to effort. . . . Once again, however, it seems clear that the effort a person is willing to make is influenced by his natural abilities and skills and the alternatives open to him. The better endowed are more likely, other things equal, to strive conscientiously, and there seems to be no way to discount for their greater good fortune. The idea of rewarding desert is impracticable" (311–12). The thought then is that the distribution of benefits based on desert is morally arbitrary because desert depends on natural endowments, and "no one deserves his place in the distribution of natural assets any more than he deserves his initial starting place in society" (311).

That differences of endowments and circumstances exist among people "is neither just nor unjust; nor is it unjust that persons are born into society at some particular position. These are simply natural facts. What is just and unjust is the way that particular institutions deal with these facts" (102). The just way is to recognize "that undeserved inequalities call for redress; and since inequalities of birth and natural endowments are undeserved, these inequalities are to be somehow compensated for. Thus . . . in order to treat all persons equally . . . society must give more attention to those with fewer native assets and to those born into the less favorable social positions. The idea is to redress the bias of contingencies in the direction of equality" (100–101).

It is the role of what Rawls calls "the difference principle" to achieve this. The difference principle represents . . . an agreement to regard the distribution of natural talents as a common asset. . . . Those who have been favored by nature . . . may gain from their good fortune only in terms that improve the situation of those who have lost out. . . . The basic structure can be arranged so that these contingencies work for the good of the least fortunate" (101–2). And the difference principle is: "Social and economic inequalities are to be arranged so that they are both (a) to the greatest benefit of the least advantaged, and (b) attached to positions open to all under conditions of fair equality of opportunity" (83).

This principle has been repeated so often, and often in such a commanding moral tone, that there is a tendency to be lulled by its familiarity into overlooking just how great a violence it does to common sense and ordinary moral convictions. Consider just two of its numerous counterintuitive consequences. Suppose that a man and a woman are both among the least-advantaged members of a society. The man is a hitherto unapprehended mugger; he has never held a job; he is vicious when he can get away with it; he has moderate native endowments, but he has made no effort to develop them. The woman is the mother of several children; she and the children have been abandoned by her husband and their father; she earns meager wages by working part-time at a menial job; she is doing her best to raise the children well; she has the same native endowments as the mugger but, unlike him, has used them to make great, although unsuccessful, efforts to improve her situation. According to the difference principle, the mugger and the mother are entitled to the same treatment. Their positions of inequality are due to contingencies that are arbitrary from the moral point of view. The mugger's viciousness and lack of effort and the mother's decency and unsuccessful efforts create no morally relevant differences between them insofar as the distribution of benefits is concerned. They are entitled to the same distributive shares.

Changing the scenario a little illustrates another consequence of

Rawls's position. The mugger continues as before, but the mother is no longer unsuccessful. Through her efforts, she considerably improves her position. She now has a moderately comfortable and secure, but by no means affluent, middle-class existence. She has a good job, she bought a house, the children are doing well at school, and they can even afford an occasional family vacation. According to the difference principle, the contingencies of life, among which are counted the mugger's lack of effort and the mother's successful effort, are to be redressed in the direction of equality. Thus on Rawls's view of justice, some of the mother's resources should be taken from her and used to support the mugger.

It may be, of course, that the ordinary moral convictions, which render these consequences of the difference principle unacceptable, are mistaken and Rawls's conception of justice is correct. But that needs to be shown, and showing it requires adducing very strong reasons indeed for the difference principle. Rawls certainly offers some reasons, and the next step is to see what they are. The difference principle is Rawls's second principle of justice. It serves two main purposes: to supplement the first principle and to strengthen the egalitarian component of the general conception of justice. The reasons for the difference principle emerge from understanding its purpose.

The first principle of justice is what Rawls calls "the equal liberty principle" "Each person is to have an equal right to the most extensive total system of equal basic liberties compatible with a similar system of liberty for all" (250). This is the first principle because it takes priority over the second. A just society, therefore, first guarantees, in accordance with the first principle, equal basic liberties to everyone and then, in accordance with the second principle, arranges inequalities to benefit those who are least advantaged, allowing inequalities to result only from conditions of fair equality of opportunity. One reason for having the second principle of justice, therefore, is to have a way of dealing with inequalities that will arise if the first principle is in place. And the second reason for having it is "that undeserved inequalities call for redress; and since inequalities of birth and natural endowments are undeserved, these inequalities are to be . . . compensated for" (100). In "the democratic interpretation of justice . . . liberty corresponds to the first principle, equality to the idea of equality in the first principle together with equality of fair opportunity [in the second principle]" (106).

The question of what reason there is for accepting the two principles of justice together however remains. Why should the most extensive equal basic liberties be guaranteed? Why should inequalities of endowments and circumstances be redressed? Why should those who are least advantaged be favored? Rawls's answer leads to the deepest level of his theory.

The intuitive idea is that since everyone's well-being depends upon a scheme of cooperation without which no one could have a satisfactory life, the division of advantages should be such as to draw forth the willing cooperation of everyone taking part in it, including those less well situated. Yet this can be expected only if reasonable terms are proposed. The two principles . . . seem to be a fair agreement on the basis of which those better endowed, or more fortunate in their social position, neither of which we can be said to deserve, could expect the willing cooperation of others when some workable scheme is a necessary condition of the welfare of all. Once we decide to look for a conception of justice that nullifies the accidents of natural endowment and the contingencies of social circumstance . . . we are led to these principles. (15)

Rawls's fundamental claim is then that the two principles of justice are the principles that are most likely to promote the well-being of individuals who willingly cooperate with one another in order to have a satisfactory life. The argument in support of this claim rests on the well-known hypothetical constructs of the original position, and the veil of ignorance.

We are to imagine," says Rawls about the original position, "that those who are engaged in social cooperation choose together, in one joint act, the principles which are to assign basic rights and duties and to determine the division of social benefits. Men are to decide in advance how they are to regulate their claims against one another and what is to be the foundation charter of their society. Just as each person must decide by rational reflection what constitutes his good . . . so a group of persons must decide once and for all what is to count among them as just and unjust. The choice which rational men would make in this hypothetical situation . . . determines the principles of justice. (11–12)

We are also to suppose that the people in the original position are "rational and mutually disinterested. This does not mean that the parties are egoists. . . . But they are conceived as not taking an interest in one another's interests. They are to presume that even their spiritual aims may be opposed. . . . Moreover, the concept of rationality must be interpreted as . . . taking the most effective means to given ends" (13–14). Some further characteristics of the people in the original position are that "each desires to protect his interests, his capacity to advance his conception of the good, no one has a reason to acquiesce in an enduring loss to himself in order to bring about a greater net balance of satisfactions" (14).

If people have these characteristics, each is likely "to design principles to favor his particular condition" (12). In that case, however, no principle would be generally acceptable, and the cooperation on which everyone's well-being depends could not be secured. To avoid this, Rawls supposes that "among the essential features of this situation is that no one knows his place in society, his class position or social status, nor does any one know his fortune in the distribution of natural assets and abilities, his intelligence, strength, and the like . . . the parties do not know their conceptions of the good or their special psychological propensities. The principles of justice are chosen behind a veil of ignorance" (1971: 12).

The veil of ignorance "ensures that no one is advantaged or disadvantaged in the choice of principles by the outcome of natural chance or the contingency of social circumstances. Since all are similarly situated and no one is able to design principles to favor his particular conditions, the principles of justice are the result of a fair agreement or bargain. For given the circumstances of the original position, the symmetry of everyone's relations to each other, this initial situation is fair between individuals" (12). If the principles of justice were reached "by this sequence of hypothetical agreements . . . it will then be true that whenever social institutions satisfy these principles those engaged in them can say to one another that they are cooperating on terms to which they would agree if they were free and equal persons whose relations with respect to another were fair. . . . The general recognition of this fact would provide the basis for a public acceptance of the corresponding principles of justice" (13).

The devices of the original position and the veil of ignorance "make vivid to ourselves the restrictions that it seems reasonable to impose on . . . principles of justice. . . . The aim is to rule out those principles that it would be rational to propose for acceptance . . . only if one knew certain things that are irrelevant from the standpoint of justice. . . . To represent the desired restrictions one imagines a situation in which everyone is deprived of this sort of information. One excludes the knowledge of contingencies which set men at odds and allows them to be guided by their prejudices" (18–19). When irrelevant considerations are excluded, then, according to Rawls, people will choose his two principles of justice.[3]

What this conception of justice does, notes Rawls, "is to combine . . . the totality of conditions that we are ready upon due reflection to recognize as reasonable in our conduct with regard to one another. Once we grasp this conception, we can . . . look at the social world from the required point of view. . . . This standpoint is . . . objective and expresses our autonomy. Without conflating all persons into one but recognizing them as distinct and separate, it enables us to be impartial. . . . Thus to see our place in society from the perspective of this position is to see it *sub specie aeternitatis*. . . . Purity of heart . . . would be to see clearly and to act with grace and self-command from this point of view" (587).

The purpose of this chapter has been to give an account of the concept of justice and of Rawls's liberal conception of justice, which is meant to be an interpretation of the concept. The concept was found to be inegalitarian because it involves the consistent distribution of desert, and, since people differ in respect to the characteristics, agreements, relations, and conduct that form the bases of desert, different people deserve different things. Rawls's conception of justice, by contrast, is egalitarian. He attempts to provide an interpretation of the concept of justice in which desert plays no significant role. It will be argued in the next chapter that this attempt fails. A conception of justice must recognize the centrality of desert, otherwise it is not a conception of justice but of something else.

CHAPTER 7

Justice without the Liberal Faith

Although the word justice occurs in the title and well over a thousand times in the text, the celebrated book *A Theory of Justice* is not about justice.

—WALLACE MATSON, "What Rawls Calls Justice"

The objections to Rawls's conception of justice will be presented in increasingly general terms. Those in the first section will be internal: they grant Rawls's assumptions and argue that even so his conclusions do not follow. The next section will deal with external objections, which call into question Rawls's assumptions themselves. Then there will follow an objection whose target is not merely Rawls's argument but the liberal faith itself, of which Rawls's conception of justice is merely one, albeit outstanding, expression. The chapter will conclude with considering the implications of these objections for liberalism as a whole.

The objections will focus on Rawls's argument in *A Theory of Justice*. There are several respects in which Rawls has revised his position, as he himself explains in *Political Liberalism* (1993: xiii–xxx). The revisions, however, do not affect his arguments for justice being egalitarian and against desert being essential to justice. Several of the objections have been advanced previously by others (see, for example, Galston 1980: 170–76; Matson 1978, 1983; Moore 1993: chapter 3; Sandel 1982: 82–95; and Sher 1987). There is no claim of originality made or implied here on behalf of these objections. What matters is that when drawn together, they constitute a strong enough case to establish the untenability of both Rawls's egalitarian conception of justice and his exclusion of desert from the concept of justice.

137

7.1 INTERNAL OBJECTIONS

The first internal objection concerns Rawls's claim that since people differ in their native endowments and the circumstances of their birth and upbringing, the advantages or disadvantages that result from these arbitrary conditions are undeserved. Common sense prompts the thought at this point that, even if these conditions are morally arbitrary and thus unacceptable bases of desert, what people make of their conditions is up to them, and that is a proper basis of desert. Capacities may be undeserved, but how they are exercised confers moral merit or demerit on agents.

As against this, Rawls argues that how people exercise the capacities they happen to have also depends on contingent conditions over which they have no control. Their efforts to develop or suppress various capacities are also consequences of contingencies, and they are as unacceptable bases of desert as is the mere possession of the capacities.[1] The objection is that even if it is assumed that Rawls is right about all this, his conclusion, that how people exercise their capacities is an unacceptable basis of desert, still does not follow.

Rawls's argument is not the deterministic claim that it is because everything human beings do depends on causes over which they have no ultimate control that no one deserves anything. He is quite clear that people can and do function autonomously and responsibly.[2] His reason for denying that effort is an acceptable basis of desert, therefore, is not that determinism makes autonomy and responsibility impossible.

Rawls's reason is rather that when people do not make the appropriate effort to exercise or suppress some morally relevant capacity, it must be that some contingency over which they have no control has prevented them from it. They are not sufficiently conscientious, morally motivated, or careful of others because they have been brutalized, deprived, or coarsened by their undeserved circumstances. People express their free, equal, and rational nature by acting autonomously according to the principles of justice. If they fail to act autonomously, something must have interfered with the expression of their nature. If it were not for the interference, they would have made the required effort because it is in their nature. So that when people exercise a capacity, their performance attests to their also having the capacity to make the required effort; and when they fail to exercise a capacity, their nonperformance testifies to their incapacity to make the required effort.

This conclusion, however, does not follow from the premises Rawls has supplied. There are many reasons, in addition to the one Rawls notices, that may lead people not to exercise a capacity they have. One may certainly be that owing to circumstances beyond their control they cannot make the required effort. Others are that, although they could make the effort, they do not because their interests lie elsewhere; they are lazy; they are rebelling; shame, guilt, or remorse leads them to punish themselves; they are carried away by love, hate, sex, ambition, indignation, or pity; and so on. These alternative sources of motivation can and often do interfere with the efforts people make. Even if Rawls is right about the source of one of these interferences, it is a serious mistake to overlook the others (see Sher 1987: 28–31).

The mistake is serious because the sources of interference he omits need not be beyond the control of agents; they need not be due to contingencies that prevent their agents from making the required effort. The agents, therefore, deserve the appropriate benefits or harms for the efforts they make or fail to make. Their efforts redound to their moral merit or demerit. Rawls's argument intending to show otherwise fails.

The second internal objection is that Rawls's argument tacitly relies on desert being a basic component of justice. He aims to establish that there is no preinstitutional desert and that institutional desert is a remote consequence of his conception of justice. Yet he ultimately appeals to the commensensical notion that desert is basic and that conceptions of justice merely spell out what form the distribution of desert should take. This commensensical notion, it will be remembered, is that justice requires that equals should be treated equally and unequals unequally in the distribution of desert, and that what people deserve are benefits or harms proportional to some characteristic, agreement, relation, or conduct of theirs.

Rawls sets out to reject this understanding of the concept of justice. "The principles of justice . . . do not mention moral desert, and there is no tendency for distributive shares to correspond to it" (1971: 311). Rawls argues instead that the principles of justice assign basic rights.[3] Justice therefore implies a conception of right, not desert.[4] Thus one way of characterizing the aim of Rawls's theory is that he intends it to replace an antiegalitarian, desert-based interpretation of justice with one that is egalitarian, rights-based. The question that brings out the force of this second objection is, What reason does Rawls give for thinking that rights are basic and desert is derivative?

The fundamental reason is reached by the reconstruction of how people think in the original position about the principles of justice that their task is to formulate. Their thinking is governed by rationality and self-interest. Because the interest of each is to formulate principles that secure the cooperation of others, self-interest leads them to seek mutual advantage, which in turn forces them toward greater and greater impartiality.

Their circumstances and rationality compel them to recognize one another as free and equal. The principles of justice spell out the consequence of this recognition, which is to accord to the participants at least the minimum they require for making what they regard as a good life for themselves. Rights define the content of this minimum.

The following consideration makes it obvious that this line of thought does not lead to the conclusion that rights rather than desert are the "final court of appeal for ordering the conflicting claims of moral persons" (Rawls 1971: 135). Even in a well-ordered and stable society there will be violations of the rights established by the principles of justice. Rawls recognizes this.[5] The violations of rights must be redressed on the basis of some principles. Whatever these principles are, however, they must be other than those which establish the rights, for they are meant to remedy rights violations. These remedial principles must be added to the principles establishing rights as part of the final court of appeal, otherwise the society could not redress injustice.

These additional principles call for the punishment of those who violate the rights of others and the compensation of those whose rights have been violated. They call for inflicting appropriate and proportional harm, such as imprisonment, on the violators and providing extra benefits to their victims so as to bring them to the level where they would have been without the injury they have suffered. Punishment and compensation, however, are nothing but giving people what they deserve on the basis of the appropriate characteristic, agreement, relation, or conduct of theirs. People have rights on these bases, and what they have rights to are the benefits or harms proportional to their bases. The appeal to rights, therefore, is not an alternative to the appeal to desert; the two go hand in hand because the specification of rights is inseparable from the specification of the benefits and harms people deserve and the basis on which they deserve them.

Desert has a place in justice, however, not merely as a basis for remedial principles, but also in the formulation of the rights-conferring principles of justice themselves. This becomes apparent if it is asked: Why should free and equal people have the same rights? The answer is the truism that they are equally deserving of them. Rawls presupposes this truism and counts on its intuitive acceptance, as indeed he is entitled to do. But he is not entitled to use the argument that presupposes the truism to call into question the truism on which it rests.

As a background to the third objection, it may be supposed that the previous criticisms have been successfully countered. The failure to deserve benefits is always attributable to the agent's nonculpable lack of the relevant capacity, and rights are basic and desert is derivative. The objection is that even if these mistaken suppositions were actually correct. Rawls would still not have succeeded in showing the reasonability of his egalitarian conception of justice, which excludes the antiegalitarian appeal to desert. If the arguments designed to show that the appeal to desert is arbitrary succeed, then they succeed also in showing the arbitrariness of Rawls's principles of justice. If, on the other hand, the arguments fail, then Rawls's case against desert fails with them (see Sher 1987: 34–36).

Remember that Rawls's claim is that because people's characteristics, agreements, relations, and conduct depend on arbitrary contingencies, claims of desert based on them are similarly arbitrary.[6] And that arbitrariness is the reason why "the principles of justice . . . do not mention moral desert, and there is no tendency for distributive shares to correspond to it" (1971: 311).

Bearing this in mind, consider the characteristics, agreements, relations, and conduct of the people Rawls places in the original position. Let it be supposed that they actually choose the principles of justice that Rawls says they will. Rawls's case requires depriving these people of almost all individuating features, but enough remain for the force of the present criticism to be felt. Rawls's people are alive; human; self-interested; rational; aware of one another's existence; familiar with the general and uncontroversial facts of human motivation and political life; subject to the circumstances of justice; capable of autonomy, cooperation, and responsibility; and aware of the past and plan for the future.

What irreparably damages Rawls's case is that each feature is arbitrary in precisely the same sense and for exactly the same reason as Rawls says are the characteristics, agreements, relations, and conduct on which claims of desert are based. For the features Rawls allows his people to have in the original position and behind the veil of ignorance depend on natural assets and contingencies that are arbitrary from a moral point of view. Rawls's people could be dead; have a mental disorder or attention deficit syndrome; be prenatally addicted to drugs; be enslaved; and so forth. That none of this is true of them is a contingency over which they have no control. But the principles of justice, which these people would choose, would not be chosen by them if it were not for these contingencies. The principles of justice are consequently just as arbitrary from a moral point of view as Rawls says claims of desert are.

Rawls's defense of egalitarian justice and his criticism of antiegalitarian justice face, therefore, the following dilemma: if desert is morally arbitrary because it is based on arbitrary contingencies, then the principles of justice are also morally arbitrary because they too are based on arbitrary contingencies; if the arbitrary contingencies on which the principles of justice depend do not deprive the principles of moral force, then the arbitrary contingencies on which desert depends do not deprive desert of moral force either. In either case, Rawls has failed to support his defense of egalitarian justice and his criticism of antiegalitarian justice.

7.2 EXTERNAL OBJECTIONS

The objections discussed in this section are external because they raise questions about some of Rawls's assumptions. The first such objection is that if Rawls were correct in thinking that claims of desert were not basic but derivative from the principles of justice according to which institutions are organized, then one of the strongest reasons for criticizing defective institutions would have to be abandoned. This reason is that the institutions are defective because they undeservedly harm people. If Rawls were right in claiming that desert is dependent on institutional arrangements, then, provided an institution functioned according to its own principles, it could not fail to give people what they deserve because its principles would define what desert is. The legitimacy of the standard practice of criticizing many institutions on the ground that the principles according to which they function lead them to cause undeserved harm shows that desert is more fundamental than are institutional arrangements.

The force of this criticism is strengthened by Henry Sidgwick's distinction between the "customary" and the "ideal" views of justice. He says that "the reconciliation between these two views . . . is the chief problem of political justice" (1981: 273). According to the first view, laws are just if they reflect the customary arrangements that prevail in a society; according to the second, laws are just in proportion as they conform to some reasonably founded ideal. The present objection may then be expressed by saying that a particularly telling objection to customary justice is that it fails to distribute desert according to ideal justice.

Now Rawls's reply would not only be to acknowledge that this is so, but to insist on it. For his egalitarian conception of justice may be viewed as an attempt to construct a reasonably founded interpretation of ideal justice. His point, that desert depends on institutional arrangements, may be expressed by saying that the arrangements he has in mind are not the customary but the ideal ones. If his principles of justice prevailed, he would say, then people would indeed get what they deserve because the principles define what desert is. That is why desert is not basic but derivative.

This rejoinder, however, has unacceptable implications. Suppose that institutions actually functioned according to Rawls's conception of justice. Ideal justice would then have become customary justice. If desert were defined by the ideal-turned-customary justice, then the prevailing system of justice would be immunized against criticism. It could not then be asked whether people are getting what they deserve because the system defines what they deserve. The system of justice would thus turn into a repressive institution, not by forbidding criticism, but by depriving people of the conceptual apparatus in which criticism could be formulated.

To avoid this noxious form of repression, it must be possible to express doubts about the ideal. And its most natural expression would be cast in the form of asking whether under Rawlsian arrangements people would be getting what they deserve. The possibility of expressing these doubts, however, is excluded by Rawls's view that desert depends on institutional arrangements. If Rawls is to avoid these repressive implications, and there is every reason to think that he would want to do so, then he must make room for the possibility of questioning the system from an independent point of view. Such questioning would raise the doubt that benefits and harms distributed according to Rawls's ideal were not based on the characteristics, agreements, relations, or conduct of the people who received them—that is, the ideal failed in giving people what they deserve. If Rawls allows for such doubts, he must recognize that desert is independent of institutional arrangements. If he does not allow for them, his ideal is dogmatically protected from rational criticism.

This objection creates another difficulty as well for Rawls. It shows that his treatment of desert violates his announced method of argumentation: reflective equilibrium. When Sidgwick says that the chief problem of political justice is the reconciliation between the customary and the ideal views of justice, he, like Rawls, has the method of reflective equilibrium in mind. A theory of justice begins with customary arrangements and then improves them in the light of some ideal. The ideal is persuasive, however, only if it appeals to people whose convictions have been influenced by the customary arrangements. Rawls recognizes this, and in making his case he frequently appeals to his readers' intuitions, which reflect customary moral convictions. But when he comes to desert, Rawls proceeds differently. He recognizes that "there is a tendency for common sense to suppose that income and wealth, and the good things in life generally, should be distributed according to moral desert" (1971: 310), but he rejects this tendency: "The principles of justice . . . do not mention moral desert" (311). Rawls is thus rejecting a substantial portion of customary justice by appealing to ideal justice. One would expect consequentialists to repudiate what is customary because it falls short of an ideal they cherish. It is surprising, however, that Rawls would do so, given his opposition to all forms of consequentialism and his commitment to maintaining the reflective equilibrium between the customary and the ideal.

A possible explanation of this inconsistency is that customary justice prompts both egalitarian and antiegalitarian intuitions. Egalitarian intuitions reflect a commitment to impartiality, whereas antiegalitarian ones express the wish that people should get what they deserve. In constructing his theory of justice, Rawls draws on egalitarian intuitions nurtured by customary justice, while rejecting antiegalitarian intuitions that are also nurtured by it. This way of proceeding may still be said to maintain a semblance of the reflective equilibrium, but no more than a semblance. It appeals to what supports Rawls's theory and rejects what does not. A less indulgent way of describing the method is that it involves cooking the results. As Rawls engagingly puts it in a slightly different context, "We want to define the original position so that we get the desired solution" (141).

The second external objection concerns the principles of justice that would be chosen by Rawls's rational and self-interested people in the original position. An enormous amount has been written about whether the principles that Rawls claims would be chosen would indeed be chosen. But the present objection proceeds differently. It grants that Rawls's two principles would be chosen, but it claims that Rawls's people would also choose a third principle. This principle, however, requires the recognition of the central role desert plays in justice, it is incompatible with the egalitarian implications of Rawls's second principle, and it calls for a considerable restriction of the scope of the first principle.

The need for a third principle follows from what Rawls himself says. He announces the surely correct precept that "conceptions of justice must be justified by the conditions of life as we know it [*sic*] or not at all" (454). Some of these conditions are what he calls, following Hume, "the circumstances of justice" (126–30). These circumstances are adverse conditions of human existence that require justice to cope with them: the lack of self-sufficiency, moderate scarcity, limited benevolence, and human vulnerability to physical and psychological harm (see the introduction to Chapter 6). When people in the original position set about to choose principles of justice, they are familiar with these circumstances.[7] Among these circumstances there is surely the fact that there will be violations of whatever principles of justice they would arrive at. The tendency to injustice must be recognized as one of the circumstances of justice.

It is an odd feature of Rawls's theory that it says very little about controlling injustice. He recognizes that there will be "inevitable deviations from justice," but he thinks that in a society arranged according to his principles the deviations "are effectively corrected or held within tolerable bounds by forces within the system" (458). He discusses only one of these forces, "the sense of justice shared by the members of the community," which sense, Rawls says, "has a fundamental role" in assuring "that the basic structure is stable with respect to justice" (458). The sense of justice no doubt exists and motivates people. But selfishness, aggression, greed, envy, prejudice, and resentment also exist, they also motivate people, and they often overwhelm such sense of justice as people may have. This being so is surely one of "the general facts about human society" that people in the original position would have to know.

If these darker aspects of human motivation did not exist, there would be no need for Rawls to place his people behind the veil of ignorance. The veil hides from people their personal situation so that they will not "exploit social and natural circumstances to their own advantage" (136); "no one knows his situation in society nor his natural assets, and therefore no one is in a position to tailor his principles to his advantage" (139). The clear implication is that if the veil did not keep people ignorant of the relevant facts, then they would seek their own advantage at the expense of others.

The sense of justice may act as a curb on injustice, but any realistic observer of the conditions of life—conditions with reference to which conceptions of justice must be justified, if at all (454)—will know that unjust motivation often overwhelms the sense of justice. Consistency requires that the people in the original position should be supposed to know this. If they do, however, then they will want to choose a third principle of justice to protect the first two principles from unjust violations. The third principle will state how injustice should be "effectively corrected or held within tolerable bounds" (458).

The generally known conditions of life are that some people act unjustly occasionally, whereas others do so habitually. A society cannot survive unless it protects itself from such actions and people. The form such protection must take is to curtail their activities. That will involve restricting their liberty and depriving them of the resources and the opportunities to act in violation of the first two principles of justice. Unjust people and actions will not be protected by the first two principles of justice. Unless a society were bent on self-destruction, it would not devote its scarce resources to encourage unjust activities and agents, not even if the agents were among its least-advantaged members; it would not keep open for them desirable positions so that they could subvert them for unjust purposes; and it would not extend to them the most extensive liberty possible, so as to provide greater scope for their injustice.

It may be said against this that Rawls's principles have the appropriate restrictions built into them. People's exercise of liberty must be "compatible with a similar liberty of others" (60), and social and political inequalities must be "to everyone's advantage" (60). The restrictions are certainly there, but their consequences are incompatible with Rawls's conception of justice.

One of these consequences is that in Rawls's presentation of his conception the restrictions appear as tertiary qualifications. The rhetoric is that in a just society there will be a great deal of freedom and equality and the vast majority of people will use their freedom and equality to pursue a plurality of autonomous conceptions of a good life. But nothing in the theory itself, as opposed to the rhetoric in which it is couched, would rule out that in a just society very many people indeed would have their freedom, resources, and opportunities severely and justifiably curtailed. This would happen to all those whose actions fall afoul of the restrictions of which Rawls makes so little. In fact, most of the resources of a just society could be used to protect the few who live according to the principles of justice.

It is, of course, an open question whether injustice would be rampant in a particular society. The unjust may be the majority or only a small minority. The important point is that Rawls assumes that injustice would be rare, he offers no safeguards in case his assumption fails, nor does he justify his assumption apart from naïve talk about the sense of justice, which glosses over human wickedness. Holding this assumption, however, is not an accidental oversight of Rawls. The assumption is the liberal faith, about which more will be said in the next section.

Another damaging consequence for Rawls's conception follows from the restrictions placed on the first two principles of justice. The consequence is that the restrictions require treating people as they deserve to be treated, and this is incompatible with the announced purpose of the two principles, which is to eliminate desert from justice. This point has been argued for already in connection with the third internal objection, so there is no need to belabor it. People who live and act according to the principles of justice are entitled to the freedom, resources, and opportunities they need, whereas those who live and act unjustly are justifiably curtailed. The term for this entitlement is desert. If Rawls had followed his methodological precept and asked "whether applying these principles would lead us to make the same judgments about the basic structure of society which we now make intuitively and in which we have the greatest confidence" (19), then he would not have arrived at the answer, contradicting what he acknowledges is common sense, that the "principles of justice . . . do not mention moral desert, and there is no tendency for distributive shares to correspond to it" (311).

The third external objection is that Rawls's exclusion of desert from the concept of justice rests on a misunderstanding of the nature of desert. That Rawls thinks that justice is not based on desert is placed beyond question by the passages in which he explicitly says so (100–104, 310–15). But in none of these passages, or elsewhere, does Rawls provide an account of what exactly it is that he is excluding when he excludes desert. To find out what Rawls means by desert, it is necessary to extrapolate from the relevant passages. What emerges is that he thinks that the basis of desert is moral virtue.[8] This view of desert, or of its basis, however, is unacceptably narrow. It comes nowhere close to an accurate representation of what desert actually is.

In the course of the earlier discussion of the nature of desert (Section 6.2), its basis was said to be some characteristic, relation, agreement, or conduct of the agent. These bases, it has been argued, create a claim of desert, and the claim is that because of some relevant characteristic, relation, agreement, or conduct of a particular agent that agent deserves some benefits or harms proportional to their basis.

Rawls's identification of moral virtue as *the* basis of desert thus involves a radical misunderstanding of the nature of desert (see Galston 1980: 170–6; Matson 1983; and Sher 1987: 34–36). Characteristics other than moral virtue may form legitimate bases of desert: the grace of a dancer, the skill of a novelist, the efficiency of an administrator, the acute diagnosis of a physician, and so forth. The bases of desert may be relations, such as between parents and children, teachers and students, benefactors and recipients, criminals and victims; agreements that hold, for example, between sexual partners, employers and employees, producers and consumers; uncharacteristic conduct, such as exceptional heroism, supererogation, savagery, or revenge; or characteristic conduct that does not reflect moral virtue, as notable acts of politeness, assiduity, creativity, and so on, which may not do so. Furthermore, the claims these bases create are not only for benefits, as Rawls supposes, but also for harms, and not only for mere benefits and harms but also for benefits and harms that are proportional to their bases.

When ordinary people hold the commonsense view that justice involves treating people as they deserve to be treated and when philosophers defend the commonsense view, they have a great deal more in mind than rewarding moral virtue. Even if Rawls were right in his extraordinary claim that desert based on moral virtue is irrelevant to justice, he would not come anywhere close to showing that desert is irrelevant to justice, for moral virtue is only one of several bases of desert. And, of course, strong reasons have already been given to show that Rawls is mistaken about the irrelevance of moral virtue as well.

The fourth external objection draws together the previous internal and external objections and derives from them the conclusion that Rawls's conception of justice is not merely defective, but that it is not a conception of justice at all. A conception of justice must be an interpretation of the concept of justice. What Rawls puts forward as a conception of justice, however, radically misinterprets the very concept of which it is supposed to be an interpretation. That it does so is the cumulative conclusion that follows from the previous objections.

The structure of the argument running through these two chapters on justice has been to begin with the concept of justice that Rawls himself acknowledges to be the commonsense one: justice is to treat equals equally and unequals unequally in respect to the distribution of desert. Genuine conceptions of justice differ because of disagreements over what is deserved and what principles should guide the distribution of appropriate benefits and harms. The next step has been to consider the nature of desert. Its bases are various characteristics, agreements, relations, or the conduct of agents, which justify the claim that a particular agent deserves some benefit or harm proportional to the underlying basis. Justice consists in agents getting what they deserve.

Opposed to this account of justice and desert has been a brief account of what Rawls proposes as a conception of justice. His conception rejects desert as a basic component of justice in favor of an egalitarian distribution scheme based on two principles of what Rawls calls justice. Rawls's conception of justice, therefore, is consciously and deliberately designed as an alternative to the commonsense concept of justice. Given this clash between the commonsense concept and Rawls's conception, either the first is a misunderstanding of justice, or the second fails to be a conception of it. The overall aim of the argument has been to provide reasons in defense of the commonsense concept of justice and to attack Rawls's conception of justice.

The internal objections showed that Rawls's conception fails in its own terms. He supposes, contrary to elementary knowledge of human psychology, that people's failure to make the efforts morality requires invariably reveals an incapacity that is beyond their control. He does not recognize that the so-called rights that the principles of justice are supposed to protect presuppose the very idea of desert that the conception is meant to deny. Rawls's conception provides reasons for thinking that claims of desert are arbitrary, but Rawls does not see that these reasons show with equal force that what he regards as claims of justice are also arbitrary.

The external objections showed that contrary to its announced method, the conception privileges an ideal of justice over what is customarily regarded as such, and Rawls protects the ideal he favors by making its criticism logically impossible from the vantage point of what is customary. Rawls fails to recognize that a conception of justice must make allowances for human wickedness and that the acceptance of the conception's

principles is compatible with a society in which there is very little freedom, equality, or justice. In objecting to desert Rawls works with such a
severely truncated version of it as to render his conclusion unacceptable
to reasonable defenders of the importance of desert to justice.

The conception is thus riddled with inconsistency, flies in the face of
common sense, violates its own methodological precepts, and, by denying
that people should get what they deserve, unintentionally promotes injustice. It fails, therefore, as a conception of justice, and the challenge it
presents to the customary commonsense concept of justice has been met.

The fact remains, however, that Rawls's conception of justice is widely
regarded as reasonable, indeed outstanding; its reputation is exceptionally high; it is used to justify a wide range of political programs; it is an
instrument of extensive social transformation; and its defenders include
numerous thoughtful people of goodwill whose acquaintance with the
conception is anything but superficial. This state of affairs requires an
explanation. The explanation is that Rawls has succeeded in translating
deep moral and political convictions that many people share into political
programs that command their allegiance. These convictions in the background are essential elements of the liberal faith. The objections that
have been raised here are likely to affect that faith as little as the objections of atheists are likely to affect the faith of religious believers. The
time has come, therefore, to face the liberal faith directly.

7.3 THE LIBERAL FAITH

In the last paragraph of *A Theory of Justice*, Rawls asks about the
original position: given that it is a hypothetical construct, "why should we
take any interest in it, moral or otherwise?" And he answers, because it
combines "into one conception the totality of conditions that we are
ready upon reflection to recognize as reasonable in our conduct with
regard to one another." That conception provides a perspective which
"expresses our autonomy": "To see our place in society from the perspective of this position is to see it *sub specie aeternitatis*. The perspective of
eternity is not a perspective from a certain place beyond the world, nor
the point of view of a transcendent being; rather it is a certain form of
thought and feeling that rational persons can adopt within the world.
And having done so, they can . . . arrive together at regulating principles
that can be affirmed by everyone" (1971: 587). Although these passages
do not quite state it, the liberal faith is just below their surface.

The liberal faith is that the perspective sub specie aeternitatis is the
perspective of autonomy; that reasonable people strive to be motivated by
it and thus to act autonomously; and that when they so act, they act ac-

cording to rational and moral principles which regulate human conduct
and which all reasonable people would accept on reflection. The liberal
faith can also be expressed negatively: the failure to act autonomously
and the failure to agree about the basic principles that ought to regulate
human conduct are failures of reason. The liberal faith is that on the level
of basic principles, the requirements of autonomy, reason, and morality
coincide; autonomous acts are expressions of reasonable and moral requirements; and conformity to these requirements is necessary for the
goodness of human lives. The liberal faith is the faith of Kant.[9]

In *A Theory of Justice*, Rawls works out the implications of the liberal
faith for justice. By placing people in the original position, he endeavors
to show how they would act if the motives to act unreasonably were removed. The original position is a device for forcing the sub specie aeternitatis perspective, and thus autonomy, on agents who ask what ought to be
the basic structure of their society. The liberal faith is to believe, against
ample contrary evidence, that if people act autonomously, then they will
act justly. It is the belief that "men's propensity to injustice is not a permanent aspect of community life" (245).

That this belief is a matter of faith is shown by its being held in the face
of the acknowledged fact that much injustice exists in all known human
societies. The discrepancy between belief and fact is attributed to the failure of autonomy. And that failure, in turn, is not taken to indicate anything adverse about human nature; it is ascribed instead to contingencies
creating defective institutions.[10]

Rawls says that the view of human nature that underlies liberalism is
"the high point of the contractarian tradition in Kant and Rousseau"
(1971: 252). According to it, "a person is acting autonomously when the
principles of his action are chosen by him as the most adequate possible
expression of his nature as a free and equal rational being" (252). These
are the principles of justice, and by "acting from these principles persons
express their nature as free and equal rational beings" (252). And because acting from them "belongs to their good, the sense of justice aims
at their well-being . . . directly. It supports those arrangements that enable
everyone to express his common nature" (476). Moreover, "the sense of
justice is continuous with the love of mankind . . . the objects of these two
sentiments are closely related, being defined in large part by the same
conception of justice. If one of them seems natural . . . so is the other"
(476).

The view of human nature at the core of the liberal faith is thus that
human beings are by their nature free, equal, rational, and they are benevolent too because they love mankind. They act autonomously when
they express their nature, and when they act contrary to freedom, equal-

ity, rationality, or benevolence, they act contrary to their nature because of the contingencies of heteronomous influences. To act autonomously, therefore, is to act benevolently in recognition of the freedom, equality, and rationality of all human beings. As a result, all who have the capacity for autonomy are to be treated according to Rawls's two principles of justice: they are to have equal liberty, equal opportunity, and resources inversely proportional to their advantages. All are to be treated in this way regardless of the uses to which they put their liberties, opportunities, and resources.[11]

It is now apparent why the rampant misuse of these goods causes no serious worry to those who hold the liberal faith. They believe that when people act autonomously, they do not misuse them. And if they misuse them, that is much the more reason to remake the prevailing institutions better to reflect Rawls's principles of justice, for it is institutions made unjust by contingencies that corrupt those who misuse the goods available to them.

One of the remarkable features of the liberal faith is that all facts about human conduct are grist to its mill. If people act benevolently in recognition of everyone's freedom, equality, and rationality, then the liberal faith in autonomy is confirmed. If they act in the opposite ways, that too confirms the liberal faith because the actions are ascribed to the influence of unjust institutions, which are said to prevent the exercise of autonomy. Thus no evidence would be taken to show that the liberal faith is mistaken. If critics adduce apparently contrary evidence, they merely demonstrate their lack of understanding of what the faithful claim. This self-immunization against criticism is, of course, part of its nature as a faith.

The strength of this faith is undeniable, as is its hold on contemporary Western thought and sensibility. Those who reject it ought to try to understand why thoughtful, reasonable, and decent people embrace it so fervently. Part of the answer is that powerful feelings are provoked by the undeserved suffering of people in societies with liberal aspirations and elsewhere. The liberal faith supplies a vocabulary in which these feelings can be articulated and thus civilized. But it does more: it also provides political programs designed to remake societies so as to lessen suffering. It gives a sense, therefore, that the feelings articulated in its terms are not merely reactive but also creative. It provides a way in which its adherents can contribute to changing life, as they see it, for the better and doing so in just those respects which provoke their adverse feelings.

Another part of the answer is that the loss of religious faith has created—is creating—a lacuna. Increasingly larger numbers of people can no longer believe that reality is permeated by a moral order and that good lives depend on conformity to it. The order, if there is one, is causal, not moral. It is indifferent to the moral standing of those who are affected by it. There is no reason to believe in cosmic justice. The moral dimension of human life is permeated by contingency, not by the moral order reassuringly posited by various religions. The implication of contingency is that reasonable and moral conduct may not lead to a good life. The good may suffer, and the wicked may flourish. The liberal faith responds to these deeply unsettling thoughts. It holds out the promise that if human beings live autonomously, they will create a social framework in which reason and morality are more likely to lead to good lives than under other arrangements, undeserved suffering will be ameliorated, and a system of human justice will replace the religious ideal of cosmic justice. The promise is not of the Garden of Eden but of a garden carved out from the moral wilderness by human effort.

These achievements of the liberal faith are surely considerable. They are inspired by high moral purpose. It is right to be disturbed by widespread undeserving suffering; it is right to try to do something about it; and it is right to want human beings to live more and more in accordance with reason and morality. These are the features of the liberal faith that make it attractive, explain its influence on contemporary thought and sensibility, and account for its command of the allegiance of people of intellect and goodwill. What is wrong with the liberal faith is that these fine ideals are ill served by it. It lowers a veil not of ignorance but of illusion, behind which is hidden the true significance of undeserved suffering, wickedness, and contingency. The liberal faith substitutes secular illusions for religious ones.

A more realistic view (see Chapters 2–3) recognizes that much undeserved suffering is due to human wickedness; that much wickedness is nonautonomous; that contingency is an ineliminable feature of human existence; that the strife for greater autonomy is itself jeopardized by contingency; that greater autonomy gives greater scope to wickedness; that contingency affects and renders unequal the moral worth of human beings; and that bettering the human condition depends on decreasing both nonautonomous and autonomous wickedness. According to this realistic view:

We are in an ethical condition that lies not only beyond Christianity, but also beyond its Kantian and its Hegelian legacies. We have an ambivalent sense of what human beings have achieved, and have hopes for how they might live (in particular, in the form of the still powerful idea that they should live without lies). We know that the world was not made for us, or we for the world, that our history tells no purposive story, and that there is no position outside the world or outside history from which we might hope to authenticate our activities. We have to acknowledge the hideous costs of many human achievements we value, including this reflective sense itself, and recognize that there is no redemptive Hegelian history or universal Leibnizian cost-benefit analysis [or, it may be added, Kantian contractarian contrivance] to show that it will come out well enough in the end. (Williams 1993: 166)

7.4 SOME PROBLEMS OF THE LIBERAL FAITH

The problems of the liberal faith have not been much addressed by liberals. But two efforts made in this direction merit discussion. One is Rawls's, the other is Annette Baier's. Rawls developed his thoughts in response to what must surely be one of the most serious criticisms of Kant's ethics. The criticism is Sidgwick's, and it is hard to know why it is not widely discussed. Sidgwick cites numerous passages to show that Kant uses "freedom" in two incompatible senses: there is "Good or Rational Freedom," on the one hand, and "Neutral or Moral Freedom," on the other (Sidgwick 1981: 512). In the first sense, "a man is a free agent in proportions as he acts rationally;" in the second sense, "man has a freedom of choice between good and evil, which is realised or manifested when he deliberately chooses evil just as much as when he deliberately chooses good." These two senses are incompatible because "if we say that a man is a free agent in proportion as he acts rationally, we cannot also say . . . that it is by his free choice that he acts irrationally" (Sidgwick 1981: 511).

When Kant talks about freedom in the context of the universal, impartial, and disinterested perspective expressed by the categorical imperative, he means good or rational freedom; when he talks about freedom in the context of moral responsibility for choosing right or wrong, he means neutral or moral freedom. Good or rational freedom expresses a moral necessity that rational agents must recognize, otherwise they are not rational. Neutral or moral freedom expresses a moral possibility that rational agents must also recognize, otherwise they are not morally responsible. The moral necessity, however, excludes the choice of evil, whereas the moral possibility allows it.

The problem this creates for Kant's ethics is not one of ambiguity that clarity and care could remove. The problem is the fundamental one that the exercise of good or rational freedom requires agents to act in abstraction of their contingent selves and circumstances, whereas the exercise of neutral or moral freedom requires them to make choices among contingent possibilities presented in contingent circumstances to their contingent selves. The claim central to Kantian ethics, that the impartial perspective will motivate rational agents in their contingent circumstances to choose good rather than evil, rests on an equivocation between the two senses of freedom. Why would the moral necessity that holds in the impartial perspective also hold in contingent circumstances? Why would agents be morally responsible if their actions are dictated by necessity? Why would impartial actions be invariably good rather than evil?

If "freedom" in Sidgwick's argument is replaced by the liberal understanding of "autonomy," then this objection to Kant's ethics becomes a fundamental challenge to the liberal faith itself. The challenge is that liberals should explain why autonomy precludes wickedness and why greater autonomy would diminish rather than enlarge the scope of wickedness.

Rawls's response is that "Sidgwick's objection is decisive, I think, as long as one assumes, as Kant's exposition may seem to allow, both that a noumenal self can choose any consistent set of principles and that acting from such principles . . . is sufficient to express one's choice as that of a free and rational being" (1971: 255). And Rawls goes on: "Kant's reply must be that though acting on any consistent set of principles could be the outcome of a decision on the part of the noumenal self, not all such action by the phenomenal self expresses this decision as that of a free and rational being. . . . Kant did not show that acting from the moral law expresses our nature in identifiable ways that acting from contrary principles does not" (255). The defect in Kant's ethics is thus acknowledged, but Rawls comes to its rescue: "This defect is made good, I believe, by the conception of the original position. The essential point is that we need an argument showing which principles . . . free and equal rational persons would choose. . . . My suggestion is that we think of the original position as the point of view from which noumenal selves see the world. . . . Our nature as [free and equal rational] beings is displayed when we act . . . [in] independence from the contingencies of nature and society" (255–56).

Rawls's attempt to use the original position to meet Sidgwick's criticism fails, however, because contingency and wickedness present problems that the liberal faith has not met. The problem with contingency is that it makes unreliable the distribution of benefits and harms according to any principle or principles designed for that purpose. The liberal response is to formulate principles in a context from which contingency has been excluded. But why should it be supposed that principles arrived at in abstraction of contingency will be applicable in contingent circumstances? How could the products of a thought experiment overcome the accidents, scarcity, misfortune, indifference, and wickedness that permeate all schemes of distribution? Rawls makes a great effort to think contingency away, but because it is part of the furniture of the world, not a product of human thought, the effort cannot succeed.

To say in response that the principles are meant to cope with contingency, not to eliminate it, is a first step toward realism and away from illusion. But for there to be a second step, it must be recognized that principles formulated in an artificial context in which contingency is allowed to play no role are ill suited to cope with contingency in real life. Realistic principles must be derived from, formulated in response to, and continually revised to fit the changing, shifting, unpredictable contingencies of actual human circumstances.

Or the response may be that in the flux of contingencies there is a permanent element: human nature. It too is affected by contingency, but it is permanent enough to establish some minimum requirements of human welfare. The exercise of autonomy is surely one of those requirements. The aim of the principles is to make it possible for people to exercise their autonomy in whatever contingent circumstances they may find themselves. Freedom, equality, rights, and the pursuit of a conception of a good life people make their own from among a plurality of possibilities are the prerequisites of autonomous functioning, which is what the principles protect. But this too is an illusion unless it is combined with the recognition that among the contingencies of life there is human wickedness. Autonomy needs to be protected not only from external threats but also from the internal one that wickedness presents. And because the internal threat is also part of human nature, protecting autonomy often requires curbing its scope. The liberal faith in the betterment of the human condition by increasing autonomy leaves wickedness out of the picture.

One philosopher who does not avert her gaze from wickedness and considers the reasonable response to it is Annette Baier (1985b). Why would reasonable people be just in the contingent circumstances of real life, she asks, when injustice surrounds them? As Hume memorably put it, the injustice of others "affords me a new reason for any breach of equity, by showing me, that I should be a cully of my integrity if I alone shou'd impose on myself a severe restraint amidst the licentiousness of others" (Hume 1960: 535). Baier agrees: "Hume's point, a valid one, is that only a fool supports widely unsupported institutions whose only good depends on their getting wide support" (1985b: 304). She then asks, "Is justice then an ideal which is committed to a perhaps groundless liberal faith?" The answer for herself is, "I shall proceed within the limits of the comforting liberal faith" (293). However, "faith, for rational persons, must appear reasonable," and what makes the liberal faith reasonable "is the great unreasonableness of any alternative to it" (294). And she goes on: "The best one can say for the reasonableness of willing to believe in the value of (possibly) unilateral moral action is that the alternative . . . must lead eventually to an outcome disastrous for all" (295). To be just in an unjust world is thus not to be the cully of one's integrity: "Apparently futile unilateral and possibly self-sacrificing action is neither futile nor unilateral. Not futile, because it keeps alive the assurance of the possibility of qualified members for a just society. Not unilateral, because the one just man has a 'cloud of witnesses', all those whose similar acts . . . keep alive the same hope" (305). The "just man *now*, in an unjust world, has no certainty, only faith and hope, that there really can and will be a just society" (307). The faith and hope, however, are reasonable because abandoning them would make matters worse.

The trouble with this defense of the liberal faith is that with small verbal changes it can be used to defend any faith. All faiths hold out the ideal of some good so as to motivate the faithful who live in a bad world; and all faiths claim that the world would be even worse if it were not for the faithful actions of the faithful. Some faiths, however, are mistaken about this. The world would actually be better without them and the actions they motivate. The question is whether or not this is true of the liberal faith. It is not to the testimony of the faithful, however, that one should turn for an answer.

The answer must surely depend on the credentials of the ideal to which the faith advertises itself as a means. But the ideal of justice advocated by the liberal faith has been shown to be defective by the internal and external objections adduced against it. The choice facing reasonable people is not between liberal justice and "an outcome disastrous to all" but between justice, the liberal misinterpretation of it, and the breakdown of justice, which would indeed be very bad.

The argument in these two chapters on justice was a defense of the concept of justice against the liberal misinterpretation of it. Justice is consistency in the distribution of deserved benefits and harms. The basis of desert is some characteristic, relation, agreement, or conduct. And the bases of desert create a claim that the people to whom they are correctly ascribed ought to receive some benefits or harms proportional to their bases.

The concept of justice must be supplemented with a conception of justice in order to provide an interpretation of desert by specifying what particular characteristics, relations, agreements, or conduct form an appropriate basis of what particular benefits or harms and how benefits and harms can be made proportional to their bases. Conceptions of justice differ because there are disagreements about the bases of desert and about the appropriateness and proportionality of fitting benefits and harms to their bases.

Justice is done, or not done, by individuals and institutions as they apply explicit or implicit principles derived from particular conceptions of justice to particular cases. The justice of individuals and institutions depends on their conformity to the prevailing conception of justice and on how well that conception interprets the concept of justice itself. Justice is thus conventional, but not merely conventional, because the requirement of the consistent distribution of deserved benefits and harms serves as an external standard by which the conventions of justice can be judged.

The concept of justice expresses the ideal that there ought to be a balance between the good and evil that people cause and receive. If cosmic justice existed, it would guarantee that this balance would be maintained over the whole course of the life of each human being. But there is no cosmic justice, and so it is left to individuals and institutions to maintain the desired moral balance, as well as they can. They will not do it very well because contingency and wickedness stand in the way.

Contingency upsets the balance in such forms as scarcity, chance, the impossibility of redressing the imbalance between crime and punishment, injury and compensation, merit and recognition in numerous cases, and so forth. Contingency, however, affects not only the distribution of desert but also its bases. It often happens that individuals have insufficient control over the characteristic, relation, agreement, or conduct that forms the basis of their desert. What people deserve and whether they get it are often placed beyond human control because of contingent circumstances. The ideal of justice nevertheless calls for decreasing the influence of contingency on human life. And that is done by trying to maintain the balance between the good and the evil that individuals cause and receive, even though contingency will impede the effort.

Such efforts, however, are further handicapped by wickedness, which is formed of habitual patterns of evil-causing actions. Wickedness is a regularly acted upon disposition to cause serious, undeserved harm. How much wickedness there is depends in part on how much injustice there is; "in part" because wickedness may take forms other than injustice. The more injustice is felt, the greater is the extent that wickedness must be supposed to have. Because few people deny the prevalence of injustice, there ought to be just as few who doubt that wickedness is extensive. But consistency does not reign in this respect, there is a great reluctance to acknowledge widespread wickedness.

One main reason for this reluctance is the mistaken supposition that the disposition to cause evil turns into wickedness only if it is freed from contingency by being autonomous. Autonomously caused evil, however, is insufficient to account for the prevalence of evil. Its prevalence cannot be explained by such people and actions, not even if undeserved harm caused by nonhuman sources is recognized as an additional source of evil (see Chapter 2). Much wickedness must be attributed to nonautonomous patterns of action, formed and fostered by contingent influences over which the agents have inadequate control. These actions nevertheless cause evil, and justice requires curbing it. But doing so depends on human agents who are themselves subject to contingency and prone to wickedness. That is why the effort to maintain the moral balance that justice requires is bound to be insufficient and why human justice is doomed to be imperfect.

This insufficiency and imperfection notwithstanding, the sustained effort to come as close as possible to the ideal of justice ought to be made. Part of doing so is to form a realistic view of the surrounding circumstances. The acknowledgment of contingency and wickedness must be part of that. But from them it follows that there is moral inequality among human beings. They have different moral worth because they succeed or fail in various degrees as individual centers from which the moral balance can alone be maintained. They may not have made themselves morally unequal, but they are unequal nevertheless because they differ in respect to the sum of good and evil their actions cause. Justice requires responding to thee differences, even if they are due to contingency and wickedness that are beyond the autonomous control of the agents. For justice is about maintaining the balance between good and evil caused and received—about giving people what they deserve.

One great fault of liberalism is that its illusions obscure this realistic view. Liberalism systematically de-emphasizes contingency, wickedness, and moral inequality. The liberal faith is comforting because it is pleasant to believe that autonomy can minimize contingency, that all human beings are basically disposed toward the good, that wickedness is due to institutions whose defects are remediable, and that because of this basic capacity for autonomy all human beings are morally equal and ought to be treated accordingly. However pleasant, these beliefs are false, and holding them is inconsistent with justice and good lives.

CHAPTER 8

Pluralism versus Liberalism

There is no consideration of any kind that overrides all other
considerations in all conceivable circumstances.

—STUART HAMPSHIRE, *Innocence and Experience*

The topic of this chapter is pluralism, another basic value of
liberalism. The criticism it will develop is that while liberals are right to
regard pluralism as a basic value, its acceptance as such is actually inconsistent with the rest of liberalism.

The central difficulty liberalism has on account of pluralism is that pluralism is committed to the view that there is no conception of a good life
and no particular value that, in conflicts with other conceptions and values, always takes justifiable precedence over them. But if liberalism is to
avoid the charge of vacuity, it must be committed to holding that in cases
of conflict the particular conceptions of a good life and values that liberals favor do take justifiable precedence over nonliberal ones.[1] The conclusion of this chapter will be that liberals cannot avoid this inconsistency.

The argument will begin with an account of the nature of pluralism
and of the incompatibility and incommensurability of many conflicting
values; it will then document the inconsistent liberal attitudes to pluralism; and it will end by considering various liberal responses, none of
which succeed in overcoming the inconsistency. These matters have been
discussed previously and in greater detail in *The Morality of Pluralism*
(Kekes 1993).

8.1 A FRAMEWORK FOR PLURALISM

Pluralism is a new approach to thinking about values.[2] Isaiah Berlin (1969a) and Michael Oakeshott (1962) began the task of formulating

it in a systematic way in the 1940s and 1950s. Due largely to Berlin's influence, pluralism has now become a recognizable label, one that is applied to and often claimed by a variety of contemporary writers.[3]

One way to approach pluralism is to begin with the generally acknowledged fact of the diversity of values. There are many different moral traditions, conceptions of a good life, and more specific moral principles, ideals, virtues, obligations, and rights. These values may be complex, inclusive, and general, such as a whole moral tradition; they may be relatively simple, exclusive, and specific, such as conscientiousness, the Golden Rule, or the professional obligations of a physician; or they may be somewhere in between, such as a particular conception of a good life, which is more specific than a moral tradition and more general than specific principles, ideals, and so forth. Moral diversity exists, then, because both general and specific values are diverse.

The diversity of values is moral, if "moral" is used in the broad sense to mean the evaluative dimension of the human aspiration to live a good life. In this sense, "moral" is used to indicate that the value in question is in some way important to living a good life. There are some values whose importance all reasonable people would recognize, whereas the importance of other values varies with moral traditions and individual conceptions of a good life; the former may be called "primary," and the latter "secondary." Primary values are important to living a good life regardless of what moral tradition or conception of a good life guides individual agents. Adequate nutrition, good health, living in a just society, and possessing self-respect are examples of primary values. Monogamy, scientific creativity, manual dexterity, and having a prestigious job are examples of secondary values. Both primary and secondary values contribute to moral diversity because there are many different primary and secondary values and because the same ones often have different importance within different moral traditions and conceptions of a good life.

The diversity of values is a fact of life that reasonable moral theories must take into account. The reason for this is that diverse values conflict with one another, and since many of the conflicting values are important to living a good life, it becomes a crucial question how such conflicts can be resolved. One way of classifying moral theories depends on how they answer it. The novelty of pluralism is that it offers a fresh answer.

There are two traditional responses, each with a long history, numerous varieties, and able defenders: monism and relativism. The monistic response is to acknowledge moral diversity and conflict but attribute them to the culpable or excusable human failings in morality, knowledge, or rationality. If people did not fail in these ways, nothing would prevent them from recognizing that there is an overriding value with reference to which diverse moral traditions, conceptions of a good life, and specific values could be compared and ranked, thus allowing moral conflicts to be resolved.

A value may be said to be *overriding* if it is:

(1) the highest, that is, in conflict with any other value it ought to take precedence over the conflicting value;

(2) universal, that is, its precedence over any other conflicting value ought to hold for all human beings;

(3) permanent, that is, its precedence over any other conflicting value ought to hold at all times;

(4) invariable, that is, its precedence over any other conflicting value ought to hold in all contexts; and

(5) either absolute, that is, it ought not to be violated under any circumstances, or prima facie, that is, it ought to hold normally but may be justifiably violated in specific circumstances if and only if the violation is required by the value in general.

If a value is not overriding, then it can be said to be *conditional.*

There are several different monistic theories because there are disagreements about what the overriding value is. It may be the utilitarian ideal of the greatest happiness for the greatest number of people, the Kantian principle of the categorical imperative, the welfare economists' goal of preference satisfaction, the contractarian list of fundamental human rights, the Platonic notion of the Form of Good, the Christian commitment to doing the will of God, and so on. The overriding value need not be single, for it may include a small number of specific values or principles. It may be some conception of the summum bonum or some principle or procedure by which specific values could be ranked. What matters to a value's being overriding is that it is the highest, universal, permanent, invariable, and either absolute or prima facie.

Moral diversity and conflict exist, according to monistic theories, because conditional values are mistaken for the overriding one, or the overriding value is falsely regarded as conditional. Such errors are made because people are ignorant of the relevant facts, prevented from reasonably judging their significance, or led astray by immoral or nonmoral considerations. On the other hand, if people were fully informed, totally reasonable, and wholeheartedly committed to morality, they would recognize the value that is overriding, they would not confuse it with conditional values, and they would resolve moral conflicts among diverse values according to it. Monistic theories, then, hold both that there is an overriding value and that it has rational and moral authority that all human beings would recognize, if their failings did not prevent it.

The relativistic response to moral diversity and conflict stands in sharp contrast to the monistic one. Relativists deny that there is an overriding value, and they deny also that any value has rational or moral authority outside of the context in which it is held. The relativistic claim, expressed positively, is that all values are conditional and that their rational and moral authority is context-dependent. Moral diversity and conflict, according to relativists, is precisely what is to be expected if values are conditional and context-dependent.

Relativists recognize, of course, that moral conflicts need to be resolved, but their resolution requires only that there be some conditional value that has been accorded rational and moral authority in the context in which the conflict occurs. The authority of that value, however, carries weight only in that context. It cannot be derived from context-independent considerations. The fact that different moral traditions and conceptions of a good life may share some values should not be taken as evidence of a context-independent standard. Agreements of this sort are due to similar responses to circumstances that happen to have been interpreted in similar ways. Moral diversity and conflict, therefore, need not be symptoms of human failings; they are often ineliminable facts of life that derive from different conditions and different interpretations of the prevailing conditions.

The novelty of pluralism emerges against the background formed of monism and relativism. The pluralistic response to moral diversity and conflict is in partial agreement and partial disagreement with some central features of both monism and relativism. Pluralists agree with relativists and disagree with monists about there being an overriding value. According to pluralists, all values are conditional. But pluralists also hold, as monists do and relativists do not, that some values have rational and moral authority not only within but also outside of the context in which they are held. According to pluralists, not all values are context-dependent.

What sets pluralism apart is the rejection of an assumption that monism and relativism share, namely, that only an overriding value could have context-independent rational and moral authority. Monists claim that *because* there is a value that possesses such authority that it is overriding; relativists claim that *because* there is no value that possesses such authority that no value is overriding. The pluralistic alternative to both is the assumption that values can be conditional and still have a context-independent rational and moral authority.

The argument for this pluralistic assumption must take the form of identifying the conditional values that possess context-independent authority. The first candidates for this are primary values. Their context-independent authority derives from the fact that they have to be recognized as important by all reasonable moral traditions and conceptions of a good life. Adequate nutrition, good health, living in a just society, and having self-respect make all lives significantly better than they would be without them, and all lives are made much worse by their lack.

This remains true even if it is acknowledged, as it should be, that there are considerable differences among moral traditions and conceptions of a good life about the precise interpretation of what is counted as nutritive, healthful, just, or worthy of self-respect. These differences result from disagreements over the criteria for including putative instances of these values within the relevant domain. But such differences do not change the fact that for human beings, constituted as they are, there are central and uncontroversial cases of primary values, which, allowing for exceptional circumstances, will count as important to living a good life.

The context-independent rational and moral authority of primary values follows from these considerations, but it does not follow that any specific primary value or that the system of primary values jointly is overriding. Primary values, whether individually or collectively, remain conditional because they may conflict with one another or with secondary values and there is no highest, universal, permanent, invariable, and either absolute or prima facie value that could be appealed to in order to resolve these conflicts. The reason for this is that some of the values that conflict in this manner are both incompatible and incommensurable. Before that topic is addressed, however, it is necessary to discuss the second candidates for conditional values that possess context-independent rational and moral authority.

These values are not specific, like the primary values just discussed, but general secondary values of certain forms. Specific secondary values, such as monogamy, scientific creativity, manual dexterity, and a prestigious job are context-dependent, and they do not normally carry authority outside of their context. They nevertheless point in the direction of some general secondary values that do have a context-independent authority.

One form that authoritative general secondary values may take is the regulation of some particular areas of life within a moral tradition. There are, of course, countless ways in which these areas can be identified, and many of the ways are themselves the products of particular moral traditions. It nevertheless remains true that there are some areas of life that all reasonable moral traditions must regulate. For instance, a moral tradition need not be committed to monogamy, but it must regulate sexual conduct to prevent inbreeding, protect the sexually immature, prohibit some forms of coercion, and assign responsibility for raising children.

Another form that authoritative general secondary values may take is that of rules governing the interaction of people belonging to a particular moral tradition. The most obvious of these are legal laws, but there are numerous other interactions governed by rules that need not be formalized, institutionalized, and articulated, as legal laws must be. These rules are intended to be impersonal by being applied in the relevant cases without regard to the individuality of the person who is subject to them. Rules governing commerce, courting, dealing with outsiders, the expression of respect and contempt, friendship and enmity, self-esteem and self-blame, and the recognition of achievement and failure and those marking the observance of significant stages of life, such as birth, maturity, marriage, old age, and death, and so on, are some examples of the relevant kind of rules.

Yet a further form that authoritative general secondary values may take is suggested by the fact that all conceptions of a good life require specific secondary values, in addition to specific primary values and the general secondary values discussed in the last two paragraphs. Moral traditions and conceptions of a good life differ both in the forms of their general secondary values and in the specific secondary values that instantiate them. But there is no difference among reasonable moral traditions and conceptions of a good life in respect to the requirement that if they are to make good lives possible, then they must make available to their adherents some specific secondary values. The general secondary value that emerges from the consideration of specific secondary values is that of there being an adequate supply of specific secondary values so that the adherents of a particular moral tradition could have the options, the richness, the individuality, and the means on which are based their sense that they are living as they want to live.

The significance of these three forms of general secondary values is that although each is conditional, each may nevertheless carry with it a context-independent rational and moral authority. Their authority derives from the same source as the authority of primary values: the importance they have to living a good life, however it is conceived. Just as human lives are better with adequate nutrition, good health, justice, and self-respect and worse without them, so also they are better if lived in a moral tradition that regulates sexual conduct to protect its present and future adherents; maintains rules that govern the ways in which conventional activities are conducted; and provides for its adherents sufficiently numerous specific secondary values, thus making it possible for them to construct from the possibilities of their moral tradition a conception of a good life that expresses their aspirations. These general secondary values must be instantiated in concrete ways. They occur in particular moral traditions not as general but as specific secondary values. The reason for stressing their generality is that, together with primary values, they make the comparison of different moral traditions possible.

Moral traditions may reasonably be judged to be better or worse on the basis of how well or badly they do in guaranteeing those primary and secondary values for their adherents which all human beings need to live a good life. There is no theoretical obstacle in the way of answering such questions as which of two moral traditions does better in fostering adequate nutrition, good health, justice, and self-respect; which provides the right amount of protection so that it is neither paternalistic nor insecure; which makes rewards proportional to the importance of contributions; which is more impartial in the formulation and enforcement of rules; and which supplies richer possibilities for living a good life.

These comparisons will rarely yield unequivocal overall answers in favor of one moral tradition. Most moral traditions, especially enduring ones, are not as obviously vile as Nazi Germany or the Communist Soviet Union. What usually happens is that of two moral traditions, one is ranked higher in some respects and the other in different respects. This makes it difficult to arrive at an overall ranking. But it is not difficult to say that Sweden is doing better at supplying primary values than is India; that Shiite attempts to regulate sexual conduct fare badly when compared with Melanesian ones; that Swiss rectitude in politics is better than Italian corruption; that African countries that actively try to eliminate female circumcision and child prostitution are in that respect better than countries that passively allow such practice to continue; that the Czechs and the Slovaks have done better at dividing what used to be their country than have the Serbs, Croats, and Bosnians; that the Belgian approach to religious coexistence is better than the Irish; or that the English attitude toward political dissent is better than the Chinese; and so forth. Not all comparisons between moral traditions yield as clear answers as these. But some are clear, and they are sufficient to establish that the rational and moral authority of some values extends beyond the context in which the values prevail.

There are two closely connected reasons however why the primary and secondary values that do have context-independent authority remain conditional and do not become overriding. The first is that while these values are important to living a good life, their authority does not extend far enough to resolve disagreements about their respective importance. Reasonable defenders of a moral tradition may acknowledge that they are doing badly at protecting some important value but go on to explain that they are subordinating it to another value that is more important. Such arguments, of course, are themselves reasonable or unreasonable, and which they are depends on the strength of reasons given for regarding one as more important than another. No value is overriding because there may be strong reasons for regarding any important value as more important than another in some particular context. The second reason is that important values conflict and there is no blueprint for resolving their conflicts always in favor of one of the conflicting values.

It may be asked, however, why there could not be a way of resolving such conflicts that rests on an authoritative ranking of their respective importance. The answer is that no such resolution is available because many conflicts occur among incompatible and incommensurable values.

8.2 INCOMPATIBLE, INCOMMENSURABLE, AND CONFLICTING VALUES

It is a common occurrence in everyday life that people must choose between two values, and if they choose one, they cannot have the other. An independent, unencumbered, self-reliant life in which people are accountable only to themselves cannot be combined with having a large family and a close marriage; commitment to and success in some discipline, profession, or institution cannot coexist with the bemused, distant, uninvolved perspective of an observer; life in politics does not go with a life of contemplation and privacy; a risk-taking, adventurous life excludes the peace of mind that derives from cautiously cherishing what one has. Breadth and depth, freedom and equality, solitude and public spiritedness, good judgment and passionate involvement, love of comfort and love of achievement, and ambition and humility exist in a state of tension, and the more there is of one, the less there can be of the other.

These conflicts do not result from circumstances pitting normally compossible values against each other. It is not as if people had to choose between their money and their life at the behest of an armed robber. For there is nothing inherent in life and money that would prevent having them together. But many other conflicts are intrinsic to the conflicting values themselves, and so a choice is forced on those who want to enjoy both. The choice need not be all or none; compromise and striking a balance are sometimes possible. It remains a fact of life, however, that as one of two conflicting values is chosen, so the agents must put up with missing out on the other.

Thus the sense of loss is a frequent experience in human lives. It need not be due to having made a poor choice. For people often feel that they have lost something important by choosing a profession, a place to live, a partner, or having or not having children, even if they are convinced that they have made the right choice and that, if they had to, they would make the same choice again. If the loss is accompanied by regret, it is about life being such as to exclude the enjoyment of all they value.

The ubiquitous conflicts of everyday experience, however, are not only between good possibilities, for bad ones may also force choices on agents. Overall commitment to a good life often requires choosing the lesser of two evils. In each situation, choice forces a normally immoral course of action on reasonable agents. They may claim that what they have done was the best under the wretched circumstances, yet the burden of having violated their moral convictions has still to be borne, although it may be lightened somewhat by the context in which the violation has occurred. It is reasonable to think ill of people who do not have scruples about doing what is normally wrong, even if they have to do it. It may be understandable and even praiseworthy in some circumstances for a politician to tell a public lie, but it would be a sign of corruption if the politician did not mind having to do so.

Part of the reason why pluralists are so interested in conflicts is that they present strong evidence for the plurality and conditionality of values. For the best explanation of these conflicts is that the conflicting values are incompatible and incommensurable, which is why they are plural and conditional.

The incompatibilty of values is partly due to qualities intrinsic to the conflicting values. Because of these qualities, some values are so related as to make living according to one totally or proportionally exclude living according to the other. Habitual gourmandizing and asceticism are totally incompatible, whereas lifelong commitment to political activism and solitude are proportionally so. The incompatibility of values, therefore, derives at least in part from the nature of the values and not entirely from the agents' attitude toward them. For a favorable attitude toward both of two incompatible values does not make them compatible. Compatibility also depends on whether the intrinsic qualities of the values exclude each other. But these qualities are only partly responsible for the incompatibility of some values. Another part is due to human nature. It is only for human beings that the intrinsic qualities of some values are incompatible. If gourmandizing were not pleasurable, it would not be incompatible with asceticism; if split personalities were the rule, solitude and political activism could be combined.

The incommensurability of values is the idea that:

(1) there is not some one type of highest value or combination of values in terms of which all other values can be evaluated by consider-

ing how closely they approximate it; for instance, happiness is not such;

(2) there is not some medium in terms of which all the different types of values can be expressed and ranked without any significant aspects left out, thus allowing for the intersubstitutability of different types of values; for instance, not all values can be so expressed and ranked in terms of preference satisfaction; and

(3) there is not some one principle or some principles that can provide an order or precedence among all values and be acceptable to all reasonable people; for instance, duties do not always take precedence over the general welfare, and vice versa.

This may be expressed by saying that incommensurability is the denial of (1) a summum bonum, (2) the fungibility of values, and (3) a canonical principle for ranking values. In arguing for incommensurability, pluralists are committed to the conjunction of (1), (2), and (3).

It is crucial to understand that what incommensurability excludes is the possibility of ranking important values which meets two requirements: it must be based on characteristics intrinsic to the values being ranked, and the ranking must be acceptable to all reasonable people. Meeting the first requirement without the second would lead to question-begging comparisons, for it would assume that a certain ranking of values is the reasonable one, which is precisely the issue. The value of telling a painful truth to a friend may be compared with the value of the friend's happiness by asking which would give more pleasure. But of course whether pleasure is the appropriate basis of comparison in this or in any case is an open question.

Similarly, meeting the second requirement without the first would also fail to yield what is needed. For even if, unlikely as it is, all reasonable people agreed to a particular ranking of two important values, their agreement may merely betoken a universally held human attitude that may be independent of the respective intrinsic merits of the values in question. Everyone may think that when push comes to shove, justice is more important than mercy, and everyone may be mistaken. In asserting the incommensurability of values, pluralists deny that both requirements could be simultaneously met.

What makes this serious from the moral point of view is that incommensurable values are often also incompatible. The values whose ranking is in dispute may be important to living a good life and yet reasonable people are prevented from realizing them because they totally or proportionally exclude each other. It is thus the coincidence of the incommensurability and incompatibility of important and conflicting values that creates what pluralists regard as an unavoidable feature of moral life.

A formal characterization of the relevant type of conflicts is as follows: two values, V_1 and V_2, conflict if there is a person, P, and V_1 and V_2 are incompatible; V_1 and V_2 are incommensurable; P wants V_1; and P wants V_2. To make the formal account concrete, let V_1 be a life in politics and V_2 be solitude or V_1 be a skeptical disposition and V_2 be passionate commitment to a cause. This account of the relevant type of conflicts must be understood in the light of several clarifications.

To keep the discussion simple, it is assumed that the conflicts are between two values. More complicated forms of conflict may occur between three or more values. Furthermore, the conflicts are relativized to persons, but not to any particular person. Conflicts are conflicts *for* persons. If there were no persons or perhaps no beings sufficiently like persons, then conflicts would not occur. The source of conflicts, therefore, is not merely that the values are incommensurable and incompatible but also that human beings are trying to realize the values together.

The recognition that this is so should be joined with the acknowledgment that people undoubtedly make mistakes in what they value, and some conflicts may be resolved by correcting such mistakes. But the conflicts that are of central interest to pluralists concern truly valuable and rightly wanted values, and yet conflicts show that they cannot be enjoyed together. The difficulty is not in the values, or in having a misguided attitude toward them, but in the conjunction of the right attitude directed toward the right value and the human situation.

The formal characterization offered above is not intended as an account of all types of conflict. It is essential to understanding the kinds of conflicts which concern pluralists that the conflicting values are both incompatible and incommensurable. They are both valued, it is totally or proportionally impossible to realize them together, and there is no basis on which their intrinsic merits could be compared.

The values that may conflict in the required manner may be different primary values, different secondary values, and primary and secondary values. These manifold conflicts are experienced by individual moral agents. And the conflicts confront agents in concrete terms. If one wants to have a lucrative job and freedom to dispose of one's time but cannot have both, what should one do? If the institution to which one feels allegiance becomes corrupted and undermines its own standards, should one opt for the standards or for the institution? If one's friend champions an unjust cause, is it justice or friendship that should prevail? In such conflicts, individuals must choose between incommensurable and incompatible values, both of which they prize.

This account of incompatibility, incommensurability, and conflict may perhaps go some way toward explaining what pluralism is, but these technical notions are not what animates the theory. Its source is a moral vision about the nature of good lives and about the political morality that is most likely to foster them. This vision is that of reasonable people whose lives are given meaning and purpose by a conception of a good life. Their lives are active, goal-directed, and imbued with a sense of what is important and what is not. The activity need not be a feverish pursuit of some glittering prize; it may be quiet, contemplative, turned toward others, even self-denying. People who live such lives know what they are about. They may reasonably regard their lives as successful if their continued engagement in the totality of the activities that their conceptions of a good life involve is on balance satisfying. They may fail, of course. Their conceptions of a good life may be faulty, so that no one could find them satisfying. They may be free of internal defects but be unsuitable for those who try to live according to them. Or they may be suitable but the conditions in which the agents live make them unattainable. The measure of their success or failure, however, is the satisfaction that individual agents derive from the totality of their activities prescribed by their conceptions of a good life.

What makes this moral vision pluralistic is the belief that there are many reasonable conceptions of a good life. These conceptions are formed of the values provided by the agents' moral traditions and of the agents' efforts to fit some of them to their individual characters and circumstances. The moral tradition in the background provides both possibilities and limits. The possibilities are among the values, and the limits are the restrictions on what possibilities are acceptable and how they may be pursued. The possibilities are reasonable if they contribute to good lives; the limits are reasonable if they protect the conditions in which as many conceptions of a good life as possible can be formed and pursued. There is a plurality of conceptions of a good life if there is a plurality of values from which they can be formed, if individuals can adapt these values to their personal situation, and if they can rank as they see fit the respective importance of the values that constitute their conceptions of a good life.

The moral vision that animates pluralism, then, is of people living in this manner. The political morality that goes with it has as its chief task the formation and protection of both the possibilities and the limits that make living thus possible. Pluralists reject monism because its possibilities are impoverished and its limits arbitrarily exclude possibilities that fail to conform to the value to which overriding status has been accorded. And pluralists reject relativism as well because it fails to recognize the need for limits beyond those which happen to have been developed within particular moral traditions. Monism is too restrictive about both possibilities and limits, whereas relativism is too permissive about both. Pluralism is intended to hold the center.

8.3 THE INCONSISTENCY OF PLURALISM AND LIBERALISM

Pluralism is a basic value of liberalism, and there is no shortage of liberals who explicitly say so.[4] It is clear that if liberals are committed to pluralism, then they must accept the conditionality and reject the overridingness of any value. Liberals must deny that any value or combination of a small number of values is the highest, universal, permanent, invariable, and either absolute or prima facie, they must deny, that is, that any single or complex value has such rational and moral authority as always to have a stronger claim than any other value with which it may conflict.

This, however, is not what liberals do. They believe that the claims of autonomy and the basic values of liberalism override the conflicting claims of other values. This belief is what makes them liberals. If they thought that the autonomous life was just one among many possible forms that good lives may take or if they thought that a society may be fine even though claims of freedom, equality, rights, and distributive justice were overridden by other values, then they would lose any title to being liberals. Liberals see this, of course, and they think that liberal values should override nonliberal ones.

For instance, Berlin and Robert Nozick think that rights are overriding, Ronald Dworkin thinks that it is equal concern and respect, John Rawls thinks that it is justice, and Joseph Raz believes that freedom is overriding.[5] Their language is permeated with talk about absolutes, inviolability, trumps, ultimate justification, fundamental prohibitions, first virtues, uncompromising claims that cannot be overridden, and so forth. How could the insistence on some value being overriding and its violation impermissible be compatible with pluralism? Indeed, how could any approach to political morality that regards some one or few values as basic be pluralistic? Surely, to regard some value or values as basic is to be committed to the claim that when it or they conflict with other values, then the basic value or values should prevail over the others. To hold, as liberals do, that the basic values are pluralism, freedom, rights, equality, and distributive justice and that they are basic because they protect the core, which is autonomy, is to hold that these values singly or jointly should always override the claims of any other value or values that conflict with them. Not to claim this is to abandon liberalism, but to claim it is to be inconsistent, because pluralism is incompatible with it. (See Gray 1993b and 1995 for a similar argument.) How do liberals respond to this problem?

8.4 LIBERAL RESPONSES

Perhaps the most widely accepted liberal response is the neutrality thesis. It is most prominent in the liberalism of R. Dworkin, Thomas Nagel, and Rawls.[6] The idea underlying the thesis is that the overridingness of the basic liberal values and autonomy is not incompatible with pluralism because these values and autonomy are presupposed by all conceptions of a good life. Overriding values and pluralism are thus conceived as obtaining on different levels: requirements that all good lives have are overriding, whereas pluralism prevails about the different conceptions of life that may be adopted once these requirements are met. If these two levels are distinguished, then the charge of incompatibility between pluralism and the overridingness of the basic liberal values and autonomy is revealed as groundless.

Before it can be shown why this response fails, it is necessary to avoid a possible misinterpretation. The neutrality thesis should not be understood as resting on the distinction between procedural and substantive values, because it is unclear how procedural and substantive values could be distinguished, and even if they could be, the argument that some values are required by all conceptions of a good life applies equally to some procedural and some substantive values. Are liberty of conscience, the obligation to pay a certain percentage of one's income in taxes, or the right to dispose of legitimately acquired wealth procedural or substantive? And if these can all be said to be procedural on the basis of some criterion yet to be formulated, is it not obvious that among the requirements of any conception of a good life are also values that liberals do not regard as basic, such as peace, a healthy environment, prosperity, law-abidingness, civility, and so on, which are surely substantive, if anything is?

Liberals would be better advised, therefore, to eschew the distinction between procedural and substantive values and rest their case, as Rawls does, on their being some primary goods.[7] It may then be said that the basic liberal values and autonomy are primary goods. The liberal response to the charge of the incompatibility of liberalism and pluralism is then that the attribution of overridingness to primary goods does not violate pluralism and the neutrality thesis because primary goods are presupposed by all conceptions of a good life. The alleged incompatibility is avoided, then, if autonomy and the basic values of liberalism are accorded overriding status as primary goods, while pluralism holds on a level beyond primary goods.

The reasons why this response is unsatisfactory emerge if the obvious point is recognized that the number of primary goods—goods required by all conceptions of a good life—is much larger than the basic liberal values and autonomy. Even if it is conceded, if only for the sake of argument, that no life can be good unless pluralism, freedom, equality, rights, distributive justice, and autonomy prevail, it remains true that good lives require countless other values as well. Some of them are a healthy environment; prevalent law-abidingness; civility, understood as a moderate degree of mutual goodwill among people living in a society; peace; at least modest prosperity; security; and so forth. It would be very difficult, if indeed possible, to enumerate all the physical, economic, physiological, political, social, and psychological requirements that are necessary for all conceptions of a good life.

It follows from this that the overridingness of autonomy and the basic liberal values cannot be defended simply by pointing at their supposed necessity for good lives, since the same is true of many other values. Liberals must therefore provide some additional reason to show why the values they favor should be accorded overriding status, while denying such status to other values equally necessary for good lives.

There are a number of alternative ways of meeting this requirement, none of which, however, could be acceptable to liberals. One is to abandon all claims to any value being overriding. Human rights, equal concern and respect, freedom, distributive justice, and so forth could all be subordinated to some other value that is more important than they in some particular context. This would certainly be consistent with pluralism. But it would be tantamount to abandoning liberalism because it would attribute to liberal values a status identical to other primary values. Liberals must believe that basic liberal values and autonomy should prevail over nonliberal values, otherwise liberalism becomes vacuous.

Another alternative is to accord overriding status to all primary values, both liberal and others. This, however, would leave liberals without a principled basis for resolving conflicts among primary values. If primary liberal values were overriding, whereas other primary values were not, then liberals would be able to resolve conflicts consistently with their beliefs. But this is precisely what the present alternative denies.

A third alternative is a variant of the first. Liberals may concede that autonomy and the basic liberal values are not always and in all possible contexts overriding. They may go on to claim, however, that in the context of contemporary industrialized democracies, autonomy and the basic liberal values should prevail over other values. Give present conditions, liberals may claim that they are more nearly right about what matters for all good lives than are their opponents. But this claim is no better than the previous two.

If this claim were true, it would reduce autonomy and the basic values of liberalism to a merely instrumental status. Its truth would imply that good lives currently just happen to require autonomy, pluralism, freedom, equality, rights, and distributive justice, but things may change and then good lives may have other requirements and be possible without those currently favored by liberals. This would deprive liberalism of one of its most powerful features, namely, the moral vision that is capable of appealing to people living in widely different moral traditions and according to widely different conceptions of a good life. The vision is supposed to capture values that all moral traditions and all conceptions of a good life should aim to protect and foster. But if liberalism is relativized to the present context, it cannot sustain that vision. Moreover, if this claim were true, it would commit liberalism to consequentialism because the justification of autonomy and the basic values of pluralism would be that they are means to good lives, which is the desirable end. Liberals would find this unacceptable because of the intrinsic problems with consequentialism and because it is incompatible with the strong, perhaps dominant, Kantian strain in liberalism.

These consequences of the possible truth of the liberal claim, that autonomy and the basic values are necessary conditions for good lives only in the present context, are beside the point, however, because the claim is actually false. It is a mistake to suppose that in the present context primary nonliberal values are somehow less necessary than liberal ones. If there were no adequately healthy environment, moderate law-abidingness, civility, peace, prosperity, security, and so forth, then autonomy, pluralism, freedom, equality, rights, and distributive justice would not prevail.

The mistake liberals make is not that of supposing that the values they favor are important when they are not; their mistake is to overlook the fact that other values are equally important. Nor is it that liberals are somehow ignorant of the importance of nonliberal values. They are certainly aware of them, but they relegate them into constituent elements of the context in which they urge that liberal values should prevail. They take them for granted, much as they take human life, sunshine, and air, overlooking the fact that the nonliberal values mentioned above, and others too, of course, are political achievements as important as any that liberals themselves stress. The nonliberal values, however, must often be maintained and protected at the expense of liberal values.

It is a prominent fact of political life in the present context that the claims of the environment, law-abidingness, civility, peace, prosperity, security, and so forth often conflict with and take justifiable precedence over the claims of autonomy, pluralism, freedom, equality, rights, and distributive justice. Their precedence is justified when they are more important for good lives, however they are conceived, than are autonomy and the basic liberal values. Liberalism is inconsistent with pluralism because pluralism recognizes the ubiquity of these conflicts and refuses to assume that they should always be settled, in the present context, or in any other, in favor of liberal values, whereas liberalism must assume it, otherwise it would be devoid of substance.

The central difficulty with appealing to the neutrality thesis in order to counter the charge that liberalism is inconsistent with pluralism is that if liberals were truly neutral, then they would cease to be liberals; while if they were not neutral, then they would cease to be pluralists.

A second response made by some liberals is to concede the impossibility of perfect neutrality and consequently of a thoroughgoing pluralism, but to claim that the core of liberalism is to try to be as neutral and pluralistic as it is possible to be. The dominant aspiration remains to have a state that takes no sides about the respective merits of the moral traditions and conceptions of a good life that exist under its jurisdiction. But this aspiration is combined with the realistic acknowledgment that some moral traditions and conceptions of a good life will have to be curtailed because those who live according to them are intent on making it impossible for others to live in other ways.

What is important, according to this liberal response, is not so much that the state should be neutral, but that it should foster a political system in which as many moral traditions and conceptions of a good life as possible could compete with one another for resources and for the allegiance of people. The chief function of the state is thus seen to be to maintain what is referred to as the dialogue or conversation among these contending visions of how life ought to be lived. The limits of neutrality and of pluralism are set by whatever is required for the continuation of politics thus conceived. These limits require curtailing moral traditions and conceptions of a good life that endanger the continuing dialogue, and they require as well the equal distribution of resources as a way of promoting its continuation. This is the liberalism of Bruce Ackerman, Charles Larmore, and Richard Rorty, all of whom have been influenced by Jürgen Habermas (1984, 1987).

A key to this response is the sharp distinction of the private and the political spheres. In the private one, individuals are committed to particular moral traditions and conceptions of a good life. In the political sphere, they are committed to the continuation of the dialogue in which their own conceptions of a good life compete with others for resources and recognition. Reasonable people would support both spheres and their sharp distinction because through them good lives for themselves and those they care about are more likely to be achieved than in any other way.

The greatest possible pluralism and neutrality ought to prevail in the political sphere, whereas in the private one, individuals may live committed lives in which pluralism and neutrality have no place.[8] It thus emerges that as the strategy behind the first liberal response to the incompatibility of liberalism and pluralism is to distinguish between two levels on which good lives must be lived, so the strategy guiding the second response is to distinguish between two spheres that good lives require. Basic liberal values are overriding because they are thought to be necessary for maintaining the distinction and thus for good lives however they are conceived.

There are two reasons why this second response fails to remove the inconsistency between liberalism and pluralism. Both are connected with the requirements of maintaining the political system in which moral traditions and conceptions of a good life compete with one another for resources and the allegiance of people. The conception of politics and the view that good lives require maintaining a pluralistic political system are, of course, congenial to pluralists. One of the reasons why pluralists must nevertheless reject liberalism is that no pluralistic political system could be maintained if it is supposed, as liberals must, that autonomy and the basic liberal values ought always to prevail over other values when they conflict. A healthy environment, law-abidingness, civility, peace, prosperity, and security are as necessary for maintaining a pluralistic political system as are autonomy and the basic liberal values. This point has been stressed in criticizing the previous liberal response, and it applies with equal force against the response presently considered.

It merely flaunts the liberal bias to pick out and emphasize of the countless requirements of a pluralistic political system just those which coincide with the liberal outlook. But then to go on and attribute overriding importance to them, even if only in a particular context, is worse than claiming dominance for liberalism while avowing pluralism, for it actually endangers the political system.

Such a system is fragile even under the best circumstances because many of the competing moral traditions and conceptions of a good life aim to attract greater resources and recruit more adherents so as to acquire ever more political power. A pluralistic political system, therefore, must continually be on guard against allowing this to happen. To this unavoidable fragility, however, various unpredictable adversities are continually added. Crime waves, demographic changes, war, bad economic times, pollution of the environment, antagonisms between various minorities or between the majority and some minority, hostile external competitors, widespread dissatisfaction with the legal system, the unwillingness of citizens to accept the burdens placed on them, epidemics, and so forth all threaten to disrupt a pluralistic political system. It cannot be reasonably supposed that the liberal policy of coping with such threats by increasing autonomy, pluralism, freedom, equality, rights, and distributive justice should always be followed. Sometimes liberal policies should prevail, but sometimes not. Maintaining a pluralistic political system may well require curtailing the autonomy, pluralism, freedom, equality, rights, and distributive justice to which liberals are committed to giving preference. That is one reason why pluralism and liberalism are inconsistent even if the conception of politics that the second response advocates is accepted.

The other reason why the second response fails is the prevalence of evil caused by human wickedness. The tacit liberal assumption is that in a pluralistic political system, a hundred flowers will bloom. There will be, to be sure, occasional people and acts that violate the system, but, the assumption is, that such violations will be occasional and manageable because people's sense of justice, altruism, and rational self-interest will separately or jointly motivate them to regard their own welfare as inseparable from that of their fellow citizens. The facts, however, belie this assumption, and it is difficult to understand how liberals could fail to see that this is so.

Contemporary America is perhaps the most pluralistic society that has ever existed. No one doubts, however, that crime is rampant, drug addiction is widespread, and that there are very many people, and their number grows daily, who live in the society but have no interest in maintaining its political system. Furthermore, the threats to the political system are not only internal but also external. There is no reason to suppose that China, Japan, Shiite Muslims, many developing countries, various organized criminals, terrorists, and ideologues would not do what they can, consistent with what they regard as their interests, to undermine the political system. Surely, a condition of maintaining the system is that it be protected from these external and internal threats.

It is suicidal to suppose that reaffirming autonomy and the basic liberal values will provide the required protection. The response that liberals are committed to make to these threats is likely to strengthen rather than weaken the threats because it champions autonomy, pluralism, freedom, equality, rights, and distributive justice for the agents who present the threats. Maintaining a pluralistic political system often requires curtailing pluralism itself, as well as autonomy and the other basic liberal values. How often they do so and how far their curtailment should go depends on the seriousness of the threats. It is, however, a dangerous illusion to suppose that the more pluralistic a society is, the more liberal it will be.

There is one last liberal response to the incompatibility of liberalism and pluralism that needs to be considered. It has been formulated by J. Donald Moon (1993). He continues in the vein of those liberals who see political life as a dialogue between competing answers to the question of how to live a good life. But Moon rejects neutrality as impracticable and insists that liberal values must be contextualized.[9] Moon thus proposes to cope with the incompatibility of pluralism and liberalism by acknowledging its existence. The proposed remedy is to reinterpret liberalism as essentially involving a self-conscious recognition of its own deficiencies and a continuous effort to try to overcome them. Liberalism, according to this view, is a political system designed for its own improvement.

Moon's proposal is compatible with pluralism. The question that must be asked about it, however, is why it is supposed to be a version of liberalism? Why should it be thought that the self-correction will always or even usually consist in policies that will improve on the existing levels of autonomy, pluralism, freedom, equality, rights, and distributive justice? It is certainly true that many societies are deficient in these respects and would benefit from correction in the direction of basic liberal values. But it is no less true that many societies are deficient in respect to pollution, war, lawlessness, poverty, civil strife, and insecurity. Correcting these deficiencies is as important and beneficial as correcting the ones liberals tend to stress, but their correction is often at the expense of pluralism and the basic liberal values. Commitment to a policy of self-correction, therefore, does not have any obvious connection with liberalism.

Moon's response to the inconsistency of liberalism and pluralism is to opt for pluralism and call that option a new version of liberalism. Calling it that, however, does not change the fact that in the emerging political system liberal values will not have a privileged position. Champions of the systems can systematically and justifiably subordinate basic liberal values to nonliberal ones if they have reason to think that the deficiencies of the system require it. This is a reasonable attitude, but it cannot be a liberal one.

Given the interpretation of pluralism proposed in this chapter and of liberalism proposed earlier, pluralism and liberalism are incompatible. Their incompatibility, however, does not stem from a conflict between specific pluralistic and specific liberal values. Their incompatibility is, so to speak, systemic. They are incompatible because pluralists reject all ideological commitments, regardless of their content, and liberalism, being a political ideology, essentially involves making such commitments.

A political ideology must champion some values as overriding, otherwise it would have no content. Contrariwise, pluralists must reject the overridingness of all values, without regard of their content, because their core belief is that there is no value that ought always to prevail over all conflicting values in all contexts.

The source of this pluralistic belief is not a relativistic doubt about the possibility of a context-independent justification of any value. Pluralists think that such justification is available for primary values and for some types of general secondary values. This justification, however, will not establish the overridingness of the values accredited by it.

It is not that the justification falls short by not being strong enough; on the contrary, the justification is as strong as it can be. The reason why it excludes overridingness is that in the pertinent political contexts there is always a plurality of values made important by their necessity for good lives, regardless of how they are conceived. What is most important is not to establish that one of these values is more important than the others, but to maintain the system in which the claims of all the values important to living a good life may be considered and weighed. It is of course true that in any particular context decisions have to be made among conflicting important values, and that these decisions will result in one value prevailing over another. But this does not make the value that prevails overriding. It prevails in that context without prejudice to what happens in other contexts.

There is a range of important political values, and provided they are rightly interpreted, the claims of each ought to be attended to in all specific political contexts. These values include pluralism, freedom, rights, equality, justice, a healthy environment, civility, law-abidingness, peace, prosperity, security, and so forth. In some contexts one and in other contexts another of these values ought to take precedence over the others. But to suppose that one or some combination of a few of these values should always and in all contexts prevail over the rest is to try to force the fluidity of life to conform to a blueprint that reflects the preferences of its designers rather than the way things are.

The arguments presented in this chapter about the incompatibility of pluralism and liberalism apply equally to all political ideologies. Liberalism shares with conservatism, socialism, communitarianism, civic republicanism, and so forth the attitude toward some values as overriding. The arguments were directed against liberalism because of its dominant position in the contemporary world and because the need to go beyond it is the topic of this book. But it should be clear that pluralists reject not just pluralism but all political ideologies that subscribe to some more or less dogmatic version of monism.

CHAPTER 9

The Sentimentalism of Benevolence

The man who works from himself outwards, whose conduct is governed by ordinary motives, and who acts with a view to his own advantage and the advantage of those who are connected with himself in definite assignable ways, produces in the ordinary course of things more happiness to others (if that is the great object of life) than a moral Don Quixote who is always liable to sacrifice himself and his neighbors. . . . [A] man who has a disinterested love for the human race—that is to say, who has got a fixed idea about some way of providing for the management of the concerns of mankind—is an unaccountable person . . . capable of making his love for men in general the ground of all sorts of violence against man in particular.

—JAMES FITZJAMES STEPHEN, *Liberty, Equality, Fraternity*

The majority of contemporary liberal thinkers attempt to justify their position by using some form of Kantian argument. Their fundamental idea is that the basic liberal commitments are to universal requirements of all good lives and that rationality requires everyone to support these requirements. This approach has been called "deontological liberalism."[1] Many of the arguments hitherto discussed have been directed against this interpretation and justification of liberalism. There is, however, another approach: the utilitarian. Its central claim is that the aim of liberalism is to maximize human welfare and minimize human suffering. The justification of the basic liberal commitments is that they are the best means to achieving this end. The utilitarian approach draws on what it regards as a basic disposition, which is identified as the love of humanity, fraternity, altruism, fellow feeling, or sympathy but which will from here on be referred to as "benevolence."

180

Defenders of the utilitarian justification of liberalism usually appeal to Hume.[2] This is doubly odd because Hume was a conservative, not a liberal, and because he defended a limited, not a general, form of benevolence. His arguments are nevertheless cited in support of liberalism, and so this approach to the justification of liberalism will be called "Humean," even though Hume would not have approved of the use that liberals make of his ideas.

The aim of this chapter is to consider whether the Humean approach succeeds as a justification of liberalism. The conclusion will be that it does not. The chief reasons for its failure are that benevolence is a misplaced attitude in numerous centrally important moral contexts and that expressing benevolence in these contexts reflects the vice of sentimentalism, which involves the falsification of reality to make it fit the agents' strong and misguided emotions.

9.1 BENEVOLENCE

Morality requires acting for the good of others. This is not the only moral requirement, and where the good of others lies is, of course, controversial. But whatever their good is, there can be no serious doubt that acting so as to bring it about is one central moral obligation. Yet the nature of this obligation is unclear because there are difficult questions about the interpretation of its aim and about the motivational sources required for realizing it. Are the others for whose good agents are obligated to act only people in agents' immediate context, members of their society, or all human beings? What leads agents to honor this obligation? Is it justice, prudence, decency, pity, benevolence, or some combination of these and other motives?

The dominant tendency in utilitarian thought is to answer these questions in terms of benevolence. It is supposed that the obligation to act for the good of others extends to all human beings and that the best hope of meeting it is by fostering benevolence. In this respect, utilitarian benevolence may be thought of as a secular version of Christian love.[3]

The relevant definition of "benevolence" in the *OED* (1961 ed.) is "disposition to do good, kindness, generosity, charitable feeling (towards mankind)." Benevolence is composed of emotive, cognitive, and motivational elements. Among them, the emotive one is primary and dominant. The fundamental drive of benevolence is a feeling that predisposes human beings to care for the good of others. It ranges from rejoicing if others flourish, through many intermediate stages, to being distressed if others suffer. The cognitive element guides and corrects the identification of people and situations in whose presence benevolent feelings are appropriate; it aims to resolve conflicts between the dictates of benevolence and those of justice, prudence, self-interest, and so forth; and it exerts critical control over the actions that benevolence prompts agents to take. This last introduces the motivational element of benevolence. It is not merely a feeling guided by critical reflection but also a disposition that moves agents to appropriate action. Hume, following in the tradition of the moral sense school (see Roberts 1973), regards benevolence, thus understood, as a basic element of human nature. Contemporary psychological research seems to support him in this view (see Brandt 1976: 429–53).

The characteristics of benevolence that have emerged so far may be summed up as follows: first, it is primarily an emotive disposition to care about the welfare of others; second, it is a morally desirable character trait, hence a virtue; third, it has a dominant emotive element but is guided by critical reflection and motivates action; and fourth, it is a basic component of human nature to be found in all human beings. The conjunction of these characteristics defines *limited* benevolence. But there is also *general* benevolence.

The difference between limited and general benevolence is the addition of universality and impartiality. Universality refers to either the possession or the object of benevolence. Limited benevolence attributes its possession to all human beings, whereas general benevolence goes beyond universal possession and claims as well that the objects of benevolence ought to be all human beings. Champions of general benevolence claim that, as a matter of fact, all human beings have limited benevolence, and, as a matter of morality, they also ought to have general benevolence. According to them, moral progress consists in expanding limited benevolence until it embraces all human beings.[4]

The universality of benevolence, however, does not completely express the moral vision of its defenders, for universality is compatible with the unequal distribution of benevolence, provided everyone gets some of it. The moral vision also requires equal or impartial distribution.[5] General benevolence may then be understood as having the four characteristics of limited benevolence as well as two other characteristics: it is universal, in being directed toward all human beings; and it is impartial, in being directed toward all human beings equally.

In the rest of this chapter, three questions will be considered about this understanding of benevolence. First, can liberalism be justified on the basis of its opposition to cruelty, which is the denial of benevolence? Second, can liberalism be justified on the basis of general benevolence? And, third, can liberalism be justified on the basis of limited benevolence? The answer to all three questions is "no."

9.2 OPPOSITION TO CRUELTY AS THE JUSTIFICATION OF LIBERALISM

To begin with the first question, if the justification of liberalism depends on the assumption that limited benevolence is a basic human disposition and that human well-being depends on making it more general, then liberalism may be interpreted as opposition to the contrary disposition, cruelty, which will be seen as the most serious threat to human well-being. Three well-known liberals argue in this way.

Judith Shklar says that "liberal and humane people, of whom there are many among us, would, if they were asked to rank the vices, put cruelty first. Intuitively they would choose cruelty as the worst thing we do" (1984: 44). And she thinks that "liberalism is the possibility of making the evil of cruelty . . . the basic norm of its political practices and prescriptions. The only exception to the rule is the prevention of greater cruelties" (1989: 30). "Liberalism," she says, "begin[s] with a *summum malum*, which all of us know and would avoid if only we could. That evil is cruelty" (29). Richard Rorty says that "we liberals" are "the people who think that cruelty is the worst thing we do" (1989: 173), and he endorses "Judith Shklar's criterion of a liberal: someone who believes that cruelty is the worst thing we do" (1989: 146). Annette Baier acknowledges an "obviously Humean bias" (1993: 437), and elsewhere she says that she proceeds "within the limits of the comforting liberal faith" (1985b: 294). She claims that "cruelty is not the worst vice for the Kantian, as it is for the Humean" (1993: 451). And she allies herself with "Judith Shklar and Richard Rorty [who] have reaffirmed the Humean moral judgment" (1993: 437).

It takes no more than a little thought to realize that this slogan—that a liberal is one who believes that cruelty is the worst thing we do—is mere verbiage that cannot withstand the most elementary questioning. Why is cruelty the worst thing we do? Why not genocide, terrorism, betrayal, exploitation, humiliation, brutalization, tyranny, and so forth? If it is said in reply that all serious evils are forms of cruelty, then the liberal becomes one who believes that serious evil is the worst thing we do. But who would disagree with that? Would not conservatives, socialists, libertarians, or anarchists also endorse that claim? Shklar's avowed inspiration is Montaigne, but she says that "Montaigne . . . was no liberal" (1989: 23), and Baier's fountainhead is Hume, who rejected Whiggish liberalism for Tory conservatism. And yet Montaigne says that "I hate cruelty . . . as the extreme of all vices" (1980: 313), and Hume says that when "angry passions rise to cruelty, they form the most detested of all vices" (1960: 605). Are Montaigne and Hume liberals then? And if they are, who is not a liberal, apart from the Marquis de Sade and a few other moral monsters? And why could a liberal not think that large-scale evils caused by benevolent motives are worse than small-scale evils caused by cruelty?

It must be said that this slogan is provoking not merely because of its intellectual vacuity but also because of the specious moralizing that informs it. It insinuates that nonliberals are less opposed to cruelty than liberals and that those who are appropriately outraged by cruelty have willy-nilly joined the ranks of liberals. It encourages the thought that liberals are right-minded and that their opponents are morally insensitive. It helps to create a climate of opinion in which it seems to be morally questionable to criticize liberalism.

If this were all, the charitable response would be to write the slogan off as one of those silly things that even good thinkers occasionally say and to talk about more important things. But matters are more complicated. Sympathy for the slogan results from unarticulated but deeply held moral attitudes. If these attitudes are made explicit, it will become apparent why they create sympathy for the slogan. It will also become apparent that the attitudes are as indefensible as the slogan itself.

One expects those who advocate making opposition to cruelty "the basic norm of . . . political practices and prescriptions" to offer a clear account of what cruelty is. But they do not. Rorty uses "cruelty" extensively in two sensitive essays of literary criticism in which he discusses Nabokov's and Orwell's attitude toward cruelty, but he nowhere explains what he understands cruelty to be (Rorty 1989: 141–68 and 169–88). Baier says that "I shall . . . leave aside the very tricky question of just what should count as cruelty." And she goes on, "I take torture to humans or animals to be paradigm cases of cruelty . . . but just how close to torture the pain inflicted in cruel treatment has to be to count as 'cruel' is impossible to get agreement on" (Baier 1993: 445).

Shklar does a bit better by actually offering two definitions. The first is "the willful inflicting of physical pain on a weaker being in order to cause anguish and fear" (1984: 8). But why does the pain have to be physical? Why does the cruel person have to be stronger than the victim? Could not a weaker person torture a stronger one? Why must cruelty cause anguish and fear? Could it not cause death or mental illness or amnesia without anguish and fear? And what if physical pain is willfully inflicted not to cause anguish and fear but to bring about the moral improvement of a miserable sinner, deviant, or heretic? Could that not be cruel?

Shklar's second definition, given several years later, is an improvement over the first. She says that cruelty "is the deliberate infliction of physical, and secondarily emotional, pain upon a weaker person or group by stronger ones in order to achieve some end, tangible or intangible, of the latter" (1989: 29). This definition is better because it allows that the pain involved in cruelty may be both physical and emotional. It also gets rid of the requirement that cruelty requires the intention to cause anguish and fear. But it retains the arbitrary proviso that cruelty can flow only from the strong to the weak. It also has the fatal consequence of making surgeons, dentists, physical fitness instructors, people fighting in self-defense, and judges imprisoning criminals all cruel. It is odd to think of liberals as those who make opposition to the perfectly reasonable activities of such people "the basic norm of . . . political practices and prescriptions."

From this portentous imprecision it is a relief to turn to the crispness of the *OED* (1961 ed.), in which cruelty is defined as "the quality of being cruel; disposition to inflict suffering; delight in or indifference to the pain or misery of others; mercilessness, hardheartedness: *esp.* as exhibited in action." It will soon be obvious that this definition needs to be supplemented, but first we should take note of what is essentially correct in it.

Cruelty requires an agent and a victim. The agent acts and the victim suffers. Part of what the agent does is to perform an action that inflicts pain on the victim. But this is not enough to make the action cruel. What the agent does also includes a state of mind in which the agent takes delight in or is indifferent to the pain that the action causes the victim. The victim suffers because of the pain the agent's action inflicts. Cruelty may then be said to include three essential elements: the agent's state of mind, the agent's action, and the victim's suffering.

Another essential feature of cruelty is that it is a disposition of human agents. To be a cruel person, an agent must habitually be in the appropriate state of mind and perform the appropriate action. But it is not necessary for being a cruel person to know that the relevant action will cause pain to the victim. For the agent's indifference to the victim's pain may be so extensive as to preclude awareness of the misery the action inflicts. Of course, if the agent takes delight in the pain of the victim, then the effect of the action must be known, otherwise it could not delight. Cruelty thus may be ascribed to human agents both when they know what they are doing and when they do not. The point of the condemnation involved in saying that an agent is cruel may be to assign blame for not knowing what the agent ought to know, namely, that his or her habitual actions regularly cause suffering.

Cruelty may also be ascribed to actions, but only in a derivative sense. Actions, to be sure, can predictably cause pain, but that is not sufficient to make them cruel. For the predictable pain they can cause may be justified as punishment, excused as the lesser of two evils, or exempted as unavoidable. To say that an action is cruel is thus to say that it is the kind of action that would be performed by a cruel agent, and that is why when actions are correctly said to be cruel, a derivative sense of "cruelty" is being used.

This much is implicit in the dictionary definition. There are, however, two respects in which it needs to be supplemented. First, it is silent on the subject of how severe the pain must be to justify calling its infliction cruel. It is clear that the pain should be serious, not trivial. People who habitually take delight in or are indifferent to causing others embarrassment, annoyance, or inconvenience may be offensive, but they are not cruel. Cruelty requires the infliction of pain that harms the victim in a way that endangers the victim's functioning as a full-fledged agent.

The second omission from the dictionary definition is that as it stands it fails to specify that the pain inflicted on the victim must be unjustified or excessive. The victim does not deserve the pain, or that much of it, and there is no morally acceptable reason for its infliction. This is what leads some opponents of capital punishment, flogging, or mutilation to call the practice "cruel and unusual." Their thought is, rightly or wrongly, that there is no morally acceptable reason to inflict that much pain even on criminals who are guilty as charged.

Given these supplements, the dictionary definition may be amended as follows: in its primary sense, cruelty is the disposition of human agents to take delight in or be indifferent to the serious and unjustified suffering that their actions cause to their victims.

9.3 IS CRUELTY THE WORST THING?

Armed with this definition, it is now possible to identify the mistaken moral attitudes that motivate the slogan that a liberal is one who believes that cruelty is the worst thing we do. These attitudes involve stressing the moral significance of one essential element of cruelty at the expense of the others, and that is their mistake. The three elements are the agent's state of mind, the agent's action, and the victim's suffering. Corresponding to them are three mistaken moral attitudes.

It must be said in favor of the Humean way of thinking, before turning to its criticism, that it is an improvement over the Kantian way at least in one crucial respect. Kantians approach moral questions from the agent's point of view. The primary consideration for them is that the agent should be motivated by good will, which is spelled out by the requirements of the categorical imperative. How the agent's actions affect others is a contingent matter that is denied to have any bearing on the moral quality of the agent's action. Since the victim's suffering is among these contingent matters, it is irrelevant to the moral quality of the action that causes it. This leads Baier to say, perhaps a trifle excitedly, that "Nietzsche's comment in the *Genealogy of Morals* . . . seems fair enough: that a bad smell of sadomasochism, the reek of blood and torture, lingers on the Categorical Imperative" (1993: 445). What Nietzsche actually says, in Kaufmann's translation, is that "the categorical imperative smells of cruelty" (1966b: Second Essay, sec. 6), but let that go. The substantive point is surely right: the Kantian attitude is remiss in not recognizing the central moral importance of the victim's suffering.

It is precisely because Humeans do recognize it that they regard cruelty as having such great moral significance. Their underlying attitude is that morality should protect the victims from the suffering that cruel agents inflict on them. No one who is committed to morality can fail to agree with them—at least so far. Their difficulties begin if it is asked how it follows from this that cruelty is the worst thing we do and why believing that makes one a liberal.

If cruelty is considered, in the Humean manner, from the victim's point of view, then there are two ways of trying to answer the question of what needs to be done to protect its victims. Each rests on a mistaken moral attitude. The first is to stress the primary importance of prohibiting the actions that cause suffering and to attribute only secondary importance to states of mind. The second is to stress the primary importance of changing the states of mind from which both cruel actions and the victim's suffering follow and to attribute secondary importance to the actions themselves, which are merely symptoms of the states of mind that motivate the actions. The problem is that whichever way is preferred, the conclusion that cruelty is the worst thing we do does not follow, and it follows even less that those who are committed to protecting the victims from cruelty thereby become liberals.

The first way is represented by Philip Hallie's writings on cruelty (1969, 1992). Hallie's attitude is the diamentrical opposite of the Kantian one. Kantians regard the consequences of cruel actions as morally irrelevant; Hallie regards everything but the consequences as morally irrelevant.[6] He concentrates on the victim's suffering and is indifferent to the agent's state of mind. There are two things that can be said in favor of this attitude. It calls attention to what Kantians ignore and what should not be ignored by anyone who cares about cruelty. The other is that the attitude has its source in passionate indignation about cruelty and consuming pity for its victims. These sentiments inform Hallie's writings and lend intensity to them. There is no doubt that his heart is in the right place. The problem is that it misleads his mind.

In the first place, it is an exaggeration to suppose that cruelty must maim or ruin its victims. It certainly damages them in serious ways, but the damage need not be as serious as Hallie claims in order to be cruel.

Many innocent victims have emerged from the cruelties of concentration camps and abusive families without being maimed or ruined. The point is not to protest against Hallie's inflated rhetoric, but to realize that if cruelty is defined in terms of maim and ruination, then a lot of cruelty, both physical and psychological, will escape identification and condemnation. The harm done by exaggeration is to create disrespect for the unexaggerated truth.

In the second place, if the agent's state of mind is ignored, then it becomes impossible to distinguish between cruelty and justified punishment, painful therapy, physically demanding training, telling hurtful truths, and similar benevolently motivated inflictions of pain. Surely, a definition of cruelty should allow that there is a moral difference between emergency amputation in wartime without anesthesia and severing a limb by chain saw so as to extract information.

In the third place, if Hallie's account were accepted, then how could cruelty be distinguished from other kinds of serious evils? If cruelty is "the activity of hurting sentient beings," then how does it differ from betrayal, fanaticism, dishonesty, expediency, greed, and so forth, which also hurt sentient beings? And if cruelty is simply serious evil in all its forms, then why does Hallie take himself to be writing about cruelty rather than about serious evil in general?

Lastly, to connect Hallie's account to the present context, it is pretty clear, although he does not explicitly say so, that he would strongly agree that cruelty is the worst thing we do. But how could it be consistently held that the agent's state of mind is morally irrelevant, that what matters is the victim's suffering, and that cruelty is the worst thing we do? The worst thing we do, given these assumptions, must surely be whatever causes the most suffering to the victim. Cruelty often does that, but why could other evils not cause greater suffering than cruelty? Paternalism, religious and ideological dogmatism, national pride, greed, Utopian aspirations, selfishness, and so forth have historically been and currently are potent causes of suffering. There is no reason to think that cruelty must always be the worst among all these and other evils.

Humeans will therefore reject Hallie's simplistic approach to cruelty. They will be guided by Hume's observation that "actions are by their very nature temporary and perishing; and where they proceed not from some cause in the character and disposition of the person, who perform'd them, they infix not themselves upon him, and neither redound to his honour, if good, nor infamy, if evil" (Hume 1960: 441). This will lead them to emphasize the importance of the agents' states of mind in trying to protect the victims of their cruelty.

This is a much more defensible attitude than either the Kantian or

Hallie's. There is a great deal to be said in favor of this attitude, and virtue theorists in contemporary moral thought are saying it. Those who hold this attitude agree with Kantians about the importance of the agent's state of mind, without dooming themselves by regarding the consequences that follow from states of mind as morally irrelevant. They may approach the evil of cruelty from the victim's point of view, as Hallie does, but they see that both the actions and the states of mind from which the actions proceed matter. They can thus do what Hallie cannot: distinguish between evil actions which are cruel and those which reflect other vices and between cruel actions that cause suffering and benevolent actions that may cause as much suffering as cruel ones. Nor is there any reason intrinsic to their position why they would have to leave "cruelty" undefined, as Rorty and Baier do, or handicap themselves with either of Shklar's terrible definitions. Humeans can in perfect consistency accept the improved version of the definition of cruelty. What, then, is wrong with their position?

Up to this point, nothing is wrong with it. Humeans rightly abhor serious and unjustified suffering being inflicted on victims. They rightly identify as one source of their suffering the states of mind of agents who take delight in or are indifferent to the suffering their actions habitually cause. They thus take due account of each of the three essential elements of cruelty: the agent's state of mind, the agent's action, and the victim's suffering. But they err nevertheless, although in a subtle and interesting way. Perhaps to avoid what they see as the mistakes of crude utilitarians, they stress the agents' state of mind, the vice, that is, from which cruel actions and the victims' suffering both follow. They are influenced by Montaigne's regarding cruelty "as the worst of all *vices*" and Hume's claim that it is "the most detested of all *vices*." That cruelty is a vice is true; that from it flow detestable actions and unconscionable suffering is also true. But why is it the most extreme, the most detestable of all vices? Why is cruelty the worst thing we do?

The answer is that it is the worst because it is the denial of benevolence, and Humeans think of benevolence as the moral master motive. Montaigne thought alike, not because he was a precocious Humean, but because he was committed to Christian love, to caritas, whose secular version benevolence is. Cruelty is the *summum malum* because it is the vice farthest away from benevolence.

It becomes obvious, however, that something is wrong with this answer if it is borne in mind that benevolence can lead to great cruelty. The way in which it can do so is explicitly allowed for by Shklar: if cruelty is "the basic norm of . . . political practices and prescriptions," then the "only exception to the rule is the prevention of greater cruelties" (1989: 30).

The great cruelties that have been caused by benevolent motives are routinely justified by the belief that they are necessary for the prevention of even greater cruelties. Their victims are the broken eggs of the ideological and religious omelettes that crusaders, inquisitors, conquistadores, commissars, SS men and, yes, women as well, have been cooking.

Shklar may reply by saying that the beliefs offered in justification of these benevolently inflicted cruelties are so obviously false that no reasonable and decent person would believe them. But even if this were conceded, there would remain numerous beliefs justifying benevolently inflicted cruelties whose truths are controversial matters among reasonable and decent people. Such beliefs underlie the controversies over abortion, capital punishment, euthanasia, welfare legislation, sex change operations, mainstreaming children with low intelligence, imprisoning marijuana users, and charging people with sex crimes on the basis of testimony that psychotherapists are said to elicit from the unconscious memories of supposed victims. It is therefore by no means clear what is benevolent and what is cruel.

Crude utilitarianism has many faults, but one of its great merits is to stress, and stress again, that the moral quality of a state of mind is determined by the kind of action that follows from it. There is no guarantee intrinsic to benevolence that it will not be misled by false beliefs and result in great cruelties. Indeed, there is ample historical evidence that this often happens. And, to put in a good word for Kant as well, he saw the fickleness of benevolence, which is why he excluded it, as well as other sentiments, from the categorical imperative.

It is not necessary, however, to side with crude utilitarians or Kantians to avoid the Humean mistake of basing morality on as insecure a foundation as benevolence. The alternative is not to exclude benevolence from morality but to stop regarding it as the moral master motive. The point is not that there is a moral master motive and Humeans mistakenly think that it is benevolence. The point is that there is no moral master motive.

Conscientiousness, justice, personal loyalties, private projects, dedication to excellence, courage, and so on and on, as well as benevolence, of course, may all motivate people in morally praiseworthy ways. But these motives, as well as benevolence, may be corrupted. Morality, therefore, is not merely or mainly a matter of making sure that agents will be in some particular state of mind when they act but of balancing the agents' states of mind, the agents' actions, and the way the actions affect other people. The balance excludes any a priori way of privileging one of these elements over the others, and it includes the weighing and harmonizing of their competing claims with a view of maximizing human welfare and minimizing human suffering.

If this is right, then cruelty is not the summum malum. Just as there is no summum bonum, so there is no summum malum. Cruelty is very bad, but it is not the worst thing. The worst thing is what causes the most evil. In different circumtances, different things will do that. There always is *a* worst thing, but there is nothing that is always *the* worst thing. Acting contrary to benevolence may have dreadful consequences. It may also have consequences that are not dreadful but just, conscientious, courageous, and so forth. If benevolence is not the moral master motive, then cruelty is not the worst thing we do. If cruelty is not the worst thing we do, then liberals would be ill advised to define their position in terms of this slogan.

Suppose, however, that the arguments that have been advanced against this slogan are all mistaken. Suppose that cruelty *is* the worst thing we do and that the first task of an acceptable political morality is to protect all citizens of a state from it. Does it follow that this political morality will be liberal? It does not. A political morality that is likely to be effective in providing protection against cruelty will tend to be conservative.

Liberals think that the state ought to provide the conditions in which its citizens can make what they regard as good lives for themselves. Decisions about what lives are good and how to go about living them depend on the citizens' exercise of their autonomy. And autonomy, in turn, depends on the availability of a plurality of conceptions of a good life among which citizens can choose, on the protection of their rights, on their freedom of choice and action, on the state guaranteeing equal concern and respect for each of its citizens, and on the state maintaining a just distribution of the goods that its citizens need. If cruelty is the worst thing we do, it is so because it endangers these conditions more than does any other threat to them. This is why a state ought to make protection against cruelty "the basic norm of its political practices and prescriptions" (Shklar 1989: 30).

The only way in which this protection can be provided, however, is by curtailing the autonomy of cruel people, and that, in turn, depends on reducing their plurality of choices and actions, restricting their rights, diminishing their freedom, not showing equal concern and respect for cruel and decent people, and not providing the goods that cruel people need to pursue their pernicious activities. It will be asked, Why does this make the state tend toward conservatism? Because if cruelty really endangers the conditions that liberals regard as essential, then interference with autonomy, pluralism, rights, freedom, equality, and distributive justice will have to be very considerable, which will tend to make the state conservative. If, on the other hand, interference with the conditions that liberals regard as essential can be kept to a minimum, then it cannot be that cruelty is as great a threat to them as to justify making its prohibition the basic norm of liberal political practices and prescriptions.

Liberals may continue to defend benevolence as the justification of liberalism by arguing that the arguments just given against it are much too indirect. Even if cruelty is not the worst thing we do, benevolence may still be the justification of liberalism, for it is the attitude that makes people receptive to the liberal values and political programs that make good lives possible. If this claim is based on general benevolence, then it raises the second of the questions whose discussion was promised earlier. If it is based on limited benevolence, then it prompts the third question. This section will deal with the second question, the next one with the third.

The arguments against general benevolence begin with Hume. He certainly defends benevolence as the basis of morality, but it is limited benevolence that he has in mind, and he explicitly rejects general benevolence: "It may be affirm'd, that there is no such passion in human minds, as the love of mankind, merely as such, independent of personal qualities, of services, or of relation to ourself" (Hume 1960: 481). The point is not the trivial one that even general benevolence must take specific forms and have specific objects. Hume thinks that human nature excludes general benevolence: "We perceive, that the generosity of men is very limited, and that it seldom extends beyond their friends and family, or, at most, beyond their native country. Being thus acquainted with the nature of man, we expect not any impossibilities from him; but confine our view to that narrow circle, in which any person moves" (1960: 602). Liberals may agree with Hume, accept the fact of limited benevolence, and go on to urge changing it, as, for instance, does Mill: "In an improving state of the human mind, the influences are constantly on the increase which tend to generate in each individual a feeling of unity with all the rest; which, if perfect, would make him never think, or desire, any beneficial condition for himself, in the benefits of which they are not included" (Mill 1979: 32). Hume's claim, however, is stronger, and it excludes Mill's "improving state of mind." He thinks that the proposed change from limited to general benevolence is both impossible and undesirable: "It is wisely ordained by nature, that private connections should commonly prevail over universal views and considerations; otherwise our affections and actions would be dissipated and lost, for want of a proper limited object" (Hume 1961: 229).

There are three arguments in favor of not even trying to extend limited to general benevolence. The first is factual: general benevolence does not exist. Human nature is so constructed that benevolence begins with the very few other people to whom the agents are intimately connected. It expands outward, but it weakens proportionally as the connection between them and others becomes more and more remote and impersonal. When it comes to the vast majority of others to whom the agents are not connected by personal ties, shared customs, and forms of life, it peters out completely. It is perfectly natural that this is so. The injunction that people should go against their natural sentiments and try, artificially, to fan their limited benevolence to embrace total strangers of whose lives and circumstances they are largely ignorant is wildly unrealistic and unrealizable. The utilitarian urging that people should act contrary to their natural inclinations comes down to a misleadingly expressed wish that human nature should be other than it is. A sound system of morality must respect facts, yet utilitarians quixotically ignore them; and they do so against Hume's advice to legislators that they "must take mankind as they find them, and cannot pretend to introduce any violent change in their principles and ways of thinking. . . . [T]he less natural any set of principles are . . . the more difficulty will a legislator meet with in raising and cultivating them" (Hume 1985: 260).

The second argument is practical. The only effective way of acting on such limited benevolence as people have is to restrict it to familiar contexts. The desire to increase the welfare or to decrease the suffering of others is not enough. It is necessary also to know how to go about doing it. But the more remote the contexts are, the less is known about them. The reasonable policy dictated by benevolence is to exercise it in contexts where its requirements are clear and to refrain from wasting scarce resources through dubious actions based on inadequate knowledge. It is, for instance, less than useless to donate money for the relief of suffering in distant parts of the world if it is not known what causes the suffering, how the money will be used, and whether there are dependable safeguards against inefficiency, corruption, and stupidity in its distribution.

These doubts have a moral point. It is not just that wasting scarce resources is an evil but also that suffering exists close to home as well. The moral choice is not between wasteful general benevolence and none at all but between wasteful general benevolence and limited benevolence that has a far better chance of relieving suffering. To put this in concrete terms, why send food to Somalia when people need it in America?

The third argument is based on moral psychology. General benevolence misdirects the moral attention of those who aspire to it. The moral life of most people consists in participation in a network of more or less personal relationships. Their obligations are set by family ties, their jobs, the roles they play in the various communities and associations to which they belong, and the laws and customs of their country. It is not easy to discharge these obligations. The difficulty is not merely that vices and temptations lead to their violations but also that the more personal the relationships that give rise to the obligations, the more active the partici- pation they require. Personal relationships are far more complex than are impersonal ones. It is much easier to be a good citizen than it is to be a good parent. Personal relationships place moral demands on the participants' sustained attention. Caring for another person requires nearly as much knowledge, understanding, and seriousness as people lav- ish on themselves. And, of course, they often fail. Benevolence motivates people to attend more carefully, to try to fail less.

It is limited benevolence, however, that motivates people in this way, not a universal and impartial wish for the good of others. In personal relationships, it is precisely to the individual qualities of the other that agents owe attention. Love is personal and partial. It is not love if it does not discriminate in favor of its object.

The trouble with general benevolence is that it directs the attention away from personal relationships and toward universality and impartiality. The more successful it is, the less there is left for everyday moral relation- ships. The more general benevolence becomes, the less capable are its agents of cherishing the individuality, the distinctness, the particularity of others that personal relationships require. Since people's primary obliga- tions are to those to whom they are personally connected, general benev- olence undermines their fulfillment of these obligations.

In the light of these three arguments against endeavoring to extend limited to general benevolence, it is right to conclude that the Humean position is "a welcome corrective to the tendency, in both Christian and utilitarian morality, to set up a quite impracticable ideal of universal be- nevolence" (Mackie 1980: 127). Doubts nevertheless remain. For it is an undeniable fact that the benevolence of all too many people is kept much too limited by selfishness, indifference to the sufferings of others, and other vices. The defense of limited benevolence and the rejection of gen- eral benevolence must therefore answer the question of how far limited benevolence should be extended before the utilitarian injunction to ex- tend it all the way can be justifiably rejected.

The required answer, however, is commonsensical and readily at hand. Limited benevolence should be extended only if there are good reasons for it, and it should be extended only so far as these reasons reach. The good reasons should take into account the facts of human nature, the practical limitations, and the existence of other moral obligations. The good reasons would have to show that the resources for acting on general benevolence are available, that their use is likely to achieve its object, and that their use to alleviate suffering at distant places should take moral precedence over their use close to home. In the absence of such reasons, the moral injunction to promote the well-being of others universally and impartially is a manifestation of sentimentalism or, worse, an immoral policy leading to the neglect of actual for spurious obligations.

It may be objected that since the world has become a global village, there is always a reason for general benevolence and always an obligation to extend limited benevolence in the direction of universality and impartiality. This objection rests on the mistaken assumption that knowledge of the sufferings of others creates an obligation to help them. Surely, knowing that many criminals have miserable lives and are afraid to enjoy the fruits of their labors, that tyrants suffer from the hostility of their subjects, or that Russian soldiers in Chechnya or Chinese soldiers in Tibet live in jeopardy of life and limb does not create an obligation to do anything to relieve their suffering. It makes a difference why people suffer.

Suppose, however, that it is known that people at distant places suffer undeservedly: children are starving, innocent people are tortured, the helpless are being exploited. These are clearly evils. Yet there is a lot of evil in the world, resources are limited, there are often great practical obstacles in the way of ameliorating evil, and suffering closer to home may have a much stronger claim on the avilable resources. Not even knowledge of undeserved suffering, therefore, creates an obligation to help.

But what if it is known that distant suffering is undeserved, it is practically feasible to alleviate it, and there are no overriding moral claims on the available resources. Is there not a moral obligation to help then? Yes, there is. It still does not follow, however, that that obligation has anything to do with extending limited benevolence universally and impartially. For the obligation may be based on justice, decency, or prudence.

It must be concluded in the light of these considerations that there are often good reasons for not extending limited benevolence universally and impartially, and that even if in some contexts there are good reasons to care about the welfare of people universally and impartially, those reasons need not rest on either limited or general benevolence. General benevolence, therefore, is an inadequate justification of liberalism.

9.5 LIMITED BENEVOLENCE AS THE JUSTIFICATION OF LIBERALISM

Liberals may concede that general benevolence is often misplaced, but they may go on to argue that limited benevolence is the foundation of morality. For if there were not some human disposition to care for the welfare of at least some other people, then moral reasons would have no appeal. The motivating force of moral reasons ultimately rests on considerations that agents find persuasive. Self-interest is one consideration, but people often go beyond self-interest, and so there must be others. Limited benevolence is another such consideration. If it did not exist, it would be inexplicable why people do many of the things they obviously do. The utilitarian justification of liberalism may then take the form of arguing that the political programs, basic values, and the core of liberalism are the best expressions of limited benevolence.

The problem with this justification is that it does not follow from the premises that are adduced in its support. It is true, as Hume claimed, that limited benevolence is a basic human motive on which human beings often act. But this is not a sufficient justification of liberalism because there are also other basic human motives, they often conflict with limited benevolence, and when people help others they may be motivated by considerations other than limited benevolence. So that even if it were true that liberalism is the best expression of limited benevolence, it would still not be true that the claims of limited benevolence, and hence the claims of liberalism, should take precedence over the claims of other basic human motives with which they conflict. The problem is that this utilitarian defense of liberalism mistakenly assumes that limited benevolence is the moral master motive.

It has already been argued (in Section 9.3) that it is a mistake to suppose that there is a moral master motive. Human beings are normally motivated by a variety of morally praiseworthy considerations, such as justice, personal ideals, conscientiousness, loyalty, and so forth. Limited benevolence is one of these, and there is no reason to assign to it a privileged status among them. To do so would be contrary to pluralism and thus inconsistent with one of the basic values of liberalism.

There are, moreover, numerous contexts in which the requirements of morality are actually violated by actions based on limited benevolence. Such are the contexts in which people are held responsible for the evil they have done, even if benevolence prompts the opposite; in which people conscientiously tell the truth, pay their debt, keep their word, and act honorably, even if the benevolent courses would be different; in which justice is done at great cost to the living, even if its recipients are dead and can no longer enjoy the fruits of benevolence.

The most telling argument against regarding limited benevolence as the moral master motive, however, derives from the occurrence of moral conflicts that people often experience in themselves between acting as limited benevolence prompts and acting as justice, honesty, and conscientiousness, fairness, or loyalty prompt. The present significance of this kind of moral conflict is that it cannot be resolved by simply asserting the overridingness of limited benevolence. For the mere fact that there are moral requirements that conflict with limited benevolence shows that it cannot be the moral master motive. Perhaps limited benevolence ought to override whatever conflicts with it. But the claim that it ought to do so requires supporting arguments.

If such arguments are available, they must appeal to some consideration that is deeper than either limited benevolence or whatever conflicts with it, since it must be shown why limited benevolence should take precedence. But then the consideration that is appealed to would have a far stronger claim to being overriding than would limited benevolence. If, on the other hand, no such argument is available for always resolving moral conflicts in favor of limited benevolence, then the claim of limited benevolence to overridingness amounts to nothing more than sentimentalist moralizing.

A similar objection rests on another type of conflict: that between incompatible moral and nonmoral requirements. The requirements of morality often conflict with the requirements of love, loyalty, politics, religion, and so forth. The point of noting this is that limited benevolence may appear on either side of the conflict. It may be a moral motive and conflict, say, with self-interest, or it may be a nonmoral motive and move the agent toward preferring the morally weaker claim of a friend to the morally stronger claim of a stranger. In such conflicts, nonbenevolent moral considerations may override benevolent nonmoral considerations. But if limited benevolence were the moral master motive, this could not or should not happen. The fact that it does happen implies that limited benevolence neither is nor ought it to be always overriding. It is justified to conclude, therefore, that limited benevolence is not the moral master motive, but merely one of several moral considerations, whose motivational force may justifiably be overridden. Since the political programs, basic values, and the core belief of liberalism are supposed to be justified as the best expressions of limited benevolence, limited benevolence is an insufficient justification because other political programs, other values, and other core beliefs may conflict with and justifiably override the liberal ones.

The objections to the utilitarian defense of liberalism are so strong and obvious that the failure to recognize their seriousness cries out for an explanation. The explanation is that this approach to the justification of liberalism is shot through with sentimentalism. The seriousness of the objections is not seen by these liberals because through their sentimentalism they contrive to hide it from themselves.

Sentimentalism is an emotional response that falsifies its object. Falsification is not just to hold a false belief but also to take an active part in getting it wrong. An emotional response is sentimental if it is based on the agents' cultivation of false beliefs about some objects and if their falseness makes their objects appear appropriate to the agents' feelings when in fact they are not. Sentimentalism inflates the significance of some unimportant feature of its object at the expense of a truly important one. What motivates it is the need to make the agents' feelings appropriate to their objects. At the root of the sentimentalism, therefore, is the mistake of trying to make the world fit the agents' feelings, rather than the other way around.

A film, novel, play, or painting is sentimental if it emphasizes some comforting feature of an otherwise distressing situation, such as focusing on instances of heroism in death camps, at the expense of the surrounding horror. The attitude toward terrorists is sentimental if it concentrates on their selfless dedication, outrage, or loyalty but not on the mayhem they cause. Love is sentimental if it exaggerates the virtues and minimizes the vices of its object.

As these examples show, the falsification involved in sentimentalism makes its objects appear better than they are. Its objects are idealized in the eyes of the beholder. It makes the past better than it was and some people are more lovable or deserving than they are; it concentrates on hope in gross inhumanity, on heroism in miserable victims, on opportunity for growth in evil. What makes this sort of falsification so insidious and recalcitrant to criticism is that it contains an element of truth. For the feature it falsifies is indeed there. It is just that its significance is small in comparison with what else is there. What if Hitler loved dogs, a terrorist had polio as a child, or a mafioso is devoted to his mentally disordered child?

The feelings that fuel the sentimentalism of this defense of liberalism have human suffering as their object, and the feelings themselves are a mixture of pity, sympathy, indignation, and guilt. The element of truth in this is that human suffering is great, and it is normal to have bad feelings about it. The much larger element of falsification is the idealization of its victims and the inflated sense of self-importance that makes guilt at inaction an appropriate feeling. Much suffering is nobody's fault; people often suffer because the consequences of their imprudence catch up with them; and inaction in response to known suffering is often justified by there being nothing that could be done or by there being more immediate demands on the agents' moral attention.

The truths about human suffering are painful. Idealizing the victims and demonizing those who know about their plight and do not act are ways of projecting these painful feelings on the wrong objects. Liberals often vent their sentimentalism on others in the form of a strident, moralizing rhetoric that falsifies the facts, thus contributes to helplessness in the face of them, and treats those who do not share the false feelings as morally corrupt. Such sentimentalism is a disservice to reason and morality alike.

CHAPTER 10

What Is Wrong with Liberalism?

We repudiated all versions of the doctrine of original sin, of there being insane and irrational springs of wickedness in most men. We were not aware that civilisation was a thin and precarious crust erected by the personality and the will of a very few, and only maintained by rules and conventions skilfully put across and guilefully preserved. We had no respect for traditional wisdom or the restraint of custom. . . . As a cause and consequence of our general state of mind we completely misunderstood human nature, including our own. The rationality which we attributed to it led to superficiality, not only of judgment, but also of feeling. . . . I can see us as water-spiders, gracefully skimming, as light and reasonable as air, the surface of the stream without any contact with the eddies and the currents underneath.

—JOHN MAYNARD KEYNES, *Two Memoirs*

Liberalism is conceived of as a political morality designed to create conditions in which people can make good lives for themselves. Its negative aim is to avoid the evils that jeopardize these conditions, and its positive aim is to identify and realize them. The core of these conditions is autonomy; the basic values that make autonomy possible are freedom, equality, rights, pluralism, and distributive justice; and the liberal political programs endeavor to implement autonomy and the basic values.

The fundamental defect of liberalism is its inconsistency. Its negative and positive aims are incompatible, several of the conditions liberals identify as necessary for good lives actually make lives worse, and many of the political programs intended to realize these conditions stand in the way of good lives.

In one sense, the negative and positive aims of liberalism are unobjectionable. Who would not favor avoiding evil and making good lives possible? These aims, however, become *liberal* only if their content is specified, only if it is explained how evil is to be avoided and how lives are to be made good. The inconsistency of liberalism becomes apparent only if its negative and positive aims are specified.

One main reason why effective criticism of liberalism is difficult is that when its specific aims are criticized, liberals retreat to the general aims to which no reasonable person can take exception. All criticisms are then deflected on the ground that they concern only insignificant details, which may be readily revised, while the overall plan, the grand design, remains intact.

In the absence of specificity, however, there is no overall *liberal* plan. The commitments to avoiding evil and making good lives possible are not liberal commitments—they are the commitments of all reasonable and decent people. The commitments become liberal only when they are specified in terms of the core belief, the basic values, and the political programs of liberalism. The details, therefore, are everything. If they are inconsistent, then liberalism is inconsistent. And they are inconsistent.

These inconsistencies occur in the liberal treatments of evil, responsibility, equality, distributive justice, and pluralism. The time has come to state them in a summary form.

10.1 THE PROBLEM OF EVIL

No liberal can fail to know that the conditions required for living a good life are regularly violated. In this respect, the present century is of a piece with the lamentable historical record of humanity.

> When we contemplate . . . the evil, the vice, the ruin that has befallen the most flourishing kingdoms which the mind of man ever created, we can hardly avoid being filled with sorrow at this universal taint of corruption. And since this decay is not the work of mere nature, but of human will, our reflections may well lead us to a moral sadness, a revolt of the good will—if indeed it has a place in us. Without rhetorical exaggeration, a simple, truthful account of the miseries that have overwhelmed the noblest nations and polities and the finest exemplars of private virtue forms a most fearful picture and excites emotions of the profoundest and most hopeless sadness. (Hegel 1953: 26)

This passage by Hegel predates Communism, Nazism, two World Wars, and the genocide of numerous peoples. The pattern it describes, however, is merely strengthened by these and other similar events subsequent to its having been written. No thinking person can fail to recognize the prevalence of evil and wickedness as a highly significant fact that must be taken into account by all political moralities.

One fundamental defect of liberalism is its naïveté about evil and wickedness. It is not that liberals are unaware of the relevant facts or that they try to ignore them. Rather, their attempts to accommodate these facts in their political morality are utterly ineffectual. The question is thus forced on those who think about, rather than within, liberalism of what could lead reasonable and decent people to make so little of such a weighty and deeply serious matter. The answer is that it is the very faith that underlies and animates liberalism that prevents liberals from proceeding otherwise. That is why keeping the faith requires liberals to tailor the facts to fit it.

The liberal response to the prevalence of evil and wickedness is to attribute it to lack of autonomy. The thought behind this response is that if people could make unforced choices, if they could favorably evaluate and understand the significance of their chosen actions, then they would not act in evil ways. Making evil and wickedness less prevalent therefore depends on increasing autonomy, which in turn depends on increasing the scope of freedom, pluralism, rights, equality, and distributive justice.

But why do liberals suppose that increasing autonomy will make evil and wickedness less prevalent? Why do they suppose that autonomous acts are more likely to be good than evil? Because liberals believe that if people are allowed to make their own decisions without external interference, if they do not have to contend with poverty, discrimination, crime, and other social ills, if they are not ignorant, indoctrinated, or enraged by injustice, if they have the time and opportunity to think about their lives and actions, then they will do what is good and not what is evil. This is the liberal faith, and it is indefensible.

It ignores the fact that the vices of selfishness, greed, malevolence, envy, aggression, prejudice, cruelty, suspicion, and laziness motivate people just as much as the virtues. It supposes, contrary to readily available contrary evidence, that virtues are autonomous and vices are not. It arbitrarily assumes that virtues are natural and basic and that vices are unnatural products of corrupting external interference without which the virtues would reign. It believes in the teeth of daily experience to the contrary that the dictates of reason and morality are bound to coincide. It flatters humanity by painting a rosy picture of its wonderful possibilities, while it inexcusably belittles the hard facts that it cannot accommodate. It is thus a sentimental falsification of reality that cannot provide the justification that liberals need for increasing autonomy and for regarding freedom, pluralism, rights, equality, and distributive justice as basic values.

Liberals will deny that they are committed to this faith. They will concede that some naïve liberals in the past have held it, but they will claim that liberals do not need it now and that they can be as hardheaded about the facts of evil and wickedness as anyone else.

In that case, however, liberals owe an explanation of why they suppose that by increasing autonomy they will succeed in making evil and wickedness less prevalent. If evil and wickedness were autonomous, then increasing autonomy would increase evil and wickedness, so this cannot be the explanation that liberals need to provide. If, on the other hand, evil and wickedness were nonautonomous, then liberals must still explain why increasing autonomy would diminish them. The liberal faith was the old explanation, but if it is disavowed, if liberals do not believe that human beings are fundamentally good and naturally virtuous, if they believe that human motives are mixed and that virtues and vices are both natural and basic, then they cannot suppose that increasing autonomy will give greater scope to virtues and smaller scope to vices. If they really do not hold the liberal faith, then they ought to believe that increasing autonomy will result in increasing evil and wickedness as well.

Liberals are thus left with a choice among three alternatives, each of which is inconsistent with their own understanding of the conditions required for living a good life. The first is keeping the liberal faith, which involves a sentimental falsification of human possibilities and a resulting incapacity to cope with evil and wickedness. The second is maintaining their commitment to increasing autonomy, which will make evil and wickedness more, rather than less, prevalent. The third is acknowledging that autonomy must be curtailed to curtail evil and wickedness, which deprives their basic values and political programs from such justification as they previously had.

10.2 THE PROBLEM OF RESPONSIBILITY

To avoid this predicament, liberals opt to acknowledge the prevalence of evil but deny the prevalence of wickedness. It is true, they concede, that the prevalence of evil results from human actions, but it is not true, in their view, that these actions reflect so adversely on their agents as to warrant ascribing wickedness to them. The reasoning behind this attempt to deny the reflexivity of evil is as follows. Liberals agree that some evil actions are autonomous and that they do make agents who regularly perform them wicked. Such evildoers, however, are few in number. Most evil actions are nonautonomous. They are done because their agents face forced choices or because they have been prevented from evaluating or understanding the significance of their actions by poverty, lack of education, exploitation, fear of crime, and similar adversities.

Such agents, being nonautonomous, should not be held responsible for their actions. They are merely causal, not moral, agents of their deeds. Moral responsibility goes without autonomy, and lack of autonomy excuses agents from being held morally responsible. Since the legitimate ascription of wickedness implies moral responsibility, agents of nonautonomous actions are not liable to it, and they cannot be said to merit the condemnation that wickedness implies.

The intended or unintended consequence of this line of argument is to derail legitimate moral concerns with evil and wickedness. It is acknowledged by liberals that the prevalence of evil is due to people whose actions habitually and predictably cause it. It must also be acknowledged by them that anyone committed to morality must be concerned with making evil less prevalent. But then liberals go on to express this concern in a way that makes evil more rather than less prevalent. For the primary interest of liberals is to determine the extent to which the people whose habitual actions predictably cause evil are autonomous. They are thus preoccupied with the psychology, circumstances, and motivation of the evildoers, and they agonize over the proper distribution of responsibility between evildoers and the influences that made them evildoers. They focus on whether it is poverty, poor education, a hostile environment, and so forth that are responsible for the evil these people cause or whether the responsibility lies with their autonomous vices.

These questions are, of course, legitimate. What is wrong with them, however, is that by giving priority to asking and answering them, liberals divert attention from matters that are far more important and have far greater moral significance. They relegate to the periphery of attention the evil that has been caused, the suffering that has been undeservedly inflicted on innocent people, and the damage that this does to the society in which it occurs.

That the morally salient question is how to curtail evil is tacitly acknowledged even by liberals. For their reason for worrying about the degree of autonomy of habitual and predictable evildoers is that they do evil; that is why the question of their responsibility arises. If it is evil that is recognized as mattering first and the assignment of responsibility for causing it only later, then the primary moral task will be seen as curtailing evil, regardless of whether it is caused autonomously or nonautonomously. A just sense of moral priorities requires facing the fact that there are people who habitually and predictably cause evil, that the prevalence of evil is due to their actions, and that they must be stopped.

One traditional task of a political morality is to formulate and enforce limits to achieve this end. Liberal political morality, however, is incapable of doing that because it restricts the sphere of legitimate moral concern to the sphere of autonomy. Nonautonomous actions are therefore non-moral, according to liberal political morality. Because liberals attribute the prevalence of evil mainly to nonautonomous actions, their political morality is by its very nature rendered incapable of dealing with the prevalence of evil, and thus it is inconsistent with their own positive aim, which is to make good lives possible. The concentration of liberals on the wrong question—on ascribing the precise degree of responsibility—is a desperate measure to show that their political morality really does care about evil, it is just that most evildoers do not come under its jurisdiction.

It compounds this problem that even if concentration on responsibility, rather than on evil, were justified, the attempt to attach responsibility solely to autonomous actions and agents would still fail. That this is so is part of the significance of collective responsibility. People may justifiably be held responsible for actions they have not performed and had no control over. This may be done if it is true of them that they have enduring identification with a group; they are committed to its values; the values are wrong; and, although they themselves have not acted according to the wrong values, they would have if they had been in the position of the fellow member of the group whose action did reflect the wrong values. Such people sustain the group, their moral identity is essentially connected with their allegiance to it, so if other members of the group cause evil by actions these agents did not do but would have done, then they come to share the responsibility for them.

The legitimacy of the ascription of collective responsibility shows that the liberal identification of responsible and autonomous actions is mistaken, even apart from the denial of the reflexivity of evil. Here, then, is a further reason for denying that autonomy is the pivot on which political morality turns and a further reason for rejecting the attitude toward evil that makes liberals incapable of coping with it.

The way out of this morass of self-inflicted ineffectuality is to recognize that a political morality may have legitimate concern with nonautonomous, as well as autonomous, actions. The task of a political morality is to provide and protect the possibilities and limits that the people of a society need to make good lives for themselves. The limits may be violated by both autonomous and nonautonomous actions. Because either may endanger the possibilities on which good lives depend, a morally acceptable political morality must be committed to curtailing both kinds of violations. And because good lives may involve both autonomous and nonautonomous possibilities, a morally acceptable political morality must recognize and foster both kinds of possibilities. If liberals are committed to these goals, they must remove autonomy from the core of their political morality. The alternative is to doom themselves to helplessneses in the face of nonautonomous evil from which the prevalence of evil mainly results.

10.3 THE PROBLEM OF EQUALITY

Another problem is that the liberal conception of equality is inconsistent with good lives. Liberals think of equality in predominantly economic terms, as the distribution of resources, broadly interpreted, that are necessary for living a good life. There are several reasons for rejecting the central liberal claim that distribution should be based on equal concern and respect for everyone.

One reason is that liberals are mistaken in thinking that the unequal distribution of resources is in itself objectionable or an obstacle to living a good life. If everyone has sufficient resources, it is not objectionable that some have more than others. What is objectionable is that some do not have enough. The equal distribution of resources, however, would not lead to everyone having enough because resources are chronically scarce and the equal distribution of scarce resources might just increase the number of those who do not have enough, and because the distribution of scarce resources diminishes the resources that can be used to produce future resources and thus makes it even less likely that people will have enough resources in the future.

Another reason against the liberal commitment to equality is that absurd policies follow from it, unless morally objectionable inequalities are distinguished from inequalities that are acceptable or neutral from the moral point of view. To draw such a distinction, however, requires asking and answering the question of why specific inequalities hold. The damaging implication of that question is that, contrary to the liberal claim, inequalities in themselves are not morally objectionable. It is a statistical necessity that in any population some people will be worst off both in specific respects and overall. This is morally objectionable only if it makes it very hard to live a good life, if their being worst off is morally unjustifiable, and if reasonable ways exist to improve these people's fortunes. The liberal commitment to equality is mistaken because it ignores these considerations.

A further reason for rejecting the liberal conception of equality is that no liberal can be committed to it consistently. The liberal rhetoric is that equality applies to everyone, but in practice liberals systematically restrict the distribution of resources to people living in a particular state. If a state were to use its resources to try to improve the lives of everyone, it would betray its most basic obligation to its citizens and it would be likely to run out of even the scarce resources it has at its disposal. If, however, a state did what all states do, and should do, and put the welfare of its citizens ahead of the welfare of noncitizens, then it would be acting contrary to the liberal conception of equality, according to which everyone should have the resources necessary for living a good life.

An additional reason is that the liberal conception of equality has the absurd consequence of having to provide equal resources in support of good and evil conceptions of a good life. To avoid this absurdity, liberals must make the case for the equal distribution of resources prima facie. They could then argue that evil conceptions of a good life provide a reason for overriding the prima facie case and withholding equal resources from them. The problem with this is that in overriding the prima facie case, liberals appeal to the moral inequality of good and evil conceptions of a good life. But because the prima facie case rests on the presumption of the moral equality of all conceptions of a good life, liberals once again stand convicted of an inconsistency. If equal resources are to be provided only for pursuing morally acceptable conceptions of a good life, then equality loses its claim to universality, generality, impartiality, disinterestedness, and neutrality. If, on the other hand, the pursuit of all conceptions of a good life, regardless of whether they are really good or evil, is to be supported by equal resources, then the inconsistency is removed, but only at the cost of absurdity.

10.4 THE PROBLEM OF DISTRIBUTIVE JUSTICE

Turning now to the reasons for rejecting the liberal conception of distributive justice, the first thing to notice about it is that it is a conscious and deliberate rejection of actual practice, common sense, the philosophical tradition, and the history of political thought regarding justice. It aims at the radical transformation of the theory and practice of justice as it has existed before the liberal attack on it. The point is not that there was justice before liberalism, and now that liberalism is dominant, there is injustice. There was and is plenty of injustice. Rather, the point is that theory and practice have been supposed to reflect an *ideal* of justice. The radicalism of the liberal conception of distributive justice consists in the rejection of that ideal. It is not an attempt at reforming theory and practice so that they would come closer to the ideal but an attempt at revolutionizing the ideal itself by changing its fundamental nature.

The traditional and commonsensical ideal of justice is that people should get what they deserve; that there ought to be a balance that makes the good and the evil people enjoy or suffer proportional to the good and the evil they have caused. The system of justice that exists in a state should aim to come as close as possible to approximating this ideal. Essential to this ideal are the notions of moral merit and demerit. Merit depends on what people have done to make lives better and demerit on what they have done to make them worse. The ideal of justice, then, is that desert should be proportional to moral merit or demerit. It is a consequence of this ideal that, since the balance of good and evil that different people cause is different, people have unequal moral merits and demerits. Given the nature of the world and of human beings, all systems of justice must take moral inequality into account.

Liberals reject this ideal because they reject desert as a basis of justice. Their conception of justice is egalitarian, and the notion of moral inequality is anathema to them. They suppose that the resources that a state has at its disposal ought to be distributed so as to assure that all people have what they need to make a good life for themselves. Because preliberal distribution has shortchanged many people, resources have to be redistributed. And the redistribution should proceed by always favoring the people who are worst off, since they suffer the most from the unequal distribution of resources.

The extraordinary feature of this conception is its deliberate refusal to ask the questions that will occur to any reasonable person who is not already committed to it. Why are the people who are worst off in that position? Is it due to misfortune or personal failings? What is the guarantee that if resources are redistributed without regard to moral merit, then wicked people will not use the resources given to them in evil ways? What is the justification for depriving people with moral merit of resources they have acquired legitimately? Why would reasonable people produce the resources necessary for redistribution if they know in advance that much of what they produce will be taken from them and given to others without regard to whether those others deserve the resources? Why should the distribution of resources proceed independently of considering the efforts people make to produce the resources? How could a state avoid self-destruction if it gives priority in its use of resources to supporting its nonproductive citizens over producing additional resources? Why would people who are worst off make an effort to improve their lot if they know that they can count on the state doing it for them without their having to do anything? How could it be maintained that good and wicked people should be given the same amount of scarce resources? How could a system that is designed to ignore what people deserve be a system of justice?

The reason why liberals do not ask these questions and the reason why they fail to see how fundamentally damaging they are is an assumption in the background. If the assumption were true, the questions would have obvious answers that would not be damaging at all. The assumption is that people are naturally good, and if they are not subject to unjust social arrangements, then they will live good rather than evil lives. The assumption is the liberal faith. It is from it that it follows that those who are worst off must have been unjustly treated; that in a just society there will be little evil; that the distribution of resources should ignore moral merit because everybody would have moral merit if there were no injustice; that the appearance of moral demerit is bound to be a symptom of injustice; and that on a fundamental level everybody is equally deserving.

The liberal faith, however, is an indefensible, sentimental, and destructive falsification of reality. It makes wishful thinking into a political program. It blinds itself to the obvious fact that some people are morally better than others and that some are morally worse. It ignores the historical record that testifies to widespread wickedness. The liberal faith absurdly denies that the good deserve better than the wicked. It deflects criticism by specious moralizing that accuses critics of immorality. It arrogates to itself the moral high ground by pretending to champion the welfare of the poor, the needy, and the unfortunate, while pursuing policies that refuse to face the causes of their misery and make it impossible to improve their lot. It fosters evil and wickedness by failing to acknowledge that their prevalence is caused by human vices; that unjust institutions result from human wickedness and that they merely encourage, but do not cause, preexisting vices; and that the remedy is to create and protect institutions that limit the indiscriminate pursuit of human possibilities. It is a faith that ought not to be held.

10.5 THE PROBLEM OF PLURALISM

The problem of pluralism that liberals face is a problem for all political moralities that are committed to some short list of values as basic. Given that commitment, the question to be answered is why those particular values, whatever they may be, are regarded as basic. Either there is or there is not an answer to this question. If there is not, then the fundamental commitments of that political morality are arbitrary. If there is an answer, then it must appeal to some even more basic value or principle or decision procedure that justifies regarding the values as basic. This answer, however, would be inconsistent with pluralism because whatever it is that the required justification is based on, it would have to be regarded as having overriding value. Because pluralism is the denial of there being any overriding value, no political morality that is committed to a short list of basic values could be pluralistic.

Liberals cannot consistently appeal to some more basic overriding value and simultaneously deny that any value is overriding, as their commitment to pluralism requires them to do. Given that liberals are committed to regarding some values as basic, their commitment is either arbitrary, because it lacks justification, or it is inconsistent with their commitment to pluralism.

One of the strengths of pluralism is that it avoids this problem. It is not committed to any values as basic, and so it does not need an overriding value to justify that commitment. Pluralists can and do recognize a very long list of values that are likely to be important; they recognize that they will conflict with one another and that these conflicts must be resolved. But pluralists think that reason will dictate different resolutions in different contexts. They will not commit themselves, as liberals do, to the indefensible a priori policy of always resolving these conflicts in favor of some particular basic values. That is why if liberals were to take their commitment to pluralism seriously, they would have to eschew their other commitments, and thus cease to be liberals.

By way of avoiding these problems, liberals may concede that autonomy cannot be defended as *the* core of liberalism. This would not mean, of course, that liberals must cease to value autonomy, but only that they could no longer rely on it to provide the fundamental reason why freedom, pluralism, rights, equality, and distributive justice are to be regarded as the basic values. They may then add autonomy to these other basic values, and thus demote it by one rank from the privileged position it was previously thought to occupy. They would thereby open up the possibility that increasing autonomy need not be regarded as having priority. They could acknowledge then that the defense of the basic values, to whose list autonomy has now been added, could on occasions require curtailing autonomy. They could argue that what has priority is to create a society in which there is as much autonomy, freedom, pluralism, rights, equality, and distributive justice as possible. And they could consistently hold that working to achieve that goal may well require curtailing any one of the basic values so as to increase the chances of their joint realization.

This defense, however, faces the insuperable difficulty that if autonomy is removed from its privileged position, then liberals need a new answer to the question that they previously answered in terms of autonomy: Why regard the values liberals favor as basic? The previous answer was that they are basic because they are necessary for increasing autonomy, and increasing autonomy is necessary for living good lives. But if increasing autonomy no longer has priority, then the question stands. Why should autonomy, freedom, pluralism, rights, equality, and distributive justice be regarded as basic values? Why are prosperity, order, civility, peace, a healthy environment, security, happiness, and law-abidingness not as important for good lives as the ones liberals think of as basic? The answer can no longer appeal to the necessity of the basic liberal values for autonomy.

Some of the basic liberal values are certainly important to good lives. The same is true, however, of many other values that liberals do not regard as basic. Furthermore, thinking about values as basic commits liberals to holding that conflicts between basic liberal and nonliberal values should always be resolved in favor of the liberal ones. But why should that be? If liberals are to give an answer that is more than an arbitrary preference for liberal values, they must appeal to some consideration other than the liberal values themselves. Autonomy was put up as such a consideration, but if it is demoted to a lesser status, then liberals need, but do not have, a better candidate.

Afterword

The central aim of this book has been to criticize liberalism. In the course of the argument, however, several constructive theses have emerged: morality and politics ought to be centrally concerned with the prevalence of evil; the evil that people habitually cause reflects on them adversely, even if they cause it nonautonomously; collective responsibility may be legitimately ascribed, if certain conditions are met; moral inequality is a plain fact of life; justice is essentially connected with desert; and pluralism excludes all overriding commitments, and consequently it is incompatible with all political ideologies that have such commitments.

One implication of these constructive theses is that any acceptable political morality must recognize their truth because the failure to do so makes it impossible to protect the conditions in which members of a society can make good lives for themselves. In a sequel to the present book, these theses will be developed and linked.

The guiding idea of the sequel is that whatever is worth saving from liberalism is contained in a version of pluralism, which is the best candidate for an acceptable political morality. This version of pluralism, however, is not a form of mitigated relativism. It is committed to the protection of the conditions that good lives require regardless of how they are conceived, provided they are within the bounds of reason. As the constructive theses listed above show, these conditions are numerous, they are far from being trivial truisms, and they have substantive moral and political implications. These implications move pluralism away from liberalism, with which it is commonly and mistakenly associated, and toward conservatism, with which it is commonly and mistakenly taken to be incompatible. Contrary to these common and mistaken assumptions, the strongest version of pluralism is a form of conservatism, the strongest version of conservatism is pluralistic, and it is their combination that will be developed in the sequel. The critical arguments in this book and the constructive arguments in the future one, however, stand—or fall— independently of each other.

Notes

Chapter 1

1. "A remarkable variety of political structures has been thought by different philosophers to embody Liberty, and a correspondingly mixed company has shared the name 'liberal'. In singling out certain main streams or schools of liberal thought, one has to be mindful of the divergences that exist even among those which can be usefully grouped together" (Cranston 1967: 461). "The word 'liberalism' has been used, since the eighteenth century, to describe various distinct clusters of political positions, but with no important similarity of principle among the different clusters called 'liberal' at different times" (this is "the sceptical thesis"; R. Dworkin 1985b: 183). "Liberalism has never been a closely integrated or firmly fixed doctrine; its proponents have held to a considerable and frequently changing variety of views and its historians and critics have regularly disagreed concerning its main ideas and tendencies" (Flathman 1989: 2). "It is probably true to say that no political cause, no one vision of society nor any political principle has commanded the respect of all liberals in any generation, let alone through the centuries" (Raz 1986: 1). "Anyone trying to give a brief account of liberalism is immediately faced with an embarrassing question: are we dealing with liberalism or liberalisms? It is easy to list famous liberals; it is harder to say what they have in common" (Ryan 1993: 291). "If we examine the range of views that are classified [as liberal] . . . we are unlikely to find any set of doctrines or principles that are held in common by all of them, any single cluster of theoretical and practical propensities that might be regarded as the *core* or the *essence* of the ideology in question" (Waldron 1987: 127).

2. "At the heart of the liberal position stand two ideas . . . *pluralism* . . . and *toleration*" (Larmore 1987: 22–23). "The plurality of distinct per-

215

sons with separate systems of ends is an essential feature of . . . [liberal] societies" (Rawls 1971: 28–29). "Society, being composed of a plurality of persons, each with his own aims, interests, and conception of the good, is best arranged when it is governed by . . . the liberalism of Kant and of much contemporary moral and political philosophy" (Sandel 1982: 1). "One who experiences sympathy with a variety of conflicting ideals of life . . . will be most at home in a liberal society" (Strawson 1974b: 44). It is "itself an argument for liberal society that that society expresses more than any other does a true understanding of the plural nature of values" (Williams 1978: xviii).

3. In discussing the connection between liberalism and freedom, Flathman writes: "Freedom is a good of great value because it is necessary to the satisfaction of a great many interests and desires, the achievement of many ends and purposes. . . . Unfreedom is a serious evil because it prevents or inhibits achievements and satisfactions and produces frustration, distress, and harm" (1989: 115). According to Rawls, the first principle of a just society is that "each person is to have an equal right to the most extensive basic liberty compatible with a similar liberty for others" (1971: 60). And Raz says, "The specific contribution of the liberal tradition to political morality has always been its insistence on the respect due to individual liberty" (1986: 2).

4. As Berlin puts it: "It is important to discriminate between liberty and the conditions of its exercise. If a man is too poor or too ignorant or too feeble to make use of his legal rights, the liberty that these rights confer upon him is nothing to him. . . . The obligation to promote education, health, justice, to raise standards of living, to provide opportunity for the growth of the arts and sciences, to prevent reactionary political or social or legal policies or arbitrary inequalities, is not made less stringent because it is not necessarily directed to the promotion of liberty itself" (1969a: liii).

5. "Freedom is not the only value that can or should determine behaviour . . . the freedom of the individual or the group may not be fully compatible with . . . co-operation, solidarity, fraternity. But beyond all these there is an acuter issue: the permanent need to satisfy the claims of other, no less ultimate, values: justice, happiness, love, the realization of capacities to create new things and experiences and ideas, the discovery of the truth. . . . These ends may clash irreconcilably. When this happens, questions of choice and preference inevitably arise. . . . The simple point which I am concerned to make is that where ultimate values are irreconcilable, clear-cut solutions cannot, in principle, be found" (Berlin 1969a: lvi and xlix–l).

6. These conditions have been identified with being the recipient of

equal concern and respect (R. Dworkin 1977a), with valid claims (Feinberg 1980), with the requirements of purposive agency (Gewirth 1978), with those that enable reasonable agents to carry out their projects (Lomasky 1987), with freedom from interference (Nozick 1974), with principles of justice chosen behind the veil of ignorance (Rawls 1971), or with the imposition of a correlative duty on others to protect the individual's interests (Raz 1986). For an overall view, see Waldron 1993.

7. This may be expressed as the "most fundamental of rights is . . . the right to equal concern and respect" (R. Dworkin 1977a: xii); "human rights are . . . moral rights which all persons have simply because they are human" (Gewirth 1982: 1); "at the baseline of value in the lives of individuals, from which all higher order inequalities of value must derive, everyone counts the same" (Nagel 1991: 12); "each person is to have an equal right to the most extensive basic liberty compatible with a similar liberty for others" (Rawls 1971: 60); or the "equal worth of individual freedom and happiness" (Vlastos 1962: 52).

8. "The core of this [i.e., the liberal] tradition is an insistence that the forms of social life be rooted in the self-conscious value affirmations of autonomous individuals" (Ackerman 1980: 196). "The most important task for which autonomy has been harnessed in contemporary political philosophy is to argue for a certain ideal of the liberal state. . . . [T]he root idea is that the state must recognize and acknowledge the autonomy of person" (G. Dworkin 1993: 361). "The liberal individual is fully rational, where rationality embraces both autonomy and the capacity to choose among possible actions on the basis of one's conception of the good as determined by one's reflective preferences. . . . As an autonomous being, the liberal individual is aware of the reflective process by which her later selves emerge from her present self, so that her preferences are modified, not in a random or uncontrolled way, but in the light of her own experiences and understanding" (Gauthier 1986: 346). "One common strand in liberal thought regards the promotion and protection of personal autonomy as the core of the liberal concern" (Raz 1986: 203). "The essence [of liberalism] is that individuals are self-creating, that no single good defines successful self-creation, and that taking responsibility for one's life and making of it what one can is itself part of the good life" (Ryan 1993: 304).

9. "I am free because, and in so far as, I am autonomous. I obey laws, but I have imposed them on, or found them in, my own uncoerced self. Freedom is obedience, but 'obedience to a law which we prescribe to ourselves', and no man can enslave himself. Heteronomy is dependence on outside factors, liability to be a plaything of the external world that I cannot myself fully control" (Berlin 1969b: 136). Or, "autonomy is a sec-

ond-order capacity of persons to reflect critically upon their first-order preferences, desires, wishes, and so forth, and the capacity to accept or attempt to change these in the light of higher-order preferences" (G. Dworkin 1993: 360). Or, an autonomous individual is "one who can step back from his moral beliefs and his desires . . . and . . . test their validity by reference to an inbuilt standard, which is his own tendency to rational coherence and consistency in thinking" (Hampshire 1983: 56). Or, I am "a subject with ends he has chosen, and his fundamental preference is for conditions that enable him to frame a mode of life that expresses his nature as a free and rational being as fully as circumstances permit" (Rawls 1971: 561).

10. Action, in the first condition, and choice, in the second condition, are left unanalyzed because the complex questions that their analyses raise are irrelevant for the present purposes. For an introduction to these questions and bibliographies for following up on them, see Donagan 1992 and Goldman and Smith 1992.

11. The gap between freedom and autonomy has been the subject of much discussion in more recent times. Benn (1988) describes those who satisfy the freedom but not the judgment component of autonomy as being in a state of autarchy, while those who satisfy both components as being autonomous. Berlin (1969b) thinks of the freedom component in terms of negative freedom, that is, an agent's freedom from external interference, and of the judgment component as positive freedom, the freedom to live in accordance with one's conception of a good life. Frankfurt (1988c) distinguishes between wanton acts, which are motivated by first-order desires, and acts expressive of fuller personhood, which are motivated by the agents' second-order desires to control their first-order desires. Hampshire (1965: 93) writes of the "distinction of desires and attitudes, which are formed as the outcome of considering the appropriateness of their objects, and which remain dependent on a conviction of appropriateness, from desires and moods that are not in this sense thought-dependent." Taylor (1976) expresses the same idea in his writing about weak and strong evaluators, where the former choose whether to act to satisfy first-order desires and the latter base that choice on the evaluation of their second-order desires. (For a survey of this literature, see Macedo 1990: chap. 6.)

Chapter 2

1. Here are some illustrations among many possible ones of the general liberal tendency to minimize or ignore the significance of evil. Ronald Dworkin says that the fundamental liberal belief is that there is "a

right to equal concern and respect" (1977: xii). But he does not address the question of why serial murderers and their victims, terrorists and their hostages, or scourges and benefactors of humanity should have a right to equal concern and respect. John Rawls distinguishes between "the unjust, the bad, and the evil man." He says that "the unjust man seeks dominion for the sake of aims . . . which when appropriately limited are legitimate. The bad man desires arbitrary power because he enjoys the sense of mastery which its exercise gives him. . . . [T]he evil man aspires to unjust rule precisely because it violates what independent persons would consent to in an original position of equality" (1971: 439). But Rawls explains neither why he thinks that there are not enough of these people to vitiate his political program nor what he proposes to do about them. After giving an account of autonomy (quite similar to the one in Section 1.5) Raz says, "Throughout the preceding remarks I was assuming, of course, that it is generally agreed that an autonomous life is not . . . evil" (1986: 394). He nowhere questions or justifies this assumption.

Stuart Hampshire writes that "unmitigated evil and nastiness are as natural . . . in educated human beings as generosity and sympathy: no more, and no less. . . . [H]igh culture and good education are not significantly correlated with elementary moral decency." Given this lamentable fact, what is to to done? Hampshire's answer is that the possibility of civilized life requires the recognition that "there is a basic level of morality, a bare minimum, which is entirely negative, and without this bare minimum as a foundation no morality directed towards the greater good can be applicable and can survive in practice. A rock-bottom and preliminary morality of justice and fair dealing is needed to keep a balance between competing moralities and to support respected procedures of arbitration between them" (1989: 8). Hampshire calls this rock-bottom justice "basic procedural justice." Hampshire is clearly right about evil and the need for basic justice, but he fails to show that liberalism can provide what is needed. Why would wicked people follow basic procedural justice? If liberals aim to increase autonomy, what stops them from increasing evil? If, on the other hand, evil is to be suppressed and basic procedural justice is to be enforced, then the autonomy of wicked people must be curtailed and nonautonomously wicked people cannot be accorded freedom, rights, equal concern and respect, and equal resources. If Hampshire's diagnosis is right, liberalism must be rejected as a remedy. If, on the other hand, the commitment to liberalism is maintained, then how could the exacerbation of the problem of evil that Hampshire correctly identified be avoided?

Judith Shklar advocates what she calls "the liberalism of fear." This kind of liberalism requires "making the evil of cruelty and fear the basic

norm of its political practices and prescriptions" (1989: 30). "The liberalism of fear in fact does not rest on a theory of moral pluralism. It does
not, to be sure, offer a *summun bonum* toward which all political agents
should strive, but it certainly does begin with a *summun malum*, which all
of us know and would avoid if only we could. That evil is cruelty and the
fear its inspires" (1989: 31). Like Hampshire, Shklar is surely right about
the need to avoid the great evils of cruelty and fear of it. What she fails to
show is why those who join her in recognizing this need would be committed to liberalism. Why could there not be a conservatism or a socialism of
fear?

2. "According to this doctrine—that virtue is knowledge—when men
commit crimes they do so because they are in error: they have mistaken
what will, in fact, profit them. If they truly knew what would profit them,
they would not do these destructive things. . . . Crime, vice, imperfection,
misery, all arise from ignorance and mental indolence or muddle. . . .
'Virtue is knowledge' means that if you know the good for man, you cannot, if you are a rational being, live in any way other than that whereby
fulfilment is that towards which all desires, hopes, prayers, aspirations are
directed. . . . To distinguish reality from appearance, to distinguish that
which will truly fulfil a man from that which mearly appears to promise
to do so, that is knowledge, and that alone will save him" (Berlin 1990b:
28–29).

3. As John Rawls puts it, "Men's propensity to injustice is not a permanent aspect of community life; it is greater or less depending in large part
on social institutions, and in particular on whether they are just or unjust" (1971: 245).

4. Rawls says that the view of human nature that underlies liberalism
is "the high point of the contractarian tradition in Kant and Rousseau,"
according to which "a person is acting autonomously when the principles
of his action are chosen by him as the most adequate possible expressions
of his nature as a free and equal rational being" (1971: 252).

Chapter 3

1. Attempting to draw a similar distinction, Susan Wolf says: "When
we hold a person deeply responsible . . . we understand her to be accountable . . . in a different way from that in which other objects may be accountable. It is only in the context of this distinctive type of accountability
that the question of whether an individual *deserves* praise or blame . . .
makes sense" (1991: 43).

2. As Wolf puts it: "Responsibility depends on the ability to act in
accordance with the True and the Good. If one is psychologically deter-

mined to do the right thing for the right reason, this is compatible with having the requisite ability. . . . But if one is psychologically determined to do the wrong thing, for whatever reason, this seems to constitute a denial of that ability. . . . [B]eing psychologically determined to perform good actions is compatible with deserving praise for them, but . . . being psychologically determined to perform bad actions is not compatible with blame" (1991: 79).

3. As Kant says, "The action to which ought applies must indeed be possible under natural conditions" (1953: A548); "a rational being can rightly say of any unlawful action which he has done that he could have left it undone. . . . For this action and everything in the past which determined it belong to a single phenomenon of his character, which he himself creates" (1949: 203); and "duty demands nothing of us which we cannot do," "when the moral law commands that we *ought* now to be better men, it follows inevitably that we must be *able* to be better," and "we ought to conform to it [our disposition]; consequently we must be able to do so" (1960: 43, 46, and 55).

4. As it has been put: "There is one commitment whose ground is intimately personal and which comes before any other personal or social commitment whatsoever: the commitment to the principled mode of life as such. One is tempted to call this the supreme moral commitment" (Falk 1968: 374–75).

5. To illustrate this tendency consider "the case of the victim of a deprived childhood . . . a man who embezzled some money, fully aware of what he was doing. . . . Yet it seems he ought not to be blamed for committing his crime, for, from his point of view, one cannot reasonably expect him to see anything wrong with his action. We may suppose that in his childhood he was given no love—he was beaten by his father, neglected by his mother. And the people to whom he was exposed when he was growing up gave him examples only of evil and selfishness. From his point of view, it is natural to conclude that respecting other people's property would be foolish. For presumably no one had ever respected his. . . . In light of this, it seems that this man shouldn't be blamed for an action we know to be wrong. For if we had his childhood, we would not have know either. . . . It is because he couldn't have had reason that this agent should not be blamed" (Wolf 1981: 233).

6. As Kant put it: "Man himself must make or have made himself into whatever, in a moral sense, whether good or evil, he is or is to become. Either condition must be an effect of his free choice; for otherwise he could not be held responsible for it and could therefore be *morally* neither good nor evil" (1960: 40).

7. As a previous critic of liberalism trenchantly observed: "It is one of

the commonest beliefs of the day that the human race collectively has before it splendid destinies of various kinds, and the road to them is to be found in the removal of all restraint on human conduct, in the recognition of a substantial equality between all human creatures, and in fraternity or general love. These doctrines . . . are regarded not merely as truths, but as truths for which those who believe them are ready to do battle, and for the establishment of which they are prepared to sacrifice all merely personal ends. Such, stated in the most general terms, is the religion of which I take 'Liberty, Equality, Fraternity' to be the creed. I do not believe it" (Stephen 1993: 52–53).

Chapter 5

1. Perhaps the most fully articulated liberal accounts of equality and distributive justice are Ronald Dworkin's and John Rawls's. But Dworkin says that "I want to argue that a certain conception of equality . . . is the nerve of liberalism" (1985b: 183), while Rawls claims that "Justice is the first virtue of social institutions . . . an injustice is tolerable only when it is necessary to avoid even greater injustice" (1971: 3–4). There is a large overlap between these two positions, but their differences warrant separate treatment.

2. In this respect, there is a shared ground between consequentialist and Kantian moral theories. Henry Sidgwick says that "the good of any individual is of no more importance, from the point of view (if I may say) of the Universe, than the good of any other" (1981: 382). And Immanuel Kant voices a similar opinion, although more floridly: "Man regarded as a person . . . is exalted above any price; for as such . . . he is not to be valued as a mere means to the ends of others or even to his own ends, but as an end in himself. He possesses, in other words, a *dignity* (an absolute inner worth) by which he exacts *respect* for himself: . . . he can measure himself with every other being of the same kind and value himself on a footing of equality with them" (1964a: 99). According to these passages, substantive equality holds between individual human beings, and it holds in respect to their worth, dignity, or welfare.

3. This position is attributable to Sidgwick. He was quoted above as saying that "the good of any individual is of no more importance, from the point of view (if I may say) of the Universe, than the good of any other." He then goes on: "unless, that is, there are special grounds for believing that more good is likely to be realized in the one case than in the other" (1981: 382). If the good is taken to be equality, then Sidgwick's claim is that unequal treatment is justifiable if it promotes equality.

4. Ronald Dworkin says, for instance, that "the right to treatment as

an equal is fundamental, and the right to equal treatment derivative. In some circumstances the right to treatment as an equal will entail a right to equal treatment, but not, by any means, in all circumstances" (1977c: 227). And also that "We must distinguish between two different principles that take equality to be a political ideal. The first requires that the government treat all those in its charge *as equals*, that is, as entitled to equal concern and respect. . . . The second principle requires that the government treat all those in its charge *equally* in its distribution of resources. . . . Sometimes treating people equally is the only way to treat them as equals, but sometimes not" (1985b: 190).

5. Some of these people are John Charvet (1981), Flew (1981), Harry Frankfurt (1988b), Friedrich Hayek (1960), Kekes (1988), J. R. Lucas (1965, 1967), Alasdair MacIntryre (1988), Wallace Matson (1983), Margaret Moore (1993), Louis Pojman (1991), and Joseph Raz (1986).

6. There are some egalitarians who themselves reject what they call "the complete life view," which this proposal favors. See, e.g., McKerlie 1989, 1992; and Temkin 1993. Their position escapes this objection, but remains vulnerable to the other.

7. R. Dworkin says that human beings' "highest order interest . . . lies in having as good a life as possible. . . . Almost everyone acts as if he or she had that interest" (1983: 26), and infers from this, not that everyone's highest-order interest matters, and matters equally, but that "the interests of the members of the community matter, and matter equally" (24). He slides from the universal claim to the particular without justification.

Kymlicka writes that "the idea that each person matters equally is at the heart of all plausible political theories" (1990: 5), and he, like R. Dworkin, takes this to mean that "the interests of each member of the community matter, and matter equally" (4). But he, again like R. Dworkin, does not explain why egalitarianism is restricted to members of a community, if the interests of all human beings matter equally.

Bruce Landesman claims that "egalitarianism . . . has as its ideal a condition of equal well-being for all persons at the highest possible level" and then adds, "Egalitarianism holds that society should be arranged so as to promote and maintain this state" (1983: 27). Once again, the universal claim is restricted to the context of a particular society.

Rawls acknowledges that "the distinction between a political conception of justice and comprehensive philosophical doctrine is not discussed in *Theory*, once this question is raised, it is clear, I think, that the text regards justice as fairness . . . as comprehensive" (1993: xvi). This "is unrealistic," and in *Political Liberalism*, "justice as fairness is presented from the outset as a political conception of justice" (xvii). The difficulty this raises is that, although the conception of justice is now restricted to "a reasonably harmonious and stable pluralist society" (xxv), the arguments for it continue to place the hypothetical contractors in the original position where they allegedly opt for egalitarian principles on the basis of considerations that do not derive from the political conditions of their particular society, but from universal features that human beings are said to have as rational and self-interested agents. Rawls thus acknowledges the unwarranted slide from the universal to the particular, but still fails to make it warranted.

Finally, Bernard Williams begins by exploring the implications of the idea of "equality of men as men" (1973b: 232), but he ends by speaking about equality in "an economically developed and dynamic society, in which certain skills and talents are necessarily at a premium" (248). He does not say why the "equality of men as men," universal equality, should be discussed in the context of a particular type of society.

Chapter 6

1. As Rawls puts it, "The primary subject of justice [is] the basic structure of society," and "Justice is the first virtue of social institutions . . . laws and institutions . . . must be reformed or abolished if they are unjust" (1971: 3).

2. This basic moral belief may be formulated in a number of different ways. One is the idea of moral equilibrium. "The aim of morality is to prevent the upsetting of the moral equilibrium. . . . Primary rules define what it is . . . to preserve the moral equilibrium. Secondary rules indicate what is to be done by whom when the balance has been upset. . . . [T]hey are determined by the concept of desert, of positive and negative moral merit" (K. Baier 1958: 130; the sentence order of the original has been reversed). Another is the idea of reciprocity. "Generally stated, reciprocity is the practice of making a fitting and proportional return of like for like—good for good and evil for evil. . . . [I]n one form or another, reciprocity is a social norm in every society of record" (Becker 1992b: 1075–76). Yet another is the idea of divine justice. "When we speak of the world as justly governed by God, we seem to mean that, if we could know the whole of human existence, we should find that happiness is distributed among men according to their deserts. And Divine Justice is thought to be a pattern which Human Justice is to imitate as far as the conditions of human society allow" (Sidgwick 1981: 280).

3. They will do so, according to Rawls, for several reasons. First, "not only do the parties protect their basic rights but they insure themselves against the worst eventualities" (176). Their basic rights will be protected by the first principle; and if they happen to be among the least-advan-

taged members of the society, then the second principle will assure that the improvement of their situation will take precedence over any other possible improvement. Second, if "the two principles are satisfied, each person's liberties are secured and there is a sense defined by the difference principle in which everyone is benefited by social cooperation. Therefore we can explain the acceptance of the social system and the principles it satisfies by the psychological law that persons tend to love, cherish, and support whatever affirms their own good. Since everyone's good is affirmed, all acquire inclinations to uphold the scheme" (177). Third, "the public recognition of the two principles . . . support[s] men's self-respect and this in turn increases the effectiveness of social cooperation. . . . [T]he two principles achieve this end. For when societies follow these principles, everyone's good is included in the scheme of mutual benefit and the public affirmation in institutions of each man's endeavors supports men's self-esteem. The two principles are equivalent . . . to an understanding to regard the distribution of natural abilities as collective assets so that the more fortunate are to benefit only in ways that help those who have lost out. . . . [B]y arranging inequalities for reciprocal advantage . . . persons express their respect for one another in the very constitution of their society" (178–79).

Chapter 7

1. Rawls says "that the effort a person is willing to make is influenced by his natural abilities and skills and alternatives open to him. The better endowed are more likely, other things equal, to strive conscientiously, and there seems to be no way to discount for their greater good fortune" (1971: 311–17).

2. "In the original position the parties agree to be held responsible. . . . The essential point . . . is that the principles that best conform to our nature as free and equal rational beings themselves establish our accountability. Otherwise autonomy is likely to lead to a mere collision of self-righteous wills" (1971: 519).

3. According to Rawls, "Each person possesses an inviolability founded on justice . . . the rights secured by justice are not subject to political bargaining or to the calculus of social interests" (1971: 3–4).

4. "A conception of right is a set of principles," writes Rawls, "general in form and universal in application, that is to be publicly recognized as a final court of appeal for ordering the conflicting claims of moral persons" (1971: 135).

5. Rawls says that "the inevitable deviations from justice are effectively corrected or held within tolerable bounds by forces within the system" (1971: 458).

6. As Rawls puts it: "no one deserves his place in the distribution of natural assets any more than he deserves his initial starting place in society" (1971: 311); that "inequalities of birth and natural endowments are undeserved" (100); and that "natural assets and the contingencies of their growth . . . are arbitrary from a moral point of view" (311).

7. The only particular facts which the parties know is that their society is subject to the circumstances of justice and whatever this implies. . . . [T]hey know the general facts about human society. They understand political affairs and the principles of economic theory; they know the basis of social organization and the laws of human psychology. Indeed, the parties are presumed to know whatever general facts affect the choice of the principles of justice" (Rawls 1971: 137).

8. Rawls identifies the commonsense view of justice, which he rejects, as holding that "the good things in life . . . should be distributed according to desert," which he takes to mean that "justice is happiness according to virtue" (1971: 310). He argues against distribution based on desert by equating it with "distribution according to virtue" (311); by claiming that "none of the precepts of justice aims at rewarding virtue" (311); and by asserting that the "criterion to each according to his virtue would not . . . be chosen in the original position" (313).

9. As Rawls puts it: "The original position may be viewed . . . as a procedural interpretation of Kant's conception of autonomy and the categorical imperative. The principles regulative of the kingdom of ends are those that would be chosen in this position" (1971: 256).

10. "Men's propensity to injustice . . . is greater or less depending in large part on social institutions, and in particular on whether they are just or unjust" (Rawls 1971: 245).

11. Rawls says that those who have the capacity to act autonomously have a "moral personality": "Moral persons . . . are capable of having . . . a conception of their good . . . and . . . a sense of justice, a normally effective desire to apply and act upon the principles of justice. . . . [T]he capacity for moral personality is a sufficient condition for being entitled to equal justice. . . . [I]t is possessed by the overwhelming majority of mankind" (1971: 505–6). Although "individuals presumably have varying capacities for a sense of justice . . . provided the minimum for moral personality is satisfied, a person is owed all the guarantees of justice" (506–7). "Those who can give justice are owed justice" (510).

Chapter 8

1. David Lloyd Thomas provides an admirably clear statement of this problem: "Liberals attempt to justify a framework of legal and social re-

quirements within which many styles of life and conceptions of what is worth while may be pursued. Liberals wish to present this as a 'neutral' framework, not biased against any particular conception of what is worth while. But they also want to say that it is, in some clear sense, the *best* framework to have: frameworks which are non-liberal are also worse ones. The dilemma for liberals is to explain how both of these claims can be true" (1988: 1).

2. The novelty of pluralism does not, of course, preclude historical anticipations; various passages in the works of Aristotle (1984b, 1984d), Michel de Montaigne (1980), David Hume (1960, 1961), John Stuart Mill (1978), William James (1987b), and Max Weber (1946) readily lend themselves to a pluralistic interpretation.

3. These writers include Annette Baier (1985a), Richard Brandt (1979), Ronald Dworkin (1977a, 1985a), Owen Flanagan (1991), John Gray (1993a), Stuart Hampshire (1983, 1989), Charles Larmore (1987), Steven Lukes (1991), Thomas Nagel (1979b, 1991), David Norton (1976), Martha Nussbaum (1986), Edmund Pincoffs (1986), John Rawls (1971, 1993), Joseph Raz (1986), Nicholas Rescher (1993), Richard Rorty (1982, 1989), Judith Shklar (1984, 1989), Michael Stocker (1990), Peter Strawson (1974), Charles Taylor (1985a, 1989), Michael Walzer (1983), and Bernard Williams (1981, 1985).

4. At the beginning of a recent article, Bruce Ackerman says, "If America cannot confront the problem of pluralism, it is finished as a nation." Part of his recommendation is to maintain "a principled reluctance to embed political commitments in any single comprehensive philosophy of life." And he closes by reciting the liberal faith that "political liberalism remains humanity's best hope in a world where cultural diversity is not only a fact of life, but a joy of living" (1994: 365 and 386). Isaiah Berlin writes: "Pluralism . . . seems to me a truer and more humane ideal than the goals of those who seek . . . great, disciplined, authoritarian structures. . . . It is truer, because it . . . recognize[s] the fact that human goals are many, not all of them commensurable, and in perpetual rivalry with one another" (1969b: 131). Larmore holds, "At the heart of the liberal position stand two ideas . . . *pluralism* . . . and *toleration*" (1987: 22–23). Nagel asserts that "I do not believe that the source of values is unitary—displaying multiplicity only in its application to the world. I believe that value has fundamentally different kinds of sources, and that they are reflected in the classification of values into types. Not all values represent the pursuit of some single good in a variety of settings" (1979b: 131–32). Rawls claims that it must be assumed that "the plurality of distinct persons with separate systems of ends is an essential feature of human societies" (1971: 29), and he reaffirms this claim: "The diversity

of reasonable comprehensive religious, philosophical, and moral doctrines found in modern democratic societies is not a mere historical condition that may soon pass away; it is a permanent feature of the public
culture of democracy. Under the political and social conditions secured
by the basic rights and liberties of free institutions, a diversity of conflicting and irreconcilable—and what's more, reasonable—comprehensive
doctrines will come about and persist," and this "fact of pluralism is not
an unfortunate condition of human life" (1993: 36–37). Raz says of the
"doctrine of political freedom" (1986: 400), which he defends and which
he takes to be the core of liberalism that it "is based on the values of
pluralism and autonomy" (1–2). Michael Sandel characterizes the central
claim of liberalism as "society being composed of a plurality of persons,
each with his own aims, interests, and conception of good, is best arranged when it is governed by . . . the liberalism of Kant and of much
contemporary moral and political philosophy" (1982: 1). Strawson thinks
of "a liberal society . . . [as one] in which there are variant moral environ-
ments but in which no ideal endeavours to engross, and determine the
character of, the common morality. . . . [Its advocate] will not argue in
favour of such a society that it gives the best chance for the truth about
life to prevail, for he will not consistently believe that there is such a thing
as the truth about life. . . . He will welcome the ethical diversity which the
society makes possible, and he . . . will [be] the natural . . . enemy of all
those whose single intense vision of the ends of life drives them to try to
make the requirements of the ideal coextensive with those of common
social morality" (1974b: 44). And, finally, Williams writes with approval
in his characterization of Berlin's thought that it is "itself an argument
for the liberal society that that society expresses more than any other does
a true understanding of the plural nature of values. . . . [O]ne who properly recognizes the plurality of values is one who understands the deep
creative role that these values can play in human life. In that perspective,
the correctness of the liberal consciousness is better expressed . . . round
the recognition that these different values do each have a real and intelligible significance, and are not just errors, misdirections or poor expressions of human nature" (1978: xviii).

5. Berlin thinks that for "the liberal tradition . . . only rights can be
regarded as absolute . . . and . . . there are frontiers, not artificially drawn,
within which men should be inviolable" (1969b: 165). R. Dworkin says
that for a "liberal . . . rights will function as trump cards held by individuals; they will enable individuals to resist particular decisions in spite of the
fact that these decisions are or would be reached through the normal
workings of general institutions that are not themselves challenged. The
ultimate justification for these rights is that they are necessary to protect

equal concern and respect" (1985b: 198). Nozick opens his book with the announcement: "Individuals have rights, and there are things no person or group may do to them (without violating their rights). . . . [T]he state may not use its coercive apparatus for the purpose of getting some citizens to aid others, or in order to prohibit activities to people for their *own* protection" (1974: ix). Rawls begins with a similarly ringing declaration: "Justice is the first virtue of social institutions. . . . Each person possesses an inviolability founded on justice that even the welfare of society as a whole cannot override. . . . [I]n a just society the liberties of equal citizenship are taken as settled; the rights secured by justice are not subject to political bargaining. . . . [I]njustice is tolerable only when it is necessary to avoid an even greater injustice. Being [a] first virtue . . . justice . . . [is] uncompromising" (1971: 3–4). Raz says that the "specific contribution of the liberal tradition . . . has always been its insistence on the respect due to individual liberty. . . . Indeed the argument of this book will demonstrate how far-reaching are the implications of political liberty, how they affect our conception of justice, equality, prosperity and other political ideals" (1986: 2).

6. Larmore provides a clear expression of this response: "In modern times we have come to recognize a multiplicity of ways in which a fulfilled life can be lived, without any perceptible hierarchy among them. And we have also been forced to acknowledge that even where we do believe that we have discerned the superiority of some ways of life to others, reasonable people may often not share our view. Pluralism and reasonable disagreement have become for modern thought ineliminable features of the idea of the good life. Political liberalism has been the doctrine that consequently the state should be neutral. The state should not seek to promote any particular conception of the good life. . . . [T]he neutrality of the liberal state . . . is not meant to be one of *outcome*, but rather one of *procedure*. That is, political neutrality consists in a constraint on what factors can be invoked to justify a political decision. Such a decision can count as neutral only if it can be justified without appealing to the presumed intrinsic superiority of any particular conception of the good life" (1987: 43–44).

7. "Primary goods . . . are things which it is supposed a rational man wants whatever else he wants. Regardless of what an individual's rational plans are in detail, it is assumed that there are various things which he would prefer more of rather than less. With more of these goods men can generally be assured greater success in carrying out their intentions and advancing their ends, whatever these ends may be. The primary goods, to give them in broad categories, are rights and liberties, opportunities and powers, income and wealth" (Rawls 1971: 92).

8. As Larmore puts it: "For the liberal, neutrality is a *political* ideal. The state's policies and decisions must be neutrally justifiable, but the liberal does not require that other institutions in society operate in the same spirit. . . . [N]eutrality as a political ideal governs the *public* relations between persons and the state, and not the *private* relations between persons and other institutions" (1987: 45).

9. "Political liberalism represents a response to moral pluralism, to a world in which there is systematic disagreement about the ends and significance of human life. Political liberals seek to forge political community by discovering norms and values that all can accept, and that can be used to regulate our common affairs. These commonalities can be found, if at all, through a strategy of political discourse, in which we attempt to "bracket" our differences by abstracting from our particular identities and ends" (Moon 1993: 219). Moon's specific contribution is that his version of liberalism "recognizes the contingency of its own constructions. . . . It recognizes that our shared principles may come into conflict with values that are not shared, and that the former may not always carry greater weight than the latter. Any formulation of common principles . . . may disadvantage or even silence certain voices, denying them the means to articulate their own needs and experience" (219–20). The remedy is to interpret political liberalism on "a model of generalized discourse which protects the integrity of the participants . . . [and] opens itself to criticism of its own presuppositions and assumptions" (97).

Chapter 9

1. " 'Deontological liberalism' . . . is indebted to Kant for much of its philosophical foundation. . . . Its core thesis may be stated as follows: society, being composed of a plurality of persons, each with his own aims, interests, and conceptions of the good, is best arranged when it is governed by principles that do not *themselves* presuppose any particular conception of the good; what justifies these regulative principles above all is not that they maximize the social welfare or otherwise promote the good, but rather that they conform to the concept of *right*, a moral category given prior to the good and independent of it. This is the liberalism of Kant and of much contemporary moral and political philosophy" (Sandel 1982: 1).

2. "I am of the opinion," writes Hume, "that tho' it be rare to meet one, who loves any single person better than himself; yet 'tis rare to meet with one, in whom all the kind affections, taken together, do not overbalance all the selfish" (1960: 487). "No man," according to Hume, "is absolutely indifferent to the happiness and misery of others. The first has a

natural tendency to give pleasure; the second pain. This every one finds in himself (1961: 219–20). Hume concedes that "our strongest attention is confin'd to ourselves; our next is extended to our relatives and acquaintances; and 'tis only the weakest which reaches to strangers and indifferent persons." But "nature provides a remedy in the judgment and understanding, for what is irregular and incommodious in the affections. . . . [T]he passions are restrained in their partial and contradictory motions. . . . Instead of departing from our interest, or from that of our nearest friends . . . we cannot better consult both these interests than by . . . maintain[ing] society, which is so necessary to their well-being . . . as well as to our own" (1960: 488–89).

3. The relevant Christian text is the second of the two "great commandments" on which "hang all the law and the prophets": "Thou shalt love thy neighbor as thyself" (Matt. 22:37–40). Kierkegaard, writing in the dominant exegetical tradition, interprets this as "your neighbour is every man. . . . He is your neighbour on the basis of equality before God: but this equality absolutely every man has, and he has it absolutely" (1962: 2). The secular version, in Henry Sidgwick's words, is: "Utilitarianism is sometimes said to resolve all virtues into universal and impartial Benevolence . . . we should aim at Happiness generally as our ultimate end, and so consider the happiness of any one individual as equally important with the happiness of any other" (1981: 241).

4. A representative expression of this view is that "the 'general object' of morality . . . is to contribute to the betterment . . . of the human predicament, primarily and essentially by seeking to countervail 'limited sympathies' and their potentially most damaging effects" (Warnock 1971: 26).

5. As Smart puts it: "The utilitarian must appeal to some ultimate attitudes. . . . The sentiment to which he appeals is generalized benevolence, that is, the disposition to seek happiness, or at any rate, in some sense or another, good consequences, for all mankind" (Smart and Williams 1973: 7).

6. Hallie says "that any understanding of cruelty should leave out the phrase 'intention to hurt'—the intention may not be there, but the maiming may be as substantial as if it were there. In this book, which emphasizes the victim, the main thing is that the maiming is done, not the accident of whether the person who does the maiming is doing it for the sake of maiming itself. Cruelty is for us the infliction of ruin, whatever the 'motives' " (1969: 14). He repeats the same point over twenty years later: "Cruelty is the activity of hurting sentient beings" (1992: 229), and he makes no mention of the state of mind of the agent.

Works Cited

Ackerman, Bruce A. (1980). *Social Justice and the Liberal State*. New Haven: Yale University Press.

———. (1994). "Political Liberalism." *Journal of Philosophy* 91: 364–86.

Arendt, Hannah. (1964). *Eichmann in Jerusalem: A Report on the Banality of Evil*. New York: Viking.

Aristotle. (1984a). *The Complete Works of Aristotle*. Jonathan Barnes. Princeton: Princeton University Press.

———. (1984b). *Nicomachean Ethics*. Trans. W. D. Ross. In Aristotle 1984a.

———. (1984c). *Rhetoric*. Trans. W. Rhys Roberts. In Aristotle 1984a.

———. (1984d). *Politics*. Trans. Benjamin Jowett. In Aristotle 1984a.

Arneson, Richard J. (1993). "Equality." In Goodin and Pettit 1993.

Baier, Annette. (1985a). *Postures of Mind*. Minneapolis: University of Minnesota Press.

———. (1985b). "Secular Faith." In A. Baier 1985a.

———. (1993). "Moralism and Cruelty." *Ethics* 103: 436–57.

Baier, Kurt. (1958). *The Moral Point of View*. Ithaca: Cornell University Press.

Barry, Brian. (1973). *The Liberal Theory of Justice*. Oxford: Clarendon.

Becker, Lawrence E., ed. (1992a). *Encyclopedia of Ethics*. 2 vols. New York: Garland.

———. (1992b). "Reciprocity." In Becker 1992a: 2:1075–78.

Beiner, Ronald. (1992). *What's the Matter with Liberalism?* Berkeley: University of California Press.

Beitz, Charles R. (1979). *Political Theory and International Relations*. Princeton: Princeton University Press.

Benn, Stanley I. (1985). "Wickedness." *Ethics* 95: 795–810.

———. (1988). *A Theory of Freedom*. Cambridge: Cambridge University Press.

Bennett, Jonathan. (1980). "Accountability." In Van Straaten 1980.

Berlin, Isaiah. (1969a). *Four Essays on Liberty*. Oxford: Oxford University Press.

———. (1969b). "Two Concepts of Liberty." In Berlin 1969a.

———. (1969c). "John Stuart Mill and the Ends of Life." In Berlin 1969a.

———. (1978a). *Concepts and Categories*. Ed. Henry Hardy. London: Hogarth.

———. (1978b). "Equality." In Berlin 1978a.

———. (1990a). *The Crooked Timber of Humanity*. Ed. Henry Hardy. London: Murray.

———. (1990b). "The Decline of Utopian Ideas in the West." In Berlin 1990a.

233

Brandt, Richard B. (1976). "The Psychology of Benevolence and Its Implications for Philosophy." *Journal of Philosophy* 73: 429–53.
———. (1979). *A Theory of the Right and the Good.* Oxford: Clarendon.
———, ed. (1962). *Social Justice.* Englewood Cliffs, N.J.: Prentice-Hall.
Brown, James. (1977). "Moral Theory and the Ought-Can Principle." *Mind* 86: 206–23.
Buruma, Ian. (1994). *The Wages of Guilt.* New York: Farrar Strauss Giroux.
Charvet, John. (1981). *A Critique of Freedom and Equality.* Cambridge: Cambridge University Press.
Christman, John, ed. (1989). *The Inner Citadel.* New York: Oxford University Press.
Cranston, Maurice. (1967). "Liberalism." In Edwards 1967: 4:458–61.
Daniels, Norman, ed. (1975). *Reading Rawls.* Oxford: Blackwell.
Donagan, Alan. (1992). "Deliberation and Choice." In Becker 1992a: 1:245–48.
Dworkin, Gerald. (1988a). *The Theory and Practice of Autonomy.* Cambridge: Cambridge University Press.
———. (1988b). "The Concept of Autonomy." In G. Dworkin 1988a.
———. (1988c). "The Value of Autonomy." In G. Dworkin 1988a.
———. (1993). "Autonomy." In Goodin and Pettit 1993.
Dworkin, Ronald. (1977a). *Taking Rights Seriously.* Cambridge: Harvard University Press.
———. (1977b). "Rights and Justice." In R. Dworkin 1977a.
———. (1977c). "Reverse Discrimination." In R. Dworkin 1977a.
———. (1983). "In Defense of Equality." *Social Philosophy and Policy* 1: 24–40.
———. (1985a). *A Matter of Principle.* Cambridge: Harvard University Press.
———. (1985b). "Liberalism." In R. Dworkin 1985a.
———. (1985c). "Why Liberals Should Care about Equality" In R. Dworkin 1985a.
Edwards, Paul, ed. (1967). *The Encyclopedia of Philosophy.* Vol. 1–8. New York: Macmillan.
Falk, W. David. (1968). "Morality, Self, and Others." In Thomson and G. Dworkin 1968.
Feinberg, Joel. (1963). "Justice and Personal Desert." In Friedrich 1963: 69–97.
———. (1970a). *Doing and Deserving.* Princeton: Princeton University Press.
———. (1970b). "Collective Responsibility." In Feinberg 1970a.
———. (1973). *Social Philosophy.* Englewood Cliffs, N.J.: Prentice-Hall.
———. (1980). *Rights, Justice, and the Bounds of Liberty.* Princeton: Princeton University Press.
Fischer, John Martin, ed. (1986). *Moral Responsibility.* Ithaca: Cornell University Press.
———. (1987). "Responsiveness and Moral Responsibility." In Schoeman 1987.
Flanagan, Owen. (1991). *Varieties of Moral Personality.* Cambridge: Harvard University Press.
Flathman, Richard E. (1989). *Toward a Liberalism.* Ithaca: Cornell University Press.
———. (1992). "Liberalism." In Becker 1992a: 2:698–702.
Flew, Antony. (1981). *The Politics of Procrustes.* Buffalo: Prometheus Books.
Frankfurt, Harry G. (1988a). *The Importance of What We Care About.* Cambridge: Cambridge University Press.
———. (1988b). "Equality as a Moral Ideal." In Frankfurt 1988a.
———. (1988c). "Freedom of the Will and the Concept of a Person." In Frankfurt 1988a.

Friedrich, Carl J., and John W. Chapman, eds. (1963). *Nomos VI: Justice*. New York: Atherton Press.

Gallie, William B. (1964). *Philosophy and the Historical Understanding*. London: Chatto and Windus.

Galston, William A. (1980). *Justice and the Human Good*. Chicago: University of Chicago Press.

———. (1991). *Liberal Purposes*. Cambridge: Cambridge University Press.

Gauthier, David. (1986). *Morals by Agreement*. Oxford: Clarendon.

Gewirth, Alan. (1978). *Reason and Morality*. Chicago: University of Chicago Press.

———. (1982). *Human Rights*. Chicago: University of Chicago Press.

Goldman, Alvin, and Holly Smith. (1992). "Action." In Becker 1992a: 1:12–14.

Goodin, Robert E., and Phillip Pettit, eds. (1993). *A Companion to Contemporary Political Philosophy*. Oxford: Blackwell.

Gowans, Christopher, ed. (1987). *Moral Dilemmas*. New York: Oxford University Press.

———. (1994). *Innocence Lost*. New York: Oxford University Press.

Gray, John. (1989). *Liberalisms*. London: Routledge.

———. (1983). *Mill on Liberty: A Defence*. London: Routledge.

———. (1993a). *Post-Liberalism*. London: Routledge.

———. (1993b). "What Is Dead and What Is Living in Liberalism?" In Gray 1993a.

———. (1995). "Agonistic Liberalism." *Social Philosophy and Policy* 12: 111–35.

Greenspan, Patricia. (1987). "Unfreedom and Responsibility." In Schoeman 1987.

Habermas, Jürgen. (1984 and 1987). *The Theory of Communicative Action*. 2 vols. Trans. Thomas McCarthy. Boston: Beacon.

Hallie, Philip P. (1969). *The Paradox of Cruelty*. Middleton: Wesleyan University Press.

———. (1992). "Cruelty." In Becker 1992a: 1:229–31.

Hampshire, Stuart. (1965). *Freedom of the Individual*. New York: Harper and Row.

———. (1983). *Morality and Conflict*. Cambridge: Harvard University Press.

———. (1989). *Innocence and Experience*. Cambridge: Harvard University Press.

Hart, Herbert L. A. (1961). *The Concept of Law*. Oxford: Clarendon.

———. (1968a). *Punishment and Responsibility*. Oxford: Oxford University Press.

———. (1968b). "Negligence, *Mens Rea*, and Criminal Responsibility." In Hart 1968a.

Haworth, Lawrence. (1986). *Autonomy*. New Haven: Yale University Press.

Hayek, Friedrich A. (1960). *The Constitution of Liberty*. Chicago: University of Chicago Press.

Hegel, Georg Wilhelm Friedrich. (1953). *Reason in History*. Trans. Robert S. Hartman. New York: Liberal Arts Press.

Hofstadter, Albert. (1973). *Reflections on Evil*. Lawrence: University Press of Kansas.

Hume, David. (1960). *A Treatise of Human Nature*. Ed. L. A. Selby-Bigge. Oxford: Clarendon.

———. (1961). *An Enquiry concerning the Principles of Morals*. Ed. L. A. Selby-Bigge. Oxford: Clarendon.

———. (1985). *Essays Moral, Political, and Literary*. Indianapolis: Liberty Press.

Irwin, Terence. (1977). *Plato's Moral Theory*. Oxford: Clarendon.

James, William. (1987a). *William James: Writings, 1902–1910*. New York: Library of America.

———. (1987b). *A Pluralistic Universe*. In James 1987a.

Jedlicki, Jerzy. (1990). "Heritage and Collective Responsibility." In Maclean 1990.

Kant, Immanuel. (1949). *Critique of Practical Reason*. Trans. Lewis White Beck. Chicago: University of Chicago Press.

———. (1953). *Critique of Pure Reason*. Trans. Norman Kemp Smith. London: Macmillan.

———. (1960). *Religion within the Limits of Reason Alone*. Trans. Theodore M. Greene and Hoyt H. Hudson. New York: Harper and Row.

———. (1964). *Groundwork of the Metaphysics of Morals*. Trans. Herbert James Paton. New York: Harper and Row.

———. (1983). *Metaphysical Principles of Virtue*. Trans. James W. Ellington. In Kant, *Ethical Philosophy*. Indianapolis: Hackett.

Kekes, John. (1984). " 'Ought Implies Can' and Two Kinds of Morality." *Philosophical Quarterly* 34: 459–67.

———. (1988). "Human Worth and Moral Merit." *Public Affairs Quarterly* 2: 53–68.

———. (1989). *Moral Tradition and Individuality*. Princeton: Princeton University Press.

———. (1990). *Facing Evil*. Princeton: Princeton University Press.

———. (1993). *The Morality of Pluralism*. Princeton: Princeton University Press.

Keynes, John Maynard. (1949). *Two Memoirs*. New York: Augustus M. Kelley.

Kierkegaard, Sören. (1962). *Works of Love*. Trans. H. Hong and E. Hong. New York: Harper.

Kipling, Rudyard. (1990). "The Gods of the Copybook Headings." In *Rudyard Kipling: The Complete Verse*. Ed. M. M. Kaye. London: Kyle Cathie.

Korsgaard, Christine M. (1992). "John Rawls." In Becker 1992a: 2:1070–75.

Kukathas, Chandran. (1993). "Liberty." In Goodin and Pettit 1993.

Kymlicka, Will. (1989). *Liberalism, Community, and Culture*. Oxford: Clarendon.

———. (1990). *Contemporary Political Philosophy*. Oxford: Clarendon.

Landesman, Bruce. (1983). "Egalitarianism." *Canadian Journal of Philosophy* 13: 27–56.

Larmore, Charles E. (1987). *Patterns of Moral Complexity*. Cambridge: Cambridge University Press.

Lloyd Thomas, David A. (1988). *In Defense of Liberalism*. Oxford: Blackwell.

Lomasky, Loren E. (1987). *Persons, Rights, and the Moral Community*. Oxford: Oxford University Press.

Lucas, J. R. (1965). "Against Equality." *Philosophy* 40: 296–307.

———. (1967). "Against Equality Again." *Philosophy* 42: 255–80.

Lukes, Steven. (1991). *Moral Conflicts and Politics*. Oxford: Clarendon.

Macedo, Steven. (1990). *Liberal Virtues*. Oxford: Clarendon.

Machan, Tibor, ed. (1974). *The Libertarian Alternative*. Chicago: Nelson-Hall.

MacIntyre, Alasdair. (1984). *After Virtue*. Notre Dame: University of Notre Dame Press.

———. (1988). *Whose Justice? Which Rationality?* Notre Dame: University of Notre Dame Press.

Mackie, John. (1980). *Hume's Moral Theory*. London: Routledge.

Maclean, Ian, ed. (1990). *The Political Responsibility of Intellectuals*. Cambridge: Cambridge University Press.

Matson, Wallace. (1978). "What Rawls Calls Justice." *Occasional Review* 89: 45–57.

———. (1983). "Justice: A Funeral Oration." *Social Philosophy and Policy* 1: 94–113.

May, Larry, and Stacey Hoffman, eds. (1991). *Collective Responsibility.* Savage, Md.: Rowman and Littlefield.

McKerlie, Dennis. (1989). "Equality and Time." *Ethics* 99: 475–91.

———. (1992). "Equality between Age-Groups." *Philosophy and Public Affairs* 21: 275–95.

McMurrin, Sterling M., ed. (1988). *The Tanner Lecture on Human Values.* Vol. 8. Salt Lake City: University of Utah Press.

Mill, John Stuart. (1978). *On Liberty.* Indianapolis: Hackett.

———. (1979). *Utilitarianism.* Indianapolis: Hackett.

Miller, David. (1976). *Social Justice.* Oxford: Clarendon.

Milo, Ronald D. (1984). *Immorality.* Princeton: Princeton University Press.

Montaigne, Michel de. (1980). *The Complete Works of Montaigne.* Trans. Donald M. Frame. Stanford: Stanford University Press.

Moon, J. Donald. (1993). *Constructing Community: Moral Pluralism and Tragic Conflicts.* Princeton: Princeton University Press.

Moore, Margaret. (1993). *Foundations of Liberalism.* Oxford: Clarendon.

Nagel, Thomas. (1979a). *Mortal Questions.* Cambridge: Cambridge University Press.

———. (1979b). "Equality." In Nagel 1979a.

———. (1991). *Equality and Partiality.* New York: Oxford University Press.

Narveson, Jan. (1988). *The Libertarian Idea.* Philadelphia: Temple University Press.

Nielsen, Kai. (1985). *Equality and Liberty.* Totowa, N.J.: Rowman and Allanheld.

Nietzsche, Friedrich. (1966a). *Basic Writings of Nietzsche.* Trans. and ed. Walter Kaufmann. New York: Modern Library.

———. (1966b). *On the Genealogy of Morals.* In Nietzsche 1966a.

———. (1974). *The Gay Science.* Trans. Walter Kaufmann. New York: Vintage.

Norton, David L. (1976). *Personal Destinies.* Princeton: Princeton University Press.

Nozick, Robert. (1974). *Anarchy, State, and Utopia.* New York: Basic.

Nussbaum, Martha. (1986). *The Fragility of Goodness.* Cambridge: Cambridge University Press.

Oakeshott, Michael. (1962). *Rationalism in Politics.* London: Methuen.

———. (1975). *On Human Conduct.* Oxford: Clarendon.

Pincoffs, Edmund L. (1986). *Quandaries and Virtues.* Lawrence: University Press of Kansas.

Plato. (1993). *The Republic.* Trans. Robin Waterfield. Oxford: Oxford University Press.

Pogge, Thomas W. (1989). *Realizing Rawls.* Ithaca: Cornell University Press.

Pojman, Louis P. (1991). "A Critique of Contemporary Egalitarianism." *Faith and Philosophy* 8: 481–504.

Rawls, John. (1971). *A Theory of Justice.* Cambridge: Harvard University Press.

———. (1993). *Political Liberalism.* New York: Columbia University Press.

Raz, Joseph. (1986). *The Morality of Freedom.* Oxford: Clarendon.

Rescher, Nicholas. (1987). *Ethical Idealism.* Berkeley: University of California Press.

———. (1993). *Pluralism.* Oxford: Clarendon.

Roberts, T. A. (1973). *The Concept of Benevolence.* London: Macmillan.

Rorty, Amelie, ed. (1976). *The Identities of Persons.* Berkeley: University of California Press.

Rorty, Richard. (1982). *Consequences of Pragmatism.* Minneapolis: University of Minnesota Press.

————. (1989). *Contingency, Irony, and Solidarity.* Cambridge: Cambridge University Press.

Rosenblum, Nancy L., ed. (1989). *Liberalism and the Moral Life.* Cambridge: Harvard University Press.

Ryan, Alan. (1993). "Liberalism." In Goodin and Pettit 1993.

————, ed. (1979). *The Idea of Freedom.* Oxford: Oxford University Press.

Sandel, Michael J. (1982). *Liberalism and the Limits of Justice.* Cambridge: Cambridge University Press.

Sartre, Jean-Paul. (1954). *Being and Nothingness.* Trans. Hazel E. Barnes. New York: Philosophical Library.

Scanlon, Thomas M., Jr. (1988). "The Significance of Choice." In McMurrin 1988.

Schoeman, Ferdinand, ed. (1987). *Responsibility, Character, and the Emotions.* Cambridge: Cambridge University Press.

Sher, George. (1987). *Desert.* Princeton: Princeton University Press.

Shklar, Judith. (1984). *Ordinary Vices.* Cambridge: Harvard University Press.

————. (1989). "The Liberalism of Fear." In Rosenblum 1989.

Sidgwick, Henry. (1981). *The Methods of Ethics.* Indianapolis: Hackett.

Smart, John J. C., and Bernard Williams. (1973). *Utilitarianism: For and Against.* Cambridge: Cambridge University Press.

Stephen, James Fitzjames. (1993). *Liberty, Equality, Fraternity.* Indianapolis: Liberty Press.

Sterba, James P. (1980). *The Demands of Justice.* Notre Dame: University of Notre Dame Press.

Stocker, Michael. (1990). *Plural and Conflicting Values.* Oxford: Clarendon.

Strawson, Peter F. (1974a). *Freedom and Resentment.* London: Methuen.

————. (1974b). "Social Morality and Individual Ideal." In Strawson 1974a.

————. (1974c). "Freedom and Resentment." In Strawson 1974a.

Swanton, Christine. (1992). *Freedom: A Coherence Theory.* Indianapolis: Hackett.

Taylor, Charles. (1976). "Responsibility for Self." In A. Rorty 1976.

————. (1985a). *Human Agency and Language.* Cambridge: Cambridge University Press.

————. (1985b). *Philosophy and the Human Sciences.* Cambridge: Cambridge University Press.

————. (1985c). "What Is Wrong with Negative Liberty." In Taylor 1985b.

————. (1989). *Sources of the Self.* Cambridge: Harvard University Press.

————. (1992). *The Ethics of Authenticity.* Cambridge: Harvard University Press.

Temkin, Larry S. (1993). *Inequality.* Oxford: Oxford University Press.

Thomson, Judith Jarvis, and Gerald Dworkin, eds. (1968). *Ethics.* New York: Harper and Row.

Tocqueville, Alexis de. (1961). *Democracy in America.* Vol. 1 and 2. Trans. Henry Reeve. New York: Schocken.

U.S. Bureau of the Census. (1994). *Statistical Abstract of the United States.* 114th ed. Washington, D.C.

Van Straaten, Zak, ed. (1980). *Philosophical Subjects.* Oxford: Oxford University Press.

Vlastos, Gregory. (1962). "Justice and Equality." In Brandt 1962.

————. (1991). *Socrates, Ironist and Moral Philosopher.* Ithaca: Cornell University Press.

Waldron, Jeremy. (1987). "Theoretical Foundations of Liberalism." *Philosophical Quarterly* 37: 127–50.

———. (1993). "Rights." In Goodin and Pettit 1993.

Walzer, Michael. (1983). *Spheres of Justice.* New York: Basic.

Warnock, Geoffrey J. (1971). *The Object of Morality.* London: Methuen.

Watson, Gary. (1975). "Free Agency." *Journal of Philosophy* 72: 205–20.

———. (1987). "Responsibility and the Limits of Evil." In Schoeman 1987.

Weber, Max. (1946). *From Max Weber.* Trans. and ed. H. H. Gerth and C. W. Mills. London: Routledge.

White, Morton. (1979). "Oughts and Cans." In Ryan 1979.

Williams, Bernard. (1973a). *Problems of the Self.* Cambridge: Cambridge University Press.

———. (1973b). "The Idea of Equality." In Williams 1973a.

———. (1978). Introduction to Berlin 1978a.

———. (1981). *Moral Luck.* Cambridge: Cambridge University Press.

———. (1985). *Ethics and the Limits of Philosophy.* London: Collins.

———. (1993). *Shame and Necessity.* Berkeley: University of California Press.

Wolf, Susan. (1981). "Asymmetrical Freedom." In Fischer 1986.

———. (1987). "Sanity and the Metaphysics of Responsibility." In Schoeman 1987.

———. (1991). *Freedom within Reason.* New York: Oxford University Press.

Zaitchik, Alan. (1977). "On Deserving to Deserve." *Philosophy and Public Affairs* 6: 371–88.

Index

241